SOVIET
UNION
MT. ARARAT
WESTERN EUPHRATES
EASTERN EUPHRATES
IRAN
KHABUR R.
RIA
Deir-ez-Zor
TIGRIS R.
EUPHRATES R.
Baghdad
IRAQ
SA'UDI ARABIA
D1064298

Allegheny College
Library

Bought from the
William Davis
Memorial Fund

That They May Have Life

SALES AGENT:
PRINCETON UNIVERSITY PRESS
PRINCETON, NEW JERSEY

378.569
P386t

THAT THEY MAY HAVE LIFE

The Story of the American University of Beirut 1866-1941

BY STEPHEN B. L. PENROSE, JR.

WITHDRAWN

NEW YORK 1941
The Trustees of the American University of Beirut

Copyright, 1941, The Trustees of the American University of Beirut

Printed in the United States of America by
Princeton University Press at Princeton, New Jersey

Dedicated to three great college presidents,
who have devoted their lives
to the end that the Near East may have Life
and have it more abundantly:

DANIEL BLISS, 1823-1916

HOWARD SWEETSER BLISS, 1860-1920

BAYARD DODGE, 1888-

73315

ALLEGHENY COLLEGE LIBRARY

INTRODUCTION

On December 3, 1941, the American University of Beirut will have completed seventy-five years of active college work. This life span has covered a period of almost incredible change in the Near East. With many of the changes the University has been intimately associated. At a time when the Near East is once more involved in a war of western nations, it is not improper to focus attention upon one of its most influential institutions.

The seventy-fifth anniversary of an institution is worthy of public celebration only if its history compasses unusual or unique developments or if the story contains elements of more than passing interest. There may be little question but that the American University of Beirut qualifies in these respects to receive wide recognition. It is perhaps unfortunate that this history has not been written earlier and that the University has not achieved a public interest which it merits.

The University seems to have a penchant for anniversaries in the midst of war. Its fiftieth birthday came in 1916 when Beirut was almost wholly shut off from communication with the western world. The half centenary was consequently marked only by a small local service in Beirut. This year conditions have been but very little better. To be sure, Lebanon is no longer a part of a belligerent Ottoman Empire as it was in 1916. Indeed, the Ottoman Empire itself has ceased to exist. But there is much the same difficulty of communication, for mails require nearly two months in transit and there is no possibility either for representatives of the University to come to America or for officers in America to visit Beirut. Again the University is isolated from the western world.

This isolation has had an inevitable effect upon the writing of this history. There are a great many records and papers on file in Beirut which would have provided valuable information to the author. Unfortunately no copies of them exist in this country and because of the uncertainties of communication and the certainties of censorship it was deemed inadvisable to attempt to transmit copies, had it been possible to make a selection from the mass of documents.

It has been necessary, therefore, to depend upon Trustees' minutes, president's reports, and such private and published records as were available in the New York office. The study of additional Beirut records would have provided a greater wealth of interesting detail. The history inevitably suffers from the necessity of dependence upon summaries between whose lines the historian must read much.

On the other hand this fact has not been without its blessings. The material at hand was so extensive that any increase in its amount would have made the task of selection more arduous even than it was, and might have resulted in the inclusion of too large an amount of detail.

The history frankly has been written from the standpoint of an American observer. It will, therefore, deserve the criticism of alumni and others very familiar with the college life, that too little space has been given to student affairs, campus anecdotes and alumni activities. It is an actual fact, however, that a whole book could and perhaps should be written from the student or alumnus point of view. In the present work it was found to be impracticable to combine the two positions without expanding the size of what is already a book of too imposing a length.

It is to be regretted that the story of the Alumni Association could not be told in greater detail. To one who reads over the files of *Al Kulliyah,* there is much of interest and inspiration to be found in the picture of the enthusiasm and self-sacrifice for the University which unfolds in its regular reports. More credit than it was possible to give is due Shehadi A. Shehadi, Philip K. Hitti, Said Pasha Shoucair, Joseph Aftimus, Faris Nimr, Samuel Bey Atiyyeh and many others too numerous to mention. In spite of pressing duties of their own, they gave magnanimously of time, energy, and money to the organization of the alumni in support of their Alma Mater. Certainly this brief word of appreciation of their efforts is but a small token of the recognition which they truly deserve.

It was impossible to secure a complete list of the Syrian and other Near Eastern faculty and staff members who served the University through the years. Their number, too, would have been considerably greater even than that of the French, English, and American teachers listed in Appendix J. The omission of the list is to be regretted, but practical considerations made it necessary.

Little has been said directly of the effect of the present war on the operation of the institution. This has been intentional, for, until the very end of the school year, little information as to military or political developments in Lebanon and Syria affecting the University reached this country. It will probably not be possible until after the war to present anything like a clear picture of events occurring in 1940-41. The administration in Beirut is experienced in the wisdom of reticence.

On the other hand, it should be said that until May 1941 there was no serious interference with the operation of the University. At the opening of the school year in 1940, neighboring governments assisted materially by permitting students to reach Beirut in spite of severe restrictions upon ordinary travel. As a result and because of the impossibility of study in Europe for Near Eastern students, the year has shown the largest enrollment in the University's history, the total number reaching 1,992.

The University on its part cooperated with local governments in the prevention of nationalistic movements by temporarily suspending all student organizations. In the place of their activities, substitute interests in which the entire student body could join were developed. At the same time students were stringently discouraged from taking part in political activities outside the campus walls.

In May 1941 the German conquest of Greece, the abortive anti-British coup d'état and subsequent warfare in 'Iraq and the apparent Nazi intention to use Syria as a point of attack upon the British in Palestine and 'Iraq, necessitated unusual measures by the faculty. Fearing the possibility that students from outside

Syria and Lebanon might soon be unable to return to their homes and might thus be stranded on the campus as they were in 1914-18 (see page 151), the administration decided to release these students with credit for the year and permit them to go home. Approximately 650 students were involved. This action was erroneously reported in American papers as a wholesale dismissal of students for political agitation.

In the middle of May the use of Syrian airdromes by Nazi planes flying to 'Iraq provoked bombing attacks by the British which resulted in extreme tension between the Vichy-controlled Mandate administration and the British Government. British consular officials were requested to withdraw from Syria and Lebanon. With them went other British subjects, among whom were a number of faculty members from the University. As the end of the school year was so close at hand, the date of Commencement was simply advanced and the year brought to an end in late May.

After the close of school and before the British and Free French moved into Syria, most of the American families in Beirut also left for Palestine and Egypt whence they hoped to be able to embark the women and children for the United States. Three families, the Browns, Paulys and Maynards, remained in Beirut with President and Mrs. Dodge. Dr. George H. Miller, Dean of the medical school, and four American nurses also stayed to keep the hospital in operation. All were in Beirut throughout the Syrian campaign.

It is hardly a matter for question that the University will reopen in the fall, though it is almost inevitable that the student body must be considerably reduced in numbers. Because of the impossibility of sending out replacements from America there will be a shortage of experienced staff members, but there is now a larger reservoir of potential native teachers than there was from 1914-18.

Military developments are likely to determine the immediate future of the institution. Its history shows that it is not unaccustomed to hardships and obstacles of a seemingly overwhelming nature. There is ground for full confidence that it will continue to function successfully and with expanding usefulness long after the clouds of war have disappeared. From them, as from the previous storm, may result a richer opportunity for service to the Near East.

* * *

The author wishes to acknowledge his deep obligation in this work to Dr. Charles A. Webster, Professor-Emeritus of Ophthalmology at Beirut, who has been connected with the College since 1895. Dr. Webster, who is at present living in Cambridge, Massachusetts, has given invaluable aid, advice, and criticism out of his profound knowledge and accurate memory of Beirut events. He has thrown much light on obscure happenings and has prevented the inclusion of several errors which without his guidance would have been allowed to stand. It is to be regretted that a larger part of the wealth of his personal reminiscence could not have been included herein.

Thanks should also be expressed to Albert W. Staub and the staff of the Near East College Association for their cooperation and real assistance, as well as to many others who have read and criticized the manuscript. The Atlantic Monthly graciously permitted the reprinting of Howard Bliss' article "The Modern Missionary," which forms Chapter XI. To it and to the Fleming Revell Company, Charles Scribner's Sons, J. B. Lippincott and Houghton Mifflin Company, the author is indebted for permission to quote from published works.

STEPHEN B. L. PENROSE, JR.

New York, N.Y.
August, 1941

CONTENTS

Part III

THE ADMINISTRATION OF BAYARD DODGE (1922-)

APPENDICES

LIST OF ILLUSTRATIONS

PART I

The Administration of Daniel Bliss

1866-1902

I. THE BACKGROUND

1. THE POLITICAL SITUATION

AT THE BEGINNING of the 19th century Syria and Palestine were provinces in the sprawling Ottoman Empire. Their governors were more or less responsible to the Sublime Porte but frequently took the responsibility very lightly. The Sultan had little more control over them than he did over Muhammed 'Ali, one of his former army officers who made himself ruler of Egypt in 1801 after Napoleon had evacuated his troops. In 1833 Turkey lost control of Syria altogether when Ibrahim Pasha, son of Muhammed 'Ali, conquered the Turkish forces and made himself governor, subject to his father's command. Had it not been for Palmerston's opposition, Ibrahim might well have made his father head of an Arab empire independent of Turkey—but England intervened. Unwilling to permit Turkey to become too weak, because it preferred a weak Turkey in control of the trade route to India rather than a strong Arab empire, the British fleet in 1840 settled the issue. Ibrahim was forced to withdraw by 1841 and Syria reverted to Ottoman control.

Ibrahim left his mark. An enlightened, idealistic ruler, he had abolished the sectarian distinctions which, under the Turks, had operated to the disadvantage of Christians and had prevented any unity among the population. The Christians (largely Maronite, Greek Catholic and Greek Orthodox) who formed a majority in the northern Lebanon but a distinct minority in Syria as a whole, were highly pleased. The Moslems were far from happy at this development and their distant cousins, the Druzes, who ruled the southern Lebanon, were actively annoyed by the assumption of equality and even superiority on the part of the Maronites. On Ibrahim's departure trouble periodically broke out between them. The Turks encouraged the dissension on the theory of "divide and rule." For their own competing purposes the French supported the Maronites, the English the Druzes.

Finally, in 1860, the long friction produced a conflagration. Terrible massacres occurred both in the Lebanon and in Damascus, with the result that some 11,000 Christians and Druzes were slain. Property damage was enormous. It was a frightful experience for the members of the American mission scattered throughout the Lebanon, even though none of the Americans was killed. After taking refuge in Beirut they worked unceasingly to provide relief for the suffering. When hostilities had finally been controlled by European intervention, the mission took the lead in starting physical and moral reconstruction.

For some time after the disorders had ceased, French troops remained in the Lebanon, thus establishing a precedent which was thereafter employed with some frequency. Under their influence and that of other European powers the administration of Syria was recast to provide a more equitable government for the various sections. By 1864 the administrative system for the area was completely revamped. Syria was divided into two provinces with governors appointed directly by the Sultan. Lebanon was constituted a separate district with a considerable measure of autonomy under the administration of a Christian governor appointed by the Sultan but acceptable to the Powers. A representative council was to be chosen as an advisory, if not legislative, body. The people of the new province were to be relieved of the heavy burden of taxation, freed from compulsory military service, and from interference with the exercise of their religious preferences.

To the American missionaries the new political order seemed to promise both a wonderful opportunity and a new obligation. If the autonomy of Lebanon were to prove successful the country must have trained leaders. That training must be such as to provide honest, intelligent and courageous men, liberal in point of view, devoted to the true interests of their country. It could not be entrusted to ecclesiastical groups controlled in Europe and devoted to the maintenance of sectarian distinctions. It was obvious that what was needed was a college of the American type which should combine a devotion to Christian ideals with the most modern principles and practices of western education. To avoid all criticism of sectarianism the proposed college should be under the control of a governing body distinct from any mission board. Separate endowment funds would, of course, be necessary. As the Civil War was then going on in America, the prospect of raising such funds there did not seem too bright. Nevertheless the value of the project warranted a serious attempt being made.

Another factor favoring the establishment of the college was the new freedom from religious interference. The opportunity for effective missionary work in the Lebanon was greatly augmented, but in order to take advantage of it more teachers and pastors were urgently needed. If the work were to be self-perpetuating the new men must be natives of the country. But how could they be trained unless there were a college adequately equipped to provide the education prerequisite to theological study? The compulsion toward the establishment of a college was thus from two points of view well-nigh overpowering.

2. THE AMERICAN MISSION

The idea of higher education for the Near East was a natural outgrowth of American missionary activity which, since 1820, had exercised an almost unbroken influence on Lebanon, Syria and Palestine. Pliny Fisk and his devoted successors under the American Board of Commissioners for Foreign Missions[1] may have failed in their immediate aim of converting the Moslems in large numbers to Christianity, but they succeeded better than they knew in accomplishing a regeneration in the spirit of the people. Through their schools, their printing press, their general interest in the largely forgotten culture of the Arab world, as well as through their deep concern with spiritual uplift, they kindled a vital flame. One recent chronicler of Arab history attributes to their labors,

[1] Now Congregationalist, the American Board was until 1837 the combined foreign mission agency of Congregational, Presbyterian and Dutch Reformed Churches. In 1837 the "Old School" Presbyterians formed a separate Presbyterian Board but the "New School" remained with the American Board until 1870 when the two branches of the Presbyterian Church reunited. The Presbyterian Board of Missions was then established and took over responsibility for all the work in Syria. The American Board agreed to give up that particular field to the Presbyterians.

more than to any other single factor, the beginnings of an Arab revival which promises to be one of the great social and cultural movements of the future.[2]

The missionaries early learned the necessity of establishing schools, for the general intellectual level of the people was very low. There were a few schools which had long before been established by the Jesuits and Lazarists but these were of a very low grade until American competition forced their improvement. Schools for girls were unheard of until Mrs. Eli Smith founded the first one in 1834. The need for native teachers and ministers forced the mission to raise yet further the upper limits of education and establish high schools, one of which, at 'Abeih in the Lebanon, became a teachers' training school dignified by the title of college. By the year 1860 Americans had founded no less than thirty-three schools. Their example had brought out at least as many more from rival ecclesiastical sources.

The language of the people was Arabic and it seemed only natural to the Americans to teach in Arabic. Having no desire, as others had, to "Frankify" the natives for imperialistic purposes, and realizing the untold wealth of the rapidly vanishing Arab culture, it seemed wiser to them to make use of it. They themselves learned Arabic and taught, preached, wrote or translated articles and books in Arabic. These were printed on the mission press, which had been moved to Beirut from Malta in 1834. Finding that the existing Arabic fount was inadequate, they designed a new one which was cast in Leipsig under the direction of Eli Smith. That design, universally known as American Arabic, has had wide use throughout the world. It was used for the magnificent translation of the Bible into Arabic, begun by Eli Smith in 1849 and completed by Dr. Cornelius V. A. Van Dyck in 1864. The press made possible the introduction of good text books for teaching as well as the reproduction of Arabic manuscripts. The American influence on the development of the Arabic language and literature, both in content and style, has been of enormous importance to the revival of Arab culture.

[2] Antonius, George: The Arab Awakening (Lippincott 1939), pp. 35-54 ff.

Education proved to be one of the most valuable tools which the American missionaries could have used in their effort to evangelize Syria and the Lebanon. The development of a college was the almost unavoidable consequence of the success which crowned the work of the primary and secondary schools, coupled with the educational background of the missionaries themselves, most of whom were graduates of privately endowed American colleges. The absolute non-existence in Asia Minor of any institution which men of such training would recognize as being of "college rank"; their awareness of the indubitable benefits of such an institution to the country, particularly if it could provide medical training as well as studies in theology, arts, and sciences; the political developments which seemed to open a new opportunity for educated natives; all these factors impelled the Americans to consider seriously the establishment of a college. Given the combination of circumstances which existed, it was inevitable that the attempt should be made.

II. PRELIMINARIES

1. IN SYRIA

THE PLAN of establishing an institution for higher education in the Lebanon must have been a common subject of conversation among the missionaries for some time before it was brought before them for action in January 1862. The prime movers in the scheme appear to have been the Rev. Daniel Bliss and the Rev. Dr. William M. Thomson. The former became the first president of the Syrian Protestant College and was in large measure responsible for its effective establishment. In a later account of the founding of the College, President Bliss described the considerations which influenced the group in their decision. His own words give the clearest picture that can be drawn:[1]

"Experience had led the missionaries to regard with little favor the plan to educate young men out of the country. The Malta College, which was designed to educate young men living in countries bordering on the Mediterranean as near their home as possible, had not been a success. Individuals, who had been more or less educated in England or on the Continent, exerted very little influence, on their return, in elevating their countrymen, but on the contrary their defective education tended rather to unfit them for usefulness by taking them out of sympathy with their own people. Quite a number of these did not return to settle in the country but remained abroad; and of those who returned not one ever became a man of influence as author, teacher, or preacher. On the other hand, several men, who had been educated in the Mission Seminary, under the care of Mr. Hebard, and at a later period in 'Abeih Academy, first under the care of Dr. Van Dyck and then of Mr. Calhoun, became prominent men and contributed to the great object for which Missions are established. But while the general demand for education increased, the course of study in the 'Abeih Academy was more or less modified to meet the specific wants of

[1] Bliss, Frederick J., The Reminiscences of Daniel Bliss (Revell, N.Y. 1920), pp. 162-8. The statement is abridged for brevity.

the Mission in furnishing common-school teachers and other native helpers, and thus became even less adapted to meet all the demands of the country than it was at an earlier period. It was manifest that to educate large numbers out of the country, even if in the course of time a foreign education should prove satisfactory, would require more money than the people could pay and more than the benevolent would furnish. It was also manifest that missionary societies, depending mainly for their support on small contributions, given for the direct preaching of the Gospel and for teaching children enough to enable them to read understandingly could not divert their funds for this higher education."

Concerning the practical plans for the college it was generally agreed that the language of instruction should be Arabic, since that was the native tongue of the prospective students. (This plan was actually followed until the diversity of tongues in the growing student body necessitated reversion to a language which could be common to all, namely English.) It was also agreed that since the money necessary for running the institution would have to be raised in America or England, an American or English board of trustees would be necessary to handle the funds and lend prestige to the undertaking so that large contributors might have confidence in it. It was felt that the college should have an English or American charter so that it might have the proper legal basis. Dr. Bliss noted that "it probably never occurred to any one even to ask the question whether such a Board of Trustees should be legalized by the Turkish Government."

To overcome the disadvantage of having a Board of Trustees some thousands of miles away, a local Board of Managers was considered a necessity. (This was established and served until 1902 when the improvement of communications had made its further existence unnecessary.) Much discussion centered on the point of whether the managers and president should be natives or foreigners. The fact that the natives themselves thought it safer to have the administration in American or English hands eventually decided the matter. Dr. Bliss records that "it was thought best that American and English missionaries and other American and English residents in Syria and Egypt should constitute the Board of

Managers, they all belonging to some branch of the Evangelical Church, and that the President should be chosen from the missionaries of the Syrian Mission."

Formal presentation of the subject was made to the Mission meeting on January 23, 1862 by Dr. Thomson who suggested that Daniel Bliss be made the "Principal." This was a surprise to Mr. Bliss, but after consulting his wife he decided to accept the new responsibility if the American Board were willing. Letters were at once dispatched to the Prudential Committee of the American Board, recommending the establishment of the college with Daniel Bliss as Principal, "it being understood that, until the expected endowment were secured, he should continue his connection with the Mission and derive support from the Board."[2]

The American Board considered the matter very seriously and agreed at length to support the plan if a number of stipulations were observed. These were summarized by Mr. Bliss as follows: "that it was most important that the establishment of the College should not jeopardize the training of a Christian ministry, a work which was as yet by no means accomplished; that as, owing to the demand of the country, the creation of a higher institution was inevitable, it was essential that the first of the kind should be established by Protestants, not by Jesuits; that the pupils should be educated with reference to the business which they might propose to follow, as ministers of the Gospel, lawyers, physicians, engineers, secretaries, interpreters, merchants, clerks, etc., thus avoiding the reproach of sending forth helpless and useless drones upon society; that, where suitable persons could be obtained, the native Arab element should be introduced as fast as possible into the professorships and other teaching positions, in all departments of the College, in order that the Syrians might have every facility for qualifying themselves to assume, at no distant day, the entire management of the institution; that care should be exercised to prevent the students from becoming denationalized; that, in the interests of the independence and self-respect of the student body, the principle of self-support should be fostered as far as possible."[3] It is interesting to note that, except where the internationalization of the College

[2] Bliss, op. cit., p. 167.

[3] Bliss, op. cit., pp. 167-8.

has required modifications, these stipulations have been scrupulously observed through the seventy-five years of the institution's history.

2. DANIEL BLISS

The man to whom was unanimously voted the presidency of the future college must have produced a profound change in the first opinion the Mission had formed of him on his arrival in 1855. A report sent to the American Board by one of the older missionaries shortly after the happy conclusion of the young couple's strenuous two months voyage to Syria was hardly enthusiastic. "The Blisses have arrived," he wrote. "Mrs. Bliss will not live a year and Mr. Bliss is not a practical man."[4] Both judgments were inconceivably erratic. Mrs. Bliss lived until 1914, and few men living have accomplished finer work with hand, head and heart than did her husband.

Had the critic known Mr. Bliss' previous history he would have been less dubious, for few of the missionaries could have had such a varied early life. It so impressed the Rev. D. Stuart Dodge[5] when he heard it described in 1868 that he wrote it down with minute detail in a notebook now in the possession of the Near East College Association.

Daniel Bliss was born August 17, 1823 in Georgia, Vermont, and spent his childhood on a farm at Cambridge, Vermont. When he was nine years old his mother died, and four years later his father moved to Madison, Ohio. The boy attended village school and worked for his brother until he was sixteen when he was forced to shift for himself. As he himself wrote in his Reminiscences, "my sojourn from that day till I had a home of my own—seventeen years after—was among strangers."[6]

Young Daniel supported himself with whatever work he could get, household chores, wood-cutting, ploughing, in the meantime gaining what schooling he could pick up. He became an apprentice

[4] Ibid., pp. 105-6.

[5] Son of William Earl Dodge, D. S. Dodge was the first professor of English at the College, secretary and later president of the Board of Trustees, great uncle of President Bayard Dodge.

[6] Bliss, op. cit., p. 29.

in a tannery and learned the trade in four years of service, at the end of which time the tannery closed. Grafting of fruit trees came next and then a place in another tannery in Geneva, Ohio. In 1846 he realized his ambition for an education by entering Kingsville Academy, where, at the age of 23, he commenced the study of Algebra, Greek, and Latin. After three months he began to teach school and later was made a pupil teacher in the Academy. By the summer of 1848 he was ready for college. That fall he achieved his highest ambition by entering Amherst.

Mr. Bliss had few funds and was compelled to earn his entire way through college, which he found no more difficult than his earlier experiences. Any job available he took, no matter how menial, but he himself wrote that "the only time I did any work that interfered with my studies was during haying time."[7] He was forced to borrow money for his senior year but was able to pay it back by teaching school during the summer after his graduation. At Commencement he stood seventh in a class of forty-two.

Amherst had a profound influence on Mr. Bliss, both through his contact with great teachers and through the deeply religious atmosphere which then permeated the campus. He joined the College Church in his freshman year and shortly thereafter became a member of the Missionary Band. In spite of the roughness of his early life he had managed to preserve a deep religious consciousness which crystallized to conviction under the inspiration of the college life.

Amherst was followed by Andover Seminary, where at graduation Mr. Bliss was chosen to give the Commencement oration, which Professor Park asked him to repeat at the Park Street Church in Boston. He was ordained at Amherst in the summer of 1855, and in rapid succession was married in November to Miss Abby Maria Wood of Amherst and sailed with her for Syria on December 12. For six years they served as missionaries in the Lebanon, first at 'Abeih, where the famous 'Abeih Academy had been founded in 1843 by Dr. Van Dyck, and then at Suq-al-Gharb, where they established their own station and conducted the Girls' Boarding School, which was moved up from Beirut.

[7] Bliss, op. cit., p. 68.

3. IN AMERICA AND ENGLAND

Mr. and Mrs. Bliss sailed for America with their family on August 14, 1862. The Mission had voted that they should go to make preliminary arrangements for the establishment of the college. They reached the United States in September and immediately proceeded to the annual meeting of the American Board of Commissioners for Foreign Missions at Springfield, Massachusetts. It is difficult to believe that what transpired there was not under the guidance of Providence. Let Mr. Bliss tell the story:

"I was appointed to speak on a resolution in regard to reinforcing the Missions, and the late Honorable William E. Dodge was to be the next speaker. As I had had no rest from the long journey from Syria, my haggard appearance seemed to enforce upon the mind of Mr. Dodge what was said of the magnitude of the work and of the necessity of reinforcing the overworked missionaries. When he spoke he used words to this effect: 'When our young brother was speaking, I was so moved that there was not a dry thread in the shirt on my back.' Mr. Dodge was unknown to us except by name at that time, but he invited Mrs. Bliss and me to dine with him at the Massasoit House. We had a private table—the company consisted of Mr. William E. Dodge, Mrs. Dodge, their son, Rev. D. Stuart Dodge and his wife. During the dinner Mr. Dodge asked Mrs. Bliss if her husband had come home on account of his health and she assured him that his health was perfect, then stated in a general way the plans for the proposed College. The conversation soon became more general and the needs and objects of the enterprise were more fully explained. Before we rose from the table Mr. Dodge said to his son, 'Stuart, that seems to me to be a good thing; we must look into it.' Subsequent events revealed the results of his remark. The fountain of benevolence in Mr. Dodge's heart was not only enlarged but a new channel was opened for his benefactions."[8]

With the active cooperation of Mr. Dodge, the American Board (under which Mr. Bliss retained his missionary status), and many other friends, the work of organization and acquisition of endow-

[8] Bliss, op. cit., p. 169.

ment funds proceeded steadily. Thanks to a New York statute passed in 1848, incorporation of a Board of Trustees could be accomplished without special act. In April of 1863 therefore the Board of Trustees of the Syrian Protestant College was incorporated, its members being William A. Booth, William E. Dodge, David Hoadley and Simeon B. Chittenden, of New York; and Abner Kingman and Joseph S. Ropes, of Boston. The act of incorporation was certified and signed by Governor Horatio Seymour and Secretary of State Horatio Ballard. (See Appendix A.) But the act of 1848 had limited the funds which such a corporation might acquire to $50,000 in real estate and $75,000 in personal estate, with annual income not to exceed $10,000. In the far-sighted estimate of the founders, that amount would not long be sufficient for such an institution as they had in mind. A special enabling act was therefore necessary.

In September 1863 Robert College in Constantinople opened its doors after some years of organization work. The aims of this institution and that in Beirut were quite similar, both sprang from the common soil of the American Board, and both shared at least two of their incorporators. William A. Booth and David Hoadley, the former the president of the American Home Missionary Board and the latter a member of it, were trustees of the Syrian Protestant College and Robert College alike. It was only natural that when an act of the legislature was to be sought in favor of one institution, it should be sought for both. Thus it was that the Trustees worked for and secured a Special Act, passed May 4, 1864, entitled "An Act Authorizing 'The Trustees of the Syrian Protestant College' and 'The Trustees of Robert College of Constantinople,' to take and hold real and personal estate." (Appendix B.) This provided that the two Boards of Trustees might acquire and hold property "notwithstanding the value thereof and the clear annual income thereof may exceed the amounts specified in the . . . . General Act."

The story of the legal negotiations behind the incorporation and the Special Act was written out by William A. Booth in 1889 when he was still President of the Board. His recital was inscribed in the Minutes of the Board at the end of Volume 2, and merits repetition.

"In the summer of 1863, Rev. Daniel Bliss, of the Syria Mission, came to me and asked my cooperation in raising a fund of $60,000, to establish an institution of higher education than they then had at Beirut.

"He said that education had proceeded so far there that it was now necessary to have a higher class institution for the education of boys and young men, and for this purpose he wished to raise this fund. I agreed to assist him, and one of the first things to be done was to obtain if possible, a charter under the Laws of the State of New York for a collegiate institution.

"I applied to Jesse Benedict, counsellor at law, to see if such a Charter could be obtained under the General Act of New York, and if so, for him to draw it up. He found it could be so established, and he prepared it. I then submitted the charter to Mr. Charles A. Davison for further correction, and he made some improvements in it. I then went to Mr. Samuel J. Tilden and told him I wanted him to give $500 to establish a College at Beirut. Mr. Tilden and I had been associated together in railroad enterprises for a number of years, and he looked a little downcast at my request; and I said, 'I want you to take this charter, revise it and make it perfect, which will be equivalent to the $500.' He smiled and said he would do it with great pleasure. He did so and made essential improvements in it; and thus was formed the charter under which the College has existed.

"The Law of New York, at that time, gave the privilege of but $75,000 to hold of each personal and real estate. It became necessary, therefore, to go to the Legislature to get the privilege of holding a larger amount. This was granted by the Legislature, and the Bill was in the hands of Governor Seymour at the adjournment. I asked Dr. Bliss if the bill was signed. He said of course it would be. I replied,—Possibly it may not be. He wrote to Albany and learned that the Governor had some objections to the Bill.

"I requested him to go to Albany and say to the Governor that the College was helped by such men as James Brown and Erastus Corning (his particular friends) and that the bill and the charter had been prepared by Mr. Tilden. He went, made his statement to the Governor, and the Governor said 'Did Mr. Tilden prepare the

ALLEGHENY COLLEGE LIBRARY

charter?' 'Yes.' . . . 'You come here at three o'clock and I will see.'

"At a quarter to three he went and the Secretary said, 'Your bill is signed.' "

The way was thus cleared for the collection of the $100,000 for endowment which had been decided upon as the immediate goal. Mr. Bliss had not been idle in his money-raising efforts during 1863 even though one can imagine the difficulties he had to face in the midst of the Civil War. At the first regular meeting of the Board of Trustees on December 28, 1863, power was given to the Treasurer, William E. Dodge, "to invest funds already on hand and such as may subsequently be received—but to an amount not exceeding $20,000—in 'United States 5-20 Bonds.' " At the same meeting acknowledgement was made of a contribution of £1000 from the "Committee of the Syrian Relief Fund" of London, which was to be paid when the College opened. At the second meeting, June 7, 1864, word had been received from the former secretary of this Committee, Rev. Herman Schmettau, to the effect that "this sum might be increased to an endowment of a Professorship of Medicine or Engineering." Mr. Schmettau stated further "that the interest in the enterprise already awakened in England could undoubtedly . . . be made to render valuable assistance in establishing the Institution."

By August first of that year, the $100,000 fund was complete, due to the generosity of the Board members at a meeting on July 21. At that time the fund amounted to $90,000, with one gift conditional upon completion by August first. The minutes for July 21 state simply, "The members of the Board present decided to make up the larger part of the deficiency—amounting to nearly $10,000—by increasing their own subscriptions. This was accordingly done and the meeting adjourned." President Bliss who had travelled nearly 17,000 miles and made 279 addresses could at last feel himself sufficiently free of obligation to visit his family in Ohio.

Because of the depreciated condition of United States currency at the time ($240 in "greenbacks" was equivalent to $100 gold) it seemed advisable to hold the $100,000 intact until conditions improved, in the meantime raising a fund in England to carry the work of the College. Accordingly President Bliss, who had been formally elected by the Board in July, set sail with his family for England early in September 1864. With the help of Mr. Schmettau, who was secretary of the then powerful Evangelical Alliance, and of other friends, Dr. Bliss[9] was able to meet and establish helpful relations with a large number of influential people. Among them might be listed Lord Colthorpe, the Earl of Shaftesbury, the Duke of Argyll, Lord Stratford de Redcliffe, Lord Dufferin, Rev. Horatius Bonar, Dr. Thomas Guthrie, Dr. Newman Hall, Samuel Morley and many others.

The completion of the American fund aroused less enthusiasm in England than it should have done because of English contempt for "greenbacks," but the project itself was so attractive that within a year and a half enough English money was raised to provide for the opening of the College. The Blisses sailed happily for Beirut and reached their home on March 2nd, 1866. The truly international venture could proceed after three and a half years of intensive effort.

4. ORGANIZATION

Little has thus far been said of the organization for administration and teaching which was developed during the period before the College opened.

The officers of the Board of Trustees, elected at the first regular meeting in December 1863, were William A. Booth, President, and William E. Dodge, Treasurer. At that meeting a preliminary set of by-laws was submitted but was laid over until it could be examined in Syria. The revised Constitution and By-laws, with its Preamble, was adopted at the second meeting on June 7, 1864, when the Syrian Board of Managers was formally elected. (Appendix C and D.)

In July 1864, at the meeting of the Board at which Dr. Bliss was formally elected President, Rev. D. Stuart Dodge was appointed Professor of Modern Languages at a salary of $1,000 a year. (Dr. Bliss was to receive as President the salary of $1,500 a year.) It

[9] Daniel Bliss was made an honorary Doctor of Divinity by his alma mater, Amherst, at the 1864 commencement exercises.

is interesting to learn from the pen of William Booth how D. S. Dodge came to join the faculty and thus establish a connection which was to prove of inestimable value to the College. Mr. Booth wrote, referring to the autumn of 1863:

"Returning from Springfield, in the cars, my wife suggested that it would be well for Stuart Dodge to connect himself with this College. We talked the matter over and both agreed that it would be a very excellent thing for Mr. Dodge and for the College.

"A few days afterward, Mr. Bliss called at my house, and my wife told him of the conversation. He came to see me about it and I expressed to him my views very fully. He conferred with Mr. and Mrs. Dodge, but they did not favor it. He then went to Boston and conferred with Dr. Anderson in regard to it, and Dr. Anderson and he came on to New York to see Mr. Dodge, Senior. Dr. Anderson stayed at Mr. Dodge's and Mr. Bliss at my house. Dr. Anderson was to try to persuade him to consent to have Mr. Stuart Dodge connect himself with the College; but Dr. Bliss came to me the next day and said he had not succeeded,—that they were determined Mr. Dodge would be a missionary. I was well satisfied that it would be wise for him to connect himself with the College and said to Mr. Bliss, 'wait a little and they will agree to it.'

"After about a month, Mr. D. S. Dodge decided that he would connect himself with the College as one of its Professors.

"From that time to the present, he has been most devoted to its interests, giving large sums of money, wise counsel and very earnest and devoted attention, and has been a most valued friend to the College."

From the very beginning, deep desire was felt to establish a medical department at the earliest possible date. During 1865, Dr. Bliss had discovered considerable interest in England in the endowment of medical professorships on a 50-50 English-American basis. The first financial efforts following the completion of the general endowment fund were concerned with the medical work. Likewise the first new appointment to be made by the Board was that of Dr. William H. Thomson of New York as professor in the Medical Department "to fill such chair as he may decide on in connection with the other Medical Professors."[10] Dr. C. V. A. Van Dyck, who had met with the Board while in New York supervising the electroplating of his Arabic Bible, was also appointed on the same conditions as Dr. Thomson, with the understanding that he should give but part time to the Medical School. A third medical appointee, Dr. John Wortabet of Aleppo, was given the chair of Anatomy and Physiology, to be occupied as soon as he could qualify himself.

It is interesting to note that these appointments followed the recommendations of the Board of Managers, meeting in April and July 1866, shortly after Dr. Bliss' return to Beirut. One other professorial appointment was at that time recommended and made, that of Rev. James Robertson of Beirut to the Professorship of Mathematics and Astronomy. Preparatory work had been taken care of by the association with the College of the two year old National School (Madrasa al-Wataniya) of Mr. Butrus Bustani.[11] There can be no question of the earnestness both on the part of the Managers and the Trustees in seeking at once to establish a complete institution of full collegiate rank.

[10] Minutes, October 4, 1866. Dr. Thomson, son of Dr. William M. Thomson of Beirut, had been recommended to take charge of the Medical School at a meeting of the Board of Managers on July 18, 1866. Unfortunately, he found himself unable to accept the appointment.

[11] Butrus Bustani (1819-83) was a remarkable Maronite scholar who became a Presbyterian, helped Eli Smith and Dr. Van Dyck with their translation of the Bible and taught many of the missionaries Arabic. He learned English, Italian, Hebrew, Aramaic, Greek, Syriac and Latin together with some French. He taught at 'Abeih and other schools, compiled an Arabic dictionary with its abridgment (Muhit al-Muhit and Qutr al-Muhit) and a monumental Arabic encyclopedia which was incredibly good.

III. THE FIRST STAGE

1. THE COLLEGE OPENS

THE SYRIAN PROTESTANT COLLEGE began actually to function on December 3, 1866 when it opened its doors to sixteen students. It must have been a devoutly thankful as well as a solemn occasion, that third of December. President Bliss presided at the opening exercises, and read the third chapter of First Corinthians. Paul's famous phrases, "I have planted, Apollos watered, but God gave the increase," and "other foundation can no man lay than that which is laid, which is Jesus Christ" must have seemed particularly appropriate to the opening of this Christian venture. The Rev. Henry Jessup and D. S. Dodge both made addresses. It is unfortunate that no further record remains of the proceedings, but their interest to future generations could not at the time have been apparent.

In his reminiscences Daniel Bliss records that during the year 1866 there was no faculty. This does not mean that there were no teachers, but only that there was no group of regularly appointed professors. The preparatory department was under the guidance of Mr. Bustani in his school. Dr. Bliss taught Philosophy and Ethics in the College while D. S. Dodge had English and Latin. The house tutor, Asâd al-Shadudi was a fine teacher of mathematics and science as well as being an Arab poet whose simple and beautiful Arabic translations of English hymns are still used throughout the Near East. Arabic was taught by a distinguished native scholar, Sheikh Nasif al-Yazeji, and French was given by Maurice Vairn, a member of a family of noted scholars. John Fraser, a Scotchman who remained for some years, taught English and astronomy. Louis Sabunji is reported to have been instructor of Turkish and Latin, but it is difficult to find much record of his services. Mr. Robertson, appointed by the Trustees to the professorship of mathematics and astronomy, resigned at the end of one year because it was too onerous a task to run a boys' school for the Scotch mission and also teach in the College.

When Doctors Van Dyck and Wortabet arrived in 1867 to teach chemistry and physiology respectively in addition to their work in the medical school, the Faculty was organized with Dr. Bliss as chairman and Dr. Wortabet as secretary. Faculty meetings were held weekly, "not," as President Bliss put it, "because there was always much business on hand but that we wished to establish the regularity of college life. All questions before us we quickly disposed of; Dr. Van Dyck would make a motion and Dr. Wortabet would second it, and I would call for a vote which was always carried unanimously."[1] The arrival in 1868 of Dr. George E. Post, Professor of Botany and Surgery did not disturb the happy unanimity of opinion.

It was the original policy of the College to use native teachers wherever possible, but at that time there were few such men of ability adequate to handle the work. Some of those engaged proved unsatisfactory and by 1870 it was apparent that additional American teachers would be necessary. Edward Van Dyck, son of Dr. Van Dyck, was on the field already and became a tutor for the year 1870-71. From America came Harvey Porter and the Rev. Edwin R. Lewis, M.D., the former as instructor in "the mental sciences and history," the latter as instructor in "the natural sciences." They were the first appointees who had had no previous knowledge of Arabic. Both men later became permanent members of the faculty, Mr. Porter serving for fifty-two years as Professor of Metaphysics, Logic and History, while Dr. Lewis became Professor of Chemistry and Geology. Henry Wortabet, son of Dr. Wortabet, joined the staff for the year 1871-72.

Of the original sixteen students, only five were in the graduating class of 1870, though three more were in the medical school, to which they transferred when it opened in 1867. The five of 1870 turned out astonishingly well, and brought great credit to their alma mater. One of them, Yaqub Sarruf, returned ten years later to teach Arabic at the College. In 1885 he went to Cairo, where, in cooperation with his friend Faris Nimr, of the class of '74, he founded two great publications—*Al Muḳattam* and *Al Muḳtataf*.

[1] Bliss, Reminiscences, p. 189.

The former, a newspaper, now has the largest circulation of any Arabic journal. The latter became the leading scientific magazine of the Arabic speaking world, a vital influence in the re-birth of Arabic culture. Sarruf remained its editor until his death in 1927.[2]

Bringing a class through to graduation was not accomplished without difficulties. The idea of going to school steadily for four years was new to Arab experience, and it was found necessary to put scholarship students on bond to remain for the full course. Furthermore, requirements were stiffer than were those to be found in other schools and strict discipline was necessary to prevent evasion and slackness. The institution of written examinations in 1869 was a horrid surprise to the students, for in other schools "examinations" had degenerated into a mere theatrical display, which was excused on the grounds that "the Jesuits began the practice and we must do the same to please and attract." Actually the fact that the College demanded serious work enhanced its reputation both among students and townspeople.

The reputation of the College was a very serious matter, for it was only too easily possible that the Turkish government might decide to close it as a useless foreign school. Rumors to that effect were not infrequent, particularly on such occasions as when a student from a prominent family was expelled for cheating. It was a great satisfaction when in the summer of 1869 Mr. Gharzuzi was made the official "Wakeel" or land agent for the College. Such an appointment had to be made by the Porte and was granted only to institutions officially recognized by the Government. Since the Syrian Protestant College had been originally founded without government permission it seemed most unlikely that it would be allowed a Wakeel, but the reputation established in three years, together with the exertion of some political influence in Constantinople, brought the desired results. Early in 1870 the Governor General, Raschid Pasha, paid the College a visit which impressed

[2] The members of the class were Kaysar Ghurayyib, M.D., English Hospital, Jaffa, d. 1919; Ibrahim Khairallah, M.D., teacher, Bahai missionary to United States, d. 1929; Na'um Mughabghab, teacher, chief of Climate Section in Egyptian Survey Department, d. 1919; Ibrahim Musawwir, in Egyptian Public Works, Chief of Translation Service, granted Imperial Order of Mejidiah, title of Bey, d. 1920; Yaqub Sarruf, Ph.D., 1890, see text above.

him very favorably. On leaving he said: "Gentlemen, if there is anything I can do for you, please always make it known."[3] That he meant what he said was shown by the rapid granting of permission to build on the new campus which was acquired that year.

The expenses of a college course were extremely difficult for a majority of the students to meet, even though fees at the S.P.C. were exceedingly low. From the opening of the College the policy was established of requiring every student to pay something even if it were not the full tuition, with the remainder to be made up from scholarship funds. To begin with, friends of the College would give the money to put a particular student through school. In 1868 the names of Arthington, Baker, Morgan and Church were noted by Mr. Dodge as providing funds for this purpose. Later on scholarships were endowed, but there seem never to have been enough of them. All through the records of the early years runs the urgent plea for more scholarship funds. In 1881 it was reported that the average annual contributions for scholarship purposes amounted to $1,199.29 and that "in addition to this sum the General Fund is liable for several permanent scholarships: viz,

The Wright-Drake Scholarship—January 11, 1875	of $1,200
The Mrs. A. M. Fahnestock Scholarship—February 11, 1875	of $1,000
The John Hall Scholarship—May 24, 1878 (Founded by the Young Men's Social and Benevolent Society of Dr. Hall's Church)	of $1,200
The Mrs. Franklin H. Delano Scholarship	of $1,200
The Mr. John Taylor Johnston Scholarship—November 5, 1879	of $1,000
The Thomas De Witt Scholarship—December 10, 1880 (Founded by Morris K. Jesup)	of $1,200
TOTAL	$6,800

Yet in this same report the statement is made: "The chief need of the College, at present, is declared to be additional scholarships. In a recent letter the fact was stated that fifteen boys from a single village in the mountains had to be refused admission, although they could pay ten liras each. (Total tuition was five liras, board and lodging twelve liras, total annual expense seventeen liras or about $75.00.) This was the more to be regretted as they lived in a

[3] D. S. Dodge's private notes.

particularly bigoted district which might have been directly reached and enlightened if these boys could have been received. Several afterwards entered the Jesuit College."

It may be imagined that the decision as to how much aid to give an Arab student was a difficult one to reach. Mr. Dodge's notes are full of references to arguments over ability to pay, bargaining attempted by students and parents even when funds were available, pointed boasts about "how my son would honor the institution if he were a student." The administration was wise, however, and was rarely misled into granting aid without careful examination of the facts.

When the facts were discovered, however, every effort was made to help the worthy student, either directly or by giving him work such as waiting on table, or tutoring Arabic. A letter from Beirut dated December 19, 1870 is interesting on this score. Mentioning the fact that 18 students entered the Literary Department that fall, it describes their financial arrangements:

> " 9 pay
> 2 paid for by Dr. Van D. and Fox
> One works on Concordance and pays (This was the Concordance to Van Dyck's Arabic Bible, prepared under Dr. Post's direction)
> One teaches Miss Jackson
> One teaches Mr. Porter
> One pays 700 piastres and rings bell
> One from Egypt, sent by Dr. Hogg
> Two board at home and pay tuition."

It was no mean feat to get students to work for their schooling, and it was never, until recent years, possible to persuade them to do much manual labor. Such work classified a man as a "fellah," a person of no caste, impossible for a college student to consider. Even to the present day the "dignity of manual toil" is not widely appreciated in Syria though the influence of the College has been amazing in overcoming the students' contempt for it.

2. THE COLLEGE CAMPUS

The first home of the College was a house rented from Butrus Bustani, whose school was next door. The building is still intact, standing close to what is now the compound of the American

Mission. After two years[4] the College moved to a much larger place with separate accommodations for a clinic and small hospital. Compared to the first quarters the new building appeared quite magnificent. As an old Arab said to Dr. Bliss: "I shall call you King Bliss, for your home is fit for the Sultan." D. S. Dodge, who reports the incident in his notes, says also that Doctors Van Dyck and Wortabet were delighted with the separate establishment for the Medical Department.

In 1870, during the Franco-Prussian War, the College moved once more, being forced by its growth to rent a still larger building in which it remained until its own campus was ready in 1872-73. This house was opposite the present Phara'un residence on the street which leads to the rear door of the Grand Serail. The hospital and clinic remained in their original quarters until 1871 when a much more satisfactory arrangement for them was made with the Prussian Hospital.

The Founders had from the first planned to put the new institution into quarters distinctly its own, but buying land in the Near East was not then, and is not now, done in a day. The fewer people who know about a deal the better the chances of success. A purchaser needs to hide from his right hand what his left hand doeth, and must permit himself to show interest only in property in which he is definitely not interested. Only thus can he hope to obtain a fair bargain in the long run.

With this in mind, it was decided by the Board of Managers and the Faculty to move entirely without knowledge of the Board of Managers or the Faculty. President Bliss and the Rev. D. Stuart Dodge were asked to work alone to find the site and conduct the negotiations. Money was at hand for the purchase, Mr. John J. Phelps of New York having made a gift of $5,000 to that end in the summer of 1867 while visiting his son-in-law, Mr. Dodge. That fact, too, was kept secret. President Bliss himself described their procedure as follows:

"For the space of a year or more, at the solicitations of property owners, or on the recommendation of friends, many places were

[4] The arrangement with Mr. Bustani was first made in 1865. It was actually in effect therefore for three years.

visited in different parts of Beirut. We rode everywhere through the city, looking as we rode. Finally, we saw the site where the College now stands and fell in love with it at sight, and immediately decided that we had found the finest site in all Beirut if not in all Syria.

". . . We employed one of the shrewdest natives, a broker, to obtain the property. He commenced at once by requesting us by no means to mention to a living soul that we desired to purchase it, or that we even knew the site. Weeks passed and nothing was heard from him. Finally he requested me to put myself casually in the way of the owner, whom I knew only by sight, but in no case to speak to him or recognize him. During many months I must have passed by his shop scores of times or met him on the street, but never looked at him. I was out not to see but to be seen,—not to court but to be courted.

"One day,—I remember it well,—we met on the crowded street. As usual, I looked right on; when I had passed on a few steps he said, 'Sir.' I turned, lifted my hat, and bowed. He continued, 'Mr. Gharzuzi tells me that you wish to buy some land for your school.' I replied, 'Mr. Gharzuzi is a land agent and wishes a commission. Good morning, sir.' I continued my walk to the first corner and then hastened to tell Mr. Gharzuzi what had happened. He clapped his hands, and said, 'Thank God, we have got him,' and so it was. After a few weeks the land was purchased."[5]

The payment was made on January 22, 1870, almost four years to a day, according to D. S. Dodge, after the site had first been selected. The Minutes of the Board of Trustees as far back as June 2nd, 1868, noted optimistically that "the opportunity has arrived . . . to secure the land." The $5,000 from J. J. Phelps, plus $1,000 from Mr. T——,[6] $1,000 from Mr. and Mrs. W. E. Dodge, and another $1,000 from D. S. Dodge were immediately forwarded to the treasurer of the Board of Managers, Mr. Heald, but the opportunity for using the money was long delayed.

No funds were on hand for building on the new property, but the faculty began at once to prepare plans. By April the rough

[5] Bliss, Reminiscences, pp. 190-1.

[6] The name is illegible; it is either Tirey, Ticey, Tiny or Terry.

design of College Hall was worked out, and in June Dr. Post had the Medical Building planned. Professor Dodge noted that locations for the different buildings had also been agreed upon, including the gate, president's house, hospital (if any), medical school, main building and dormitory. If one realizes that the land was innocent of any buildings, streets, or roads, being simply a place for refuse and a haunt of jackals, one can the better appreciate the vision that was required.

Professor Dodge went to America during the summer of 1870 to press a campaign for building funds and additional endowment for the literary department. At a meeting of the Trustees in November it was voted to secure a fund of $100,000 for buildings and another $100,000 for endowment. D. S. Dodge was appointed to take charge of the campaign in America and it was recommended that President Bliss go to England as soon as possible to seek funds there. It was not, however, until 1874 that the visit to England was accomplished.

By June 1, 1871, enough money had been collected in America to make it seem advisable to proceed at once with "the construction of the first and most important buildings, trusting that further subscriptions will provide for the other buildings."[7] Final plans were ordered prepared, and President Bliss was sent to Constantinople to consult with President Cyrus Hamlin of Robert College who had just completed the first building for that institution, superintending the whole procedure himself. The Trustees felt sure that Dr. Bliss must likewise become a builder, and wanted him to have the benefit of Dr. Hamlin's experience.

Preliminary work was begun during the summer and early fall. The ground for the main building (College Hall) was broken on November 28, 1871, five days after Professor Dodge's arrival with the plans. The corner-stone was laid on December 7, 1871, by William E. Dodge, treasurer of the Board of Trustees, who came from New York to be present for the ceremony. On January 23, 1872, ground was broken for the Medical Building.

At the College Hall service, President Bliss also laid a cornerstone of another sort. In his introductory remarks he defined the

[7] Minutes, Board of Trustees, June 1, 1871.

purpose of the College in words which will be repeated as long as the institution lives:

"This College is for all conditions and classes of men without regard to color, nationality, race or religion. A man white, black, or yellow; Christian, Jew, Mohammedan or heathen, may enter and enjoy all the advantages of this institution for three, four, or eight years; and go out believing in one God, in many gods, or in no God. But it will be impossible for anyone to continue with us long without knowing what we believe to be the truth and our reasons for that belief."[8]

It took almost two years to complete the three buildings in the original plan: College Hall, a small office and refectory building (a small part of the present Dodge Hall) and the Medical Hall. President Bliss records that it was not until March 13, 1874 that the risky task of hanging the bell in the tower of College Hall was accomplished, with most of the students pulling on the ropes. But the College moved into the new campus long before the tower clock and bell, a gift from William E. Dodge, were installed. The opening of the year 1873-74 found the buildings occupied. The Syrian Protestant College was ready for a new life.

For years after the purchase of the first property small segments of land adjacent to the original property or connecting it with other parcels were bought up as occasion offered. One central, key plot, known as the Fig Orchard, could not be reasonably acquired until 1899—a patient wait of twenty-nine years! Writing of these land purchases in 1913 in the Alumni magazine, *Al Kulliyah,* President-emeritus Bliss said: "Where the money came from for the most part I do not know; not from the Endowment Fund certainly. I am rather sure that the stubs of Dr. Dodge's private cheque book would reveal the secret."[9] Relatively few were the occasions on which this great-hearted man openly gave money; his and his family's generosity have been matched only by their modesty.

The completion of the first three buildings was followed shortly by the construction of an observatory, completed in 1874 and enlarged in 1880. It was known as the Lee Observatory, in honor of

[8] Bliss, op. cit., p. 198.

[9] Al Kulliyah, 5:1, p. 9 (November 1913).

Mr. Henry Lee of Manchester, England, who had given £150 for the building. Dr. Van Dyck was delighted at having at last adequate facilities for his meteorological observations and instruction in astronomy. The major part of the equipment in the observatory was his own property, which he loaned to the College for many years, adding to it whenever the income from his medical practice was sufficient to do so and still buy apparatus for the medical school and chemistry laboratory. The astronomical instruments were bought from him for £500 in 1883.

A house for the president had been among the early plans for construction but funds did not become available for it until 1877. Then Mr. Frederick Marquand donated $5,000 for that purpose, but because of the Russo-Turkish War, which threatened for a time to involve England, Mr. Marquand requested a postponement of construction. In spite of assurances that Syria was unlikely to become involved, the work was delayed until after the peace treaty of San Stefano was signed in 1878. Then "Marquand House," as it is still known, was erected and was occupied by the president in the fall of 1880.

3. THE PREPARATORY SCHOOL

The arrangement with Butrus Bustani, whereby his "National School" should take care of preparatory work for the S.P.C., was not very satisfactory in practice. The chief difficulty arose from the fact that the College preparatory students, while living under the same roof and attending the same classes as Mr. Bustani's regular pupils, were yet subject to different rules and regulations. Discipline was very hard to maintain, to say the least. After two years of slowly developing friction, the plan of cooperation was given up and the College moved to the more commodious quarters which its growth had necessitated.

From 1868 until 1872 the College tried to get along without a preparatory department, or at least without taking in boarding students of preparatory grade. The training of students for college entrance was left to the numerous schools established in Beirut and its vicinity. But as the College grew in reputation, students began to come from a distance for whom preliminary schooling was necessary. The College had no boarding facilities for them, nor could many of the Beirut schools take care of them, either physically or educationally. "It is a matter of regret," said President Bliss in his annual report of 1872, "that the various schools in Syria do not sufficiently prepare students to enter the Literary—much less the Medical—Department of the College. It is especially difficult to provide for applicants who come from a distance and must be received into a preliminary boarding school. . . . Last year a number of pupils from distant places, anxious to enter the College, but unprepared, were turned away with the means in hand and asking to remain to complete the necessary preparation. There are now several applying from other cities, whom we shall also be compelled to reject, unless we can make some provision for them."

The faculty therefore recommended that a preparatory department should be organized and should be permitted to occupy space in the new buildings then under construction. The Board of Managers was willing only that the experiment be tried for the year 1872-73. It was found to be so successful, however, that they voted in 1873 to continue preparatory work on the College campus. This action was "cordially approved" by the Trustees at their fall meeting.

No arrangements had been made for a teaching staff for the preparatory department, the hope being expressed that advanced students might be used for instruction purposes. It soon became apparent, however, that this plan would not work. Such students were not qualified to teach in English and because of the increasing number of students who did not speak Arabic as their native tongue, as well as the difficulty of securing adequate texts in Arabic, English was rapidly becoming essential as the language of instruction. Professor Dodge had found it necessary to return to America in 1874, leaving the English Department sadly undermanned, and Professor Isaac M. Hall was sent out in 1875 to take his place. During the same year the study of English was made obligatory upon all students. Within the year it was found necessary to constitute the preparatory school as a separate department and to secure a teacher from America who would devote his whole

ORIGINAL FACULTY OF THE SYRIAN PROTESTANT COLLEGE

Standing, L. to R.: D. S. Dodge, Geo. E. Post, Edwin R. Lewis, Harvey Porter. Seated: C. V. A. Van Dyck, Daniel Bliss, John Wortabet

COLLEGE HALL, THE FIRST BUILDING

ALLEGHENY COLLEGE LIBRARY

THE FIRST GRADUATING CLASS (1870)
L. to R.: Sarruf, Khairallah, Ghurayyib, Mr. Fraser, Mughabghab, Musawwir

THE ORIGINAL MEDICAL BUILDING

ALLEGHENY COLLEGE LIBRARY

time to that work. Joshua B. Crane, a graduate of Brown University, went out in the fall of 1876 to fill the position, with the title of Tutor of English. His presence made it possible to establish the practice of using English as the principal language of instruction in both the preparatory and collegiate departments. (The Medical School continued to give its work in Arabic until 1883.)

Mr. Crane has the distinction of being the first of a long series of young men, recently graduated from college, who have been sent out as assistants or tutors (now called "staffites" at Beirut) on a definite three year contract. His salary was to be £100 a year "with expenses both ways paid, and board and lodging in the College except during the summer vacation."[10]

The definite organization of the preparatory department provided the College with a branch which has ever since proved of great value, and which, within three years of its establishment, outstripped its fellows in the number of students enrolled. The annual report for the year 1879 shows an enrollment of 38 in the preparatory department, compared to 33 in the collegiate and 37 in the medical sections. By the year 1880 new accommodations for the preparatory school were an absolute necessity.

In the summer and fall of that year, an extension was made of the small building containing the refectory and offices, which by that time was flanked by "the new, broad avenue constructed by Midhat Pasha" (now Rue Bliss), the land for which was donated by the College. The length of the building was increased and a second story was added. "This," according to the Trustees' Minutes, "supplies a noble study room capable of seating 100 scholars, two large dormitories with fifty beds, and several rooms for recitations, tutors and a much needed reception room for visitors. The building has a small tower and presents a somewhat irregular shape but makes a fine addition to the College group."

Walter S. Lewis (not to be confused with Professor Edwin R. Lewis), was made principal of the Preparatory Department on the expiration of Mr. Crane's contract in 1879 but when his health failed after one year of service he was succeeded by Frederick J. Bliss, eldest son of President Bliss. Under young Bliss' guidance

[10] Minutes, Board of Trustees, June 1878.

and that of his successor, Franklin E. Hoskins, the preparatory school prospered as did the College. Such pressure was put on the available accommodations that the construction of yet another building was required. D. Stuart Dodge once more proved to be a friend in need by providing more than £4000 for the erection in 1884-85 of the Ada Dodge Memorial Hall, in memory of his daughter. Attached to the earlier building, Dodge Hall gave ample space for the needs of the College for several years. It accommodated the preparatory department until 1898, when the highest class was moved into Jesup Hall. In 1900 the entire department was transferred to the newly constructed Daniel Bliss Hall.

4. THE MEDICAL SCHOOL

Medical work at the Syrian Protestant College got under way a year later than the literary department, but it developed very rapidly and bade fair to outstrip its associate. Medicine in the Near East had been in an unbelievably backward state for generations. The demand for competent physicians and surgeons was consequently immense. When a good medical school was established it was only natural that it should attract great attention and arouse keen interest among all who learned of it. The medical work was early supported by subscriptions in England, where a Mr. John Heugh of Tunbridge Wells had originated a plan for the establishment of medical professorships. Dr. George Post built up an endowment of $11,500 for the chair of surgery in the year which elapsed between his appointment to the post in November 1867 and his occupation of it in the fall of 1868. In 1873, his distinguished father, Dr. Alfred C. Post, established a fund of $18,000 to be used at a later date, with accumulated interest, "for the purchase or erection of a Hospital in Beirut in connection with the Medical Department of the College or for such other purposes as the Donor or his son, Professor George E. Post, M.D., may decide."[11]

In 1867 there were practically no medical text books in Arabic. The professors in the new medical school were faced with the

[11] Minutes, November 11, 1873. By 1881 the Post Hospital Fund amounted to $32,000 and part of the income was being used for lectureships.

necessity of writing their own texts, and for the first few years their students were obliged "to copy the manuscripts of the works which were then in course of preparation by their teachers."[12] In 1870 the "Theodore Publication Fund" was established by William A. Booth, president of the Board of Trustees, in memory of his young son, to assist in getting these and other manuscripts into print. Thereafter the students were relieved of their heavy copy work.

The Beirut medical school required from the very beginning a four-year course of study. At that time few medical schools, even in America, offered more than a three-year course,—Harvard being one of the few exceptions. It is apparent that there could never have been any question about the intention to do a high quality of medical work at Beirut and results have shown that the intention was from the first translated into accomplishment.

The first class to graduate from the medical school was that of 1871, containing six members.[13] Of the requirements which they had to meet before getting their diplomas the President's annual report dated June 27, 1872, contained an interesting statement. It is well worth quoting at length:

"The method and thoroughness of the examination produced a salutary effect both upon the students of the College and upon the community at large. In accordance with the regulations of the Institution, all members of the Class were examined by the Medical Faculty upon the studies of the entire course of four years. The answers at this time, both oral and written, in connection with the standard of scholarship attained at previous examinations, determined, in the case of each student, whether he should be allowed to appear before the final examining Board.

"The examination by the Faculty resulted in requiring two members of the class to spend another year in studying the branches in which they were especially deficient and they accord-

[12] Sa'di, Lutfi M., Al Hakim C. V. A. Van Dyck, Isis, No. 73, pp. 31-2, May 1937. Dr. Sa'di, a graduate of the A.U.B. Medical School, is now a practising physician in Detroit, Michigan. For much of the material in this section the writer is indebted to Dr. Sa'di's research.

[13] These were Selim Diab, Selim Fureij, Nasir Hatim, Yusuf Hajjar, Rashid Shukrallah and Shibly Shumeil.

ingly entered the present graduating Class and will present themselves again for examination in due course.

"The Board of Examiners for Diplomas was composed of the Medical Faculty and Dr. Brigstocke, as Lecturer, with the three Medical Gentlemen appointed by the Board of Managers, viz: Drs. Metheny, Murad Bey and Pestalozzi. . . .

"The nine candidates were examined one by one and at the close of each examination a secret ballot was taken. Six young men were successful and three were rejected. The latter could not understand how they should have passed the previous examination before the Faculty and fail now. The reason is apparent: The Examining Board cannot take into account the former College standing of any student, but must decide upon his merits from his ability to answer their questions.

"Those who did not obtain a 'Diploma' were, for a time, sorely disappointed and indignant, but the College has risen in popular estimation. It is now felt that we are rigid and impartial in our requirements and will confer the honors of the Institution only upon those who deserve them. . . .

"The six young Physicians, who were graduated, readily found professional employment, and one or two of them are already engaged in extended and remunerative practice."

To teach medicine and surgery without a hospital or clinical material was naturally an impossibility for men with the standards of the Beirut medical faculty. For a few years the College maintained a small hospital and dispensary in its rented quarters. For the few patients who could be accommodated the students themselves took turns acting as nurses. It was recognized as a makeshift arrangement pending the acquisition of a satisfactory hospital building, which would probably have been long delayed by the difficulty in acquiring the necessary funds. Fortunately a happy development made a new hospital building unnecessary. It is described thus by Dr. Sa'di in his biography of Dr. Post:[14]

"Now, it so happened that during the early sixties of the 19th Century the Knights of St. John had built, at Beirut, on an excellent site near the west end of the town, a fine and spacious hospital.

[14] Sa'di, Lutfi M.—Life and Works of G. E. Post, Isis, No. 77, pp. 392-3, May 1938.

In this 'Prussian Hospital,' as it was commonly called, the Directress and nurses were German Deaconesses of the Kaiserswerth Sisterhood, and the medical officer in charge was a German physician, Dr. Lorange, descendant of French Huguenots who had emigrated to Germany after the revocation of the Edict of Nantes. This arrangement did not work well: there were clashes between Dr. Lorange and the Deaconesses; complaints were made by both parties; the Knights upheld the Deaconesses; and the upshot of the matter was that Dr. Lorange's connection with the Hospital came to an end.

"This was an extraordinary opportunity for the Syrian Protestant College, and it was promptly seized. The College offered to the Knights of St. John the gratuitous services of its medical faculty in exchange for the privilege of using, for the instruction of medical students, the clinical material afforded by the out-patient department of the hospital and by the public wards of its in-patient department. The Knights were disposed to favor this proposal and Dr. Post was sent to Berlin to represent the College in the discussions required for settlement of the details of the agreement that was reached in due time to the advantage of all parties concerned. This agreement continued in force until America joined the Allies against the Germans towards the close of the Great War of 1914-18." (Actually it terminated January 2, 1918, eight months after America's entrance into the War. Six months notification was required by the contract. The date was the 2nd of January because Sister Anna would not permit such a thing to happen on New Year's Day. The arrangement was first made in 1871 and ratified in 1872.)

The advantages of this connection for the College are too obvious to need mention, especially when it is noted that the hospital was but five minutes' walk from the new campus, that it was fairly well equipped and could house more than sixty in-patients. From the Hospital's point of view the benefits, too, were numerous. Chief among them was, of course, the medical staff acquired. For one doctor of somewhat doubtful capacity, three men were substituted whose quality would have been recognized anywhere, in any country. Doctors Van Dyck, Wortabet and Post were men of whom the world knows too little. It was the unbelievable good fortune of the College to have in charge of its medical school from the start men of such unusual qualifications as to knowledge, capacity, skill, breadth of interest and real vision.

Cornelius Van Alen Van Dyck (1818-95) has already been mentioned as the translator of the Bible into Arabic, a task which alone could secure his fame. The son of a New York country practitioner, Dr. Henry L. Van Dyck, and his wife, Catherine Van Alen, both of pure Dutch stock, Cornelius attended Kinderhook Academy and studied medicine under his father, before going to Jefferson Medical College in Philadelphia, from which he received his M.D. in 1839. In 1840 he was sent to Syria by the American Board as a medical missionary of the Dutch Reformed Church, and after studying theology he was ordained by his colleagues. He was, par excellence, an educator and scientist, establishing schools, writing and reviving numerous books in Arabic, of which language he made himself complete master. His influence on the written Arabic was great. Some years after his death, a learned Moslem Sheikh of Al Azhar University, Cairo, told Van Dyck's daughter: "Your father taught me, by his published writings, that it is possible to write good Arabic, correct in grammar and in idiom, in a style so simple and so clear as to be easily understood by any intelligent reader, whether learned or unlearned."[15]

Dr. Van Dyck visited America but twice after going to Syria. On the first occasion (1854) he acquired an interest in and knowledge of microscopy. On the second (1865-67), made in connection with the printing of the Bible, he found time to study ophthalmology and qualified himself to teach this subject, so important in the eye-tortured Near East. His work in the S.P.C. began as professor of Internal Medicine and General Pathology with Ophthalmology provisionally attached. He also taught Chemistry until Professor Lewis arrived. Thereafter, he offered courses in Astronomy and Meteorology, and directed the observatory. Astronomy was Dr. Van Dyck's hobby and to it he devoted most of his leisure. "He inaugurated the practice of taking and recording regular meteorological observations at stated intervals each day. Before

[15] Sa'di, L. M., C. V. A. Van Dyck, Isis, No. 73, p. 36.

long, arrangements were made with the Turkish authorities to send telegraphic reports of these observations twice daily to the Imperial Observatory at Constantinople, whence they were communicated, in due course, to the Imperial Meteorological Bureau at Vienna."[16]

In addition to these occupations, Dr. Van Dyck was Director of the Mission Press, supervising all publications and especially new editions of his Bible. He was also editor of the Mission's weekly Arabic paper, the *Neshrah*. Still he found time to write numerous Arabic texts on Chemistry, Internal Medicine, Physical Diagnosis, Trigonometry and Astronomy, while translating with a critical commentary, the great Al Razi's (850-932) classical Arabic treatise on small-pox and measles. His private medical practice was large at all times. Small wonder is it that he was widely known as "Al-Hakim," a title applying equally to a physician and a philosopher.

In comparison to Van Dyck, Dr. John Wortabet (1827-1908) does not shine with such brilliant luster though he, too, was an able physician, a distinguished Arabic scholar and a devoted missionary and teacher. He was the son of a former Armenian priest, Gregory Wortabet, who was in 1827 a friend of the famous Dr. William Goodell of the American Board. John Wortabet was born in Sidon, and studied medicine in America and theology in Scotland. Returning thence to Syria he was, in May 1853, ordained in the village of Hasbeiya, where he remained as pastor for about five years. Returning to Scotland he published a valuable work, "The Religions of Syria," which was for many years the only authoritative book on the subject. He was sent back to Aleppo as representative of a Scottish missionary society and was serving there when he was chosen in 1866 to be professor of Anatomy and Physiology in the Beirut Medical School. He asked for a year in England and America to qualify himself for the position and was appointed by the Trustees in October 1866 with the understanding that the appointment should be effective as soon as he was considered qualified. In America he continued the study of medicine, receiving his M.D. from the New York University Medical College

[16] Ibid., p. 33.

on March 1, 1867. He was on hand for the opening of the medical school in Beirut in the fall of 1867.

For fifteen years Dr. Wortabet devoted his full time to teaching, taking on from time to time additional courses as need demanded. His outstanding characteristics as a teacher were recalled many years later by a former student to have been his thoroughness and persistence. Dr. Charles A. Webster, who knew Dr. Wortabet in the years before his death in 1908, writes that he "most highly respected and esteemed him."[17] Dr. Henry H. Jessup, pillar of the Syrian Mission, said of him that "he was a man of great industry, an exact scholar, and successful physician. He was especially kind to the sick poor, and had a wide reputation throughout Syria."[18] Dr. Jessup reported that in June of 1867, immediately after Dr. Wortabet's appointment to the medical school, "I endeavored to persuade (him) . . . to accept the pastorship of the Beirut Church, but he absolutely refused."[19] He was unquestionably the one native of Syria who possessed the necessary endowments for that difficult pastorship at the time. It was not until 1890 that another qualified Syrian was found.

Dr. Wortabet resigned from the medical faculty in 1882 but continued teaching as a lecturer at several periods. From 1882-85 he taught Pathology and Anatomy; from 1885-86 and 1889-90 he lectured on Practice of Medicine; in 1895-96, during Dr. Graham's absence from the country, he gave the course on Internal Medicine and took charge of the clinical work of the hospital. Some years later he became the first chairman of the executive committee which established the Lebanon Hospital for Mental Diseases at Asfuriyeh.

In addition to preparing texts on Anatomy, Physiology and Public Health in Arabic (1873-81), Dr. Wortabet took the time, with the aid of his son Henry, who was a member of the College staff in 1871, to compile an exhaustive Arabic-English dictionary. This thorough and scholarly work was of the greatest value and required numerous editions, enlargements, and revisions to satisfy

[17] Personal letter to the writer, June 2, 1940.

[18] Jessup, Henry H., "Fifty Three Years in Syria," 2 vols. (Fleming H. Revell, 1910), vol. II, p. 781.

[19] Ibid., Vol. I, pp. 312-13.

the constant demands for it by students. The latest revision by Dr. Harvey Porter, who collaborated with the Wortabets on the original, appeared in the summer of 1913, four years after the author's death.

George Edward Post (1839-1909) made his first contact with the Near East through the mission field, as did his colleagues. The son of a distinguished surgeon who was for many years professor of surgery in the University Medical College of New York, George Post apparently planned from boyhood to be a missionary. His theological training at Union Seminary was taken concurrently with his medical work at the University Medical College. The latter course was completed in 1860, but Post was not ordained by the Fourth Presbytery of New York until 1861.

The Civil War prevented Dr. Post from going at once to the mission field, and for two years he served as chaplain and surgeon with the 15th Regiment of New York Volunteers. The application characteristic of his later life was shown during this period, when he worked for and acquired his doctorate in Dental Surgery at the Baltimore College of Dentistry while fulfilling his duties with the army.

On November 28th, 1863, Dr. Post was sent as a medical missionary to Syria where he was stationed at Tripoli. After four years of service, during which he became proficient in Arabic, his health became poor and he returned to the United States. He had been nominated for the Chair of Surgery at the S.P.C. in November 1867, but his release from the American Board was not finally obtained until January 17, 1868. Dr. Post immediately accepted the new appointment and devoted the rest of that year until the fall to raising an endowment for the Chair of Surgery. On November 30th he sailed for Beirut where he commenced at once his work as professor of Surgery, Materia Medica, and Botany.

Like both his colleagues, Dr. Post was of necessity and inclination a prolific writer in Arabic, both on scientific and religious subjects. In addition to texts on Botany (1871), Surgery (1873), and Materia Medica (1874) he had the patience and skill necessary for the compilation of a monumental botanical study "The Flora of Syria and Palestine" (1884), which still remains a standard work.[20] His first Arabic book was a treatise on Vertebrate Animals (1869). From 1873-77, despite his other duties, he directed the compilation of an Arabic Concordance to the Van Dyck Arabic Bible, to the accuracy of which Dr. George Sarton of Harvard attests.[21] During approximately the same period Dr. Post edited a medical journal for graduates of the medical school. From 1894-1901 he translated and edited a two volume Dictionary of the Bible to accompany the Concordance. Throughout his connection with the College he was curator of the museum and built up its collections from nothing to a highly exemplary condition.

"Surgery was Post's chosen vocation and for it he had conspicuous natural aptitude. He was a bold, skillful and resourceful operator, very dextrous in his manipulations and he enjoyed his work."[22] He was a very skillful lithotomist and the extensive collection of vesical calculi in the American University of Beirut surgical museum is a tribute to his numerous operations of this type, which totalled at least 700 up to the turn of the century. The field of his operations was practically unlimited, even extending to surgery of the eye, in the removal of cataracts from which he was particularly successful.

Architecture was a hobby of this indefatigable man and in it he shared some of the talent of his distinguished cousin, George B. Post. The University is indebted to him for the design and for the superintendence of construction of the old Medical Hall and Post Hall. Of the latter fine building he was the sole architect. After his plans had been accepted by the faculty, they were sent, at the request of the Trustees, to New York to be submitted for examination and testing to a professional architect. The architect pronounced them thoroughly sound and stated that they could not be improved. Post Hall stands today as Dr. Post originally designed it.[23]

[20] The Flora was published in English by the College in 1883 and again in 1896. In 1932 a two-volume edition, revised and enlarged by John E. Dinsmore of the American Colony, Jerusalem, was published by the A.U.B.

[21] Bibliography attached to Dr. Sa'di's article, Isis, No. 77, p. 412 (1938).

[22] Sa'di, L. M., Life and Works of G. E. Post, p. 393.

[23] A statement was published in Beirut to the effect that Dr. Post also designed and supervised the construction of the Children's Pavilion, the Eye Pavilion and the Wo-

Dr. Post was in large measure the College diplomat. It was he who went to Berlin to make the hospital arrangements. It was likewise he who in 1903 was sent to Constantinople to reinforce the diplomatic pressures which finally succeeded in persuading the Ottoman Government to send an Imperial examining commission to Beirut so that medical students might obtain their diplomas without having to go to Constantinople for examination. President Bliss had tried in 1871 on his visit to Constantinople to persuade the Porte to allow the College to give diplomas fully recognized by the Imperial Medical College. This was not permitted, though the College was subsequently constituted "a Branch of the Imperial College—graduates to stand on the same footing as those of the Imperial College—our students to go to Constantinople, remain and return at the expense of the Porte—to be examined there and receive their Diplomas without paying the usual fee of £5.—to have the right to enter the Military or Navy Medical Service, but not to be forced into either."[24]

The matter of the Imperial diploma was an important one, for without it the medical graduates were subject to persecution by licensed competitors and even to arrest by the authorities. Subhi Pasha, the Governor General, did not cause any trouble when in 1872 he was shown the diploma of Ibrahim Mesharka, but he may have been awed by the size of it, the red seal and blue ribbon, and the writing in Latin and Arabic. In 1873 however, Asa'ad Haddad was haled into court by four physicians on a charge of malpractice, for opening an abscess of a diseased hip-joint. Khourshid Pasha tried to disallow favorable witnesses before the Mejliss, but failed, possibly because Asa'ad happened to have numerous powerful friends.[25] It was, however, an uncomfortable situation, which might be subject to too frequent repetition. The final settlement

man's Pavilion. Actually these were designed respectively by Dr. Moore, Dr. Webster, and Dr. Dorman, each of whom had charge of the construction of his own project. The medical professors were all architects and contractors as occasion demanded.

[24] President's Annual Report, June 27, 1872, pp. 142-3. The statement is the summary of a recommendation from the Imperial Medical College to the Grand Vizier, which was shown to the American Minister in Constantinople on February 16, and reported by him to Beirut. The necessary Vizierial Order was not given until 1873 or '74, and the arrangement never worked satisfactorily.

[25] Both incidents related by D. S. Dodge in his copious notes.

of the matter, after thirty-three years of intermittent negotiation, must have been a great relief to the College.

Another medical problem of a different sort was the difficulty at first experienced in acquiring cadavers for dissection. Moslem law prohibited such dissection, on the belief that the dead retain their senses.[26] The matter was discussed in faculty meeting on January 6, 1869 when Dr. Post reported that he was trying to stimulate a little quiet grave robbing but was having difficulty because of fear of a public outbreak or of the authorities. On February 15 of the same year, however, Mr. Dodge reported with some enthusiasm that "we have more 'subjects' offered than we want," and went on to tell of a "mountain Princess" being taken from her tomb by overzealous "helpers." She was returned to it in short order and without untoward incident.

In 1872 a two-year course in pharmacy was added to the medical school, thanks to the additional facilities offered by the Prussian Hospital. Permission was secured for the pharmacy graduates to get their Imperial diplomas in Constantinople in the same manner as the medical graduates. The granting of these Vizierial orders, together with the occupation of the new campus and the arrangement with the Prussian Hospital expanded the appeal of the medical school so that its enrollment increased markedly.

Professor Dodge noted that the number of students entering the College in 1871 was but eighteen compared to forty-four in 1872. The greater proportion of this increase was in the literary department, but many medical students took their first training in that part of the College. They were encouraged to do so by the action of the Board of Managers in June 1872 which halved the medical tuition for graduates of the literary department. In December of 1872, of a total of fifty medical students who had attended the College, fifteen had come from the literary department. Thus was a broad basic education for doctors encouraged. The principle has since been recognized by all first-class medical schools.

It seems incredible that a good medical school could be maintained with only three professors, but for a number of years Van

[26] Mr. Dodge noted that this belief probably originated with the Prophet's statement: "Men are asleep, and at death they awake."

Dyck, Post, and Wortabet carried the full load in addition to their other duties. There was considerable danger of their overworking and as early as 1869 Mr. Booth, president of the Board of Trustees, while visiting in Beirut warned against putting too much pressure on the medical faculty. Mr. Dodge's notes often refer anxiously to the health of Dr. Van Dyck or Dr. Post and to the terrible situation the College would face if either of them had to give up his work.

In 1872 the situation was somewhat relieved by the appointment of Dr. Richard W. Brigstocke, an English medical practitioner of Beirut, as lecturer on "Obstetrics, Diseases of Women and Children, and Medical Jurisprudence." The acquisition of good hospital facilities and a proper nursing staff and dispensary was also a great improvement. In 1880 Dr. William Thomson Van Dyck, third son of C. V. A. Van Dyck, joined the staff as Lecturer on Materia Medica, Hygiene and Zoology. The younger Van Dyck had been a student in the S. P. C. Medical School from 1875-78, but had received his M.D. from the University Medical College in New York just before accepting his new appointment.

Development of the medical school proceeded normally under the increased staff until in 1881-82 there was a total of 62 students. But at the end of that year an event occurred which nearly wrote "finis" to the medical work of the College. The results were far-reaching, one of the more immediate being that Arabic was given up as the language of instruction for medicine.

At commencement in 1882 Professor Edwin R. Lewis was selected to give the annual address to the students. The title of his address is not now known, but in it, according to the Trustees minutes, "he appeared so distinctly to favor the theories of Darwin, that several of his associates and of the Managers of the College were constrained to express alarm at the utterance of such views by a Professor of the Institution."[27] The alarm was so violent that the matter was submitted to the Trustees, whose president, Mr. Booth, expressed the opinion "that neither the Board of Managers, the Faculty, nor the Board of Trustees would be willing to have anything that favors what is called 'Darwinism' talked of or taught in the College." After examining a copy of the address,

[27] Special meeting, December 1, 1882.

hearing Dr. Alfred C. Post's report on its implications, and listening to a report by Dr. Henry H. Jessup, of the Mission, on the repercussions in Syria, the Board voted to accept Professor Lewis' resignation, which had been offered.

Opinion on the subject in Beirut apparently was not unanimous, for the two Van Dycks, Dr. Brigstocke, and later Dr. Wortabet all resigned in sympathy with Dr. Lewis. This left Dr. Post as the only full-time professor, though Dr. Wortabet agreed to remain for a time as a lecturer until a substitute could be found. Apparently some fifteen medical students showed their disapproval by "insubordinate conduct" and were suspended. During the rest of the year it was reported that Dr. Van Dyck and Dr. Lewis attempted "to sustain the rebellious students of the Medical Department by instructing them outside the College." Finally, however, almost all of them returned "after signing the apology and pledge of good behavior, demanded by the Faculty and Board of Managers."[28]

At commencement in 1883 Professor Porter gave the annual address, dealing with the intellectual sciences, "the high position and office of the human mind" and stating definitely that "by no possible theory can it be regarded as a naturalistic growth from animal instincts." Rev. Dr. Dennis, Secretary of the Board of Managers, reported that "the address was received with applause and was regarded as a satisfactory antidote to the statements made by Dr. Lewis at the previous Commencement."

The controversy nearly ruined the Medical School, and for a year there was some doubt about the wisdom of maintaining it. However, late in 1883, such unanimously favorable expression from the Managers, the missionaries and other friends of the College had been received by the Trustees, that they proceeded at once to fill the vacancies on the faculty. Dr. Charles F. Dight of Ann Arbor, Dr. Thomas W. Kay of Baltimore and Dr. Robert J. Neal of Ann Arbor were sent out in time for the opening of the year

[28] Minutes, January 16, 1884. It should be noted that the faculty resignations were probably based on principles of "academic freedom" rather than on agreement with Dr. Lewis. Dr. Van Dyck maintained his connection with the Mission till his death. W. T. Van Dyck returned to teach in 1915.

1883-84. The Medical School was again on its feet after a serious internal ailment.

The new professors, however, knew no Arabic and could hardly be expected to learn it in time to begin their duties. The only solution of the problem they posed was to make English the language of instruction for the medical work, as it already was in the collegiate and preparatory departments. Incidentally, by that time the growth of medical literature had become so rapid and the original textbooks were becoming so outmoded that keeping up the Arabic translations promised to become a hopeless task. It is probable that the change in language would have had to come within a short time, even had the faculty revision not taken place. As it was, it appeared that the first phase of the College development had reached an abrupt end, to be succeeded by a new period of progress.

IV. RELIGION IN THE COLLEGE

THE SYRIAN PROTESTANT COLLEGE was never under the control of any mission board, though the majority of the local Managers were members of the Syrian Mission (Presbyterian after 1870). Nevertheless it was and is a missionary institution in the sense that it has always sought to create in its students an appreciation of and devotion to the values of the Christian life. By precept as well as example it has taken pains to bear out Daniel Bliss' dedicatory statement, which ends: "It will be impossible for anyone to continue with us long without knowing what we believe to be the truth and our reasons for that belief."

Though the College never sought to force conversion upon its students and received with equal favor Moslem, Jew, Druze, Maronite, Orthodox or Catholic, it provided every opportunity for the students to learn the truth as Protestant Christianity saw it. Attendance at morning and evening prayers was required of all students, as it was at the Sunday preaching service. All boarding students attended regular Bible classes on Sunday afternoons and a midweek prayer meeting. The courses in moral philosophy and metaphysics taught by the President were required of all seniors, and even in courses whose content was not specifically religious, Christian principles were emphasized wherever possible. Thus studies in English often utilized translation from the English Bible, which frequently led to discussion of fundamental religious problems. Dr. Bliss seems to have had a particularly happy facility at provoking such discussions without forcing them.

As D. S. Dodge noted, however, after describing one of Dr. Bliss' classes, "so much must depend on the personal intercourse with the teachers." All the early professors, like Dodge himself, Bliss, Post, Lewis, Van Dyck and Wortabet, were ministers as well as teachers and were trained in theology. Younger assistants were not always so well prepared and great care had to be exercised in choosing them. Mr. Fraser, for example, failed to measure up, and was permitted to leave the staff in 1870 because of his unorthodox

MARQUAND HOUSE
(The President's Home)

COLLEGE HALL AND ADA DODGE HALL
(Old photo)

ALLEGHENY COLLEGE LIBRARY

JESUP HALL
(Now used as a medical dormitory)

STUDENTS COMING FROM THE CHAPEL

ALLEGHENY COLLEGE LIBRARY

religious views, which Mr. Dodge charitably explained on the grounds of the man's unhappy early experience with narrow beliefs in Scotland.

The unfortunate Lewis affair of 1882 impelled the Trustees to require the signing of a "declaration of principles," provided for in Article VIII of the Constitution but never theretofore demanded. They considered this declaration to be "an indispensable pre-requisite to entering upon the functions of 'adjunct-professor'," the lowest permanent faculty rank.[1] They requested the Board of Managers to prepare such a creed, which embraced "the divine inspiration, authority, and sufficiency of the Holy Scriptures: the right and duty of private judgment in the interpretation of the Holy Scriptures: the unity of the Godhead and the Trinity of the Persons therein: the utter depravity of human nature in consequence of the fall: the incarnation of the Son of God, His work of atonement for the sins of mankind, and His mediatorial intercession and reign: the justification of the sinner by faith alone: the work of the Holy Spirit in the conversion and sanctification of the sinner: the immortality of the soul, the resurrection of the body, the judgment of the world by our Lord Jesus Christ, with the blessedness of the righteous, and the eternal punishment of the wicked: the divine institution of the Christian ministry and the obligation and perpetuity of the ordinances of baptism and the Lord's Supper, and the sacredness of the Lord's Day which is to be duly honored: the whole body of evangelical doctrine as contained in the inspired Word of God, and represented in the consensus of Protestant creeds, as opposed to the erroneous teachings of the Romish and Eastern Churches. We also declare our hearty sympathy with and pledge our active cooperation in advancing the chief aim of this institution which as a missionary agency is to train up young men in the knowledge of Christian truth, and if possible, secure their intelligent and hearty acceptance of the Bible as the Word of God and of Christ as the only Saviour and at the same time inspire them with high moral purposes and consecrated aims in life.

[1] Trustees Minutes, January 29, 1883.

"We further pledge ourselves to the inculcation of sound and reverent views of the relation of God to the natural universe, as its Creator and Supreme Ruler, and to give instruction in the special department assigned to us, in the spirit and method best calculated to conserve the teachings of revealed truth and demonstrate the essential harmony between the Bible and all true science and philosophy.

"In view of the responsibility of the instruction of the young and the influence of personal example, we recognize the importance of unusual care in maintaining a high standard of Christian consistency in life and conduct with reference to all the moral questions of the day."[2]

With regard to instructors and other appointees not on the permanent faculty, the Trustees strongly recommended, "that only those should be nominated or employed, who are—if possible—not merely members of Evangelical Churches, but in full sympathy with the spiritual and missionary aims of the College and with the religious doctrines and sentiments of those who direct or support it, as well as the wide Christian constituency it represents. No effort should be spared to make this institution—what it was originally established to be—a fountain of sound and Scriptural teaching in science, morals and religion:—and the Board of Trustees would especially emphasize the importance, at the present time, of inculcating right views respecting the observance of the Sabbath, the inspiration of the Scriptures, Temperance, and the various phases of modern scientific inquiry."[3]

For a number of years the "Declaration of Principles" was signed by all new appointees to the permanent staff. It gradually fell into disuse, and in 1902 Howard S. Bliss stated that the requirement of it was contrary to his conscientious convictions. He implied that if he were to be elected to succeed his father as president, he would prefer to have the Declaration eliminated from the requirements for professorial candidacy. The Board of Trustees then went on record as follows: *"Whereas,* it is the conviction of the Board of Trustees that the Evangelical and missionary character of the Col-

[2] Quoted in H. H. Jessup's "Fifty Three Years in Syria," Vol. II, pp. 707-8.

[3] Minutes, January 29, 1883.

lege is adequately guarded by the careful selection of suitable candidates for Professors and Instructors; by the various religious exercises and influences of the Institution and by the oversight of the Board of Managers and the final authority lodged in the Board of Trustees:—and *whereas,* the sentiment and practice of the different Ecclesiastical Bodies are increasingly opposed to insistence to subscription to doctrinal tests; and *whereas,* to demand from Professors and Teachers in an undenominational institution acceptance of a form of 'Creed' or detailed statement of doctrines, seems undesirable and, at the same time, in the circumstances of this College, unnecessary, therefore, be it *Resolved*:—that, while retaining the present 'Declaration of Principles' as a general expression of the religious belief of the founders of the College, subscription to this 'Declaration' be no longer required."[4]

During the early years of the College most of the students were nominally Christian though few were Protestant. Many of them joined the native Protestant churches as the result of their college experience, and in general the strengthening of character and deepening of religious consciousness among the students was noteworthy. This moral influence, strong as ever after seventy-five years, once led the famous Rustum Pasha to say to Dr. Bliss: "I do not know how much mathematics, nor how much of history, philosophy or science you teach at your Syrian Protestant College, but I do know this: that you make *men,* and that is the important thing. I wish I had one of your graduates to put into every office in my province. I would then have a far better government than I now have."[5]

Evidence is plentiful of the Christian influence which college life at Beirut exerted upon the students throughout the history of the Syrian Protestant College. References are frequently made in the Trustees' minutes to such events as the revival of 1885, when "all of the Senior class, all but one of the Junior, eight Sophomores and sixteen Freshmen had expressed a Christian hope, and most

[4] Trustees Minutes, January 30, 1902.

[5] Al-Kulliyah, V, 6:167. Reported by President-Emeritus Bliss. By birth an Italian nobleman, Rustum Pasha was for many years one of the finest public servants of the Sultan. For several years he was Governor-General of the Province of Lebanon and later served as Turkish Ambassador to the Court of St. James.

of them had united with the Church at Beirut or elsewhere." More than half the boys in the preparatory department did likewise. There the study of the Bible was particularly emphasized and "every pupil has committed to memory the whole or part of 'One Hundred Texts,' prepared for the Irish Church Missions and illustrating the leading doctrines of the Gospel. 'Pilgrim's Progress' has been read with one class of Cypriotes (students from Cyprus) and the New Testament in ancient Greek with the other."[6]

The decision to maintain the medical school after the difficulties of 1882 was no doubt influenced by the excellent missionary record of earlier medical graduates. The Trustees noted in 1884 that such men were to be found in Cairo, Gaza, Jaffa, Es-Salt, Brummana, Mersine, Zahleh, Beirut, Cyprus and at other points. Some not officially connected with any missionary society were known to be doing good service as Christian laymen. Five years later it was reported that two medical graduates had gone to East Africa as representatives of the Church Missionary Society.

In 1886 a Young Men's Christian Association was organized in the College, but being left too largely in student hands it was not a success and came to an unfortunate end in 1891. The Sabbath School, on the other hand, was under the control of the faculty and was a very great success. The funds which it raised were regularly given to missionary work in various parts of the world, in particular helping a Dutch Reformed mission in Basra, to which the Sunday School gave a boat.

John R. Mott visited the College in 1895 and held a series of meetings on the campus. He later wrote of his experience: "By far the most important place I visited was the S.P.C. at Beirut, where I spent a week, holding in all seven meetings,—six with the students and one with the teachers. Most of my addresses were on subjects bearing on the practical promotion of the spiritual life.

"Two evangelistic meetings were also held. After each of them, I gave young men an opportunity to come to my room for interviews about the matter of personal religion. I devoted over two hours each night to this absorbing work, giving each inquirer ten

[6] Minutes, January 27, 1886.

minutes. Even giving so short a time to each, I was unable to see all of the earnest seekers. . . .

"The S.P.C. is one of the three most important institutions in all Asia. In fact, I know of no college, which has, within one generation, accomplished a larger work, and which today has a larger opportunity.

"It has practically created the medical profession in the Levant. It has been the most influential factor in promoting popular education in Syria and in other parts of the East. It has been and is the center for real Christian and scientific literature and learning in all that region.

"Fully one-fourth of the graduates of the Collegiate Department have entered Christian work either as preachers or as teachers in Christian schools. Surely the men, who by their foresight and generosity laid the foundations of this College and carried it to its present position, have been divinely guided."[7]

At the time of Dr. Mott's visit a College society for Christian fellowship was organized on what was known as the Paris or "International" basis, omitting the name Young Men's Christian Association which was still in rather bad odor as a result of the abolition of the student organization in 1891. The new society was under the supervision of the faculty, being sponsored particularly by Professor West, Dr. Webster, and Mr. Nicely. For a year or more the group was so extraordinarily successful in influencing the religious life of the student body, that at the end of 1896 it became possible again to assume the name of Young Men's Christian Association. Membership in the new association included both Protestant and non-Protestant Christian students and faculty, while non-Christians were admitted as associate members after taking a special pledge. Until the outbreak of war in 1914 forced its discontinuance, the Young Men's Christian Association remained the largest and most influential student organization in the College. Its interests and activities remained truly religious throughout its existence.

The successful development of the S.P.C. early attracted Moslems and Jews to the student body, but the number who entered

[7] Quoted in Minutes, January 22, 1896.

and remained throughout the course was small until after the turn of the century. Even as late as 1894, when there was a total of 235 students enrolled, only five Moslems and two Jews were to be found in the preparatory department which had an enrollment of 136. This failure to draw non-Christians was caused in part by the consistent refusal of the Trustees to relax in any way the rules governing attendance at prayers, Bible classes, preaching services and the Sabbath School, or to permit the establishment of a separate kitchen and dining-room for Jewish students. Although both Mohammedans and Jews promised to send large numbers of students if they were permitted special exemptions, the Trustees, particularly under the guidance of their first president, William A. Booth,[8] held that this would mean a deviation from the principles upon which the College was founded. They believed that when it became apparent that the College would make no exceptions to its principles, the non-Christians would entertain greater respect for it and would eventually send their sons to it. The matter came before the Trustees in 1888 and again in 1895, but throughout the presidency of Mr. Booth the decision remained the same. Both Moslem and Jewish students were rejected if they would not agree to take part in the compulsory religious exercises.

Considerable difference of opinion was entertained on this score even in the Mission, for many experienced people felt that the Trustees were in error: that they underestimated the strength of Islam and its opposition to the practices of Christianity, and that they erred in thus denying the benefit of a higher education to groups which must inevitably, for generations, form the majority of the population of the Middle East. It was felt, too, that even if Moslem and Jewish students should be excused from Christian services, they would be bound to learn what Christian principles were and see their value through four or more years of intimate contact with the practice of them. Eventually minor modifications were introduced which permitted a larger attendance of Moslems and Jews, with a resultant widening of the College influence. Whether that widening was gained at the expense of depth is not to be proved. It will always remain a matter of individual opinion.

[8] Mr. Booth was president of the Board from 1863-96 when he died at the age of 91.

THE THEOLOGICAL SEMINARY

Mention was made in the first chapter of the high school established at 'Abeih by Dr. Van Dyck in 1846. In 1849 it became 'Abeih Seminary, with Simeon H. Calhoun, the "saint of the Lebanon" as its director from that date until 1875. During the latter half of this period it served as a training school for native helpers in the mission work, and because of this rather specialized interest the establishment of the more general education offered by the Syrian Protestant College was deemed advisable. 'Abeih Seminary could then devote itself more completely to the theological field, and in 1868 theological instruction was actually begun in summer sessions under the leadership of Calhoun, H. H. Jessup and W. W. Eddy.

Almost immediately the question arose as to whether it would not be better to associate the theological school with the S.P.C. because of the mutual benefits which might be derived through such a connection. D. S. Dodge noted during the summer of 1868 that the College had offered the Mission the use of its buildings and boarding department for the theological work. He listed as advantages of the proposal that 'Abeih Seminary had had an unfortunate record of failure in theological training and that this reputation might attach to the new work then being started. The Beirut location would be better because it was the center of the mission and there would always be teaching assistance available if needed; college classes, particularly in English, would be open to theological students; the College would serve to quicken the minds of the theologians while they would add to the sanctity of the College; the College would gain in reputation, the Seminary in dignity; the College library would be a great help, etc. etc.

The Mission, however, could not come to a decision about the association of the two institutions until ten years later, when the Presbyterian Board "agreed to close 'Abeih Seminary and send annually a number of students to the College." The College faculty agreed to accept such students on payment by the Mission of ten Turkish liras each, "this amount simply covering the cost of board, and the expense of supplying tuition and accommodations being met by the College."[9]

In 1881 the Presbyterian Board proposed to erect a building in Beirut to house the theological seminary, which was at that time under the guidance of the Reverend James S. Dennis. The Trustees at once voted to donate a plot of ground abutting on Midhat Avenue, and expressed their view that a vigorous theological seminary was not only a necessity to the Mission but was vital to the fulfillment of one of the chief purposes of the College: "to aid in raising up a thoroughly educated native ministry."[10] The Presbyterian Board accepted the grant of land and began construction, more than half of the funds for which were contributed by members of the Board of Trustees of the College.

The building was completed in 1883[11] and was occupied that fall by a class of eleven students, all of whom took their meals in the College refectory and attended some classes in the College. In 1888 it was reported by Dr. Dennis that of six men receiving theological school diplomas, three had completed the full college course before entering the seminary and three had taken a partial course. The relations between the two institutions were very cordial and the association seemed to fulfill the high hopes which had earlier been expressed for it.

Unfortunately, by the year 1891 the supply of theological students ran very low, and as many of the graduates of the school had chosen to enter business or professions other than the ministry, the Mission decided to discontinue the work in Beirut. The theological work was transferred as a summer school to Suq-al-Gharb, "where it continued until 1905, when it was reopened in Beirut on the new mission premises adjoining Dale Memorial Hall."[12] The Theological Hall, after standing idle for two years, was rented as a faculty residence and was finally bought by the College in 1898 for

[9] Minutes of Trustees, June 19, 1878.

[10] Minutes, January 26, 1882. The donation agreement stipulated that the land could not be sold or used by the Mission for any other purpose and in case the Theological School should be given up, the land should revert to the College without cost.

[11] An excellent description of the building, by Dr. Webster, appears in Al-Kulliyah, XVI, 7:163-64.

[12] H. H. Jessup, op. cit., Vol. II, p. 470.

the sum of $8,000. The building was named Jesup Hall in honor of Mr. Morris K. Jesup, then chairman of the Board of Trustees who had given $5,000 toward the purchase price. The Presbyterian Board had consented to the sale at such a low figure in recognition of the fact that two of the College Trustees, A. L. Dennis and William E. Dodge, Sr., had each contributed $5,000 to the original cost of construction and that the Reverend James S. Dennis, who had given $2,000, was then a member of the Board of Managers and favored the sale. The $3,000 remaining after Mr. Jesup's gift was provided in equal shares by Mrs. W. E. Dodge, Sr., W. E. Dodge, Jr., and D. S. Dodge. Jesup Hall has since been used by the College, first to house the upper class of the ever-growing preparatory school, then the College Junior class, and finally those medical students who desired private rooms.

It must not be supposed that the closing of the Theological School produced any diminution in the religious activities of the College. On the contrary, those which have been described were continued and expanded, being provided in 1891 with a suitable setting. In that year the present Chapel or Assembly Hall was erected through the generosity of Mr. Elbert B. Monroe, son-in-law of Frederick Marquand, who had provided the funds for erecting the President's House and had contributed to the provision of the original chapel in College Hall. Mr. Monroe noted the inadequacy of the existing chapel when he visited the campus in 1886, and began to consider the idea of replacing it with a more suitable place of worship. He accepted membership on the Board of Trustees in 1887, and the following year made a gift of some $30,000 for the new building, the plans for which were prepared without charge by Mr. George B. Post, architect cousin of Dr. George E. Post. Mr. Monroe provided the organ and all the equipment for the Chapel, or "Mahfell" as it was then called. Work was completed in time for the commencement exercises of 1891, which inaugurated the service of this beautiful addition to the physical and spiritual assets of the College.

Three years later, when Mr. Monroe died, the Trustees adopted a minute in his memory, part of which, referring to the Chapel, reads as follows: "This spacious edifice, made of stone taken from the College grounds and in the style of later English architecture, stands in the center of the campus, a fitting memorial of the wisdom, liberality and spiritual aims of its founder.

"It not only furnishes the larger accommodations so long needed for Daily Prayers, Sabbath worship and various public occasions, but, as Mr. Monroe wished, it both represents and fosters the religious life of the Institution."[13] That it continues to fulfill his desires to the present day is a matter of pride to those who have been connected with the S.P.C. and its offspring, the American University of Beirut.

It is impossible to evaluate the Christian influence of such an institution as the College in terms of theological studies, religious exercises, even by the number of graduates in pursuits directly connected with the church. There have been critics of the missionary value of the institution who have failed to realize this fact. On the other hand, there have been more who, like the sainted Dr. Maltbie Babcock, could speak of the College as the institution "which crowns the Christian work of our Presbyterian Missions in Syria." Dr. Babcock's reaction to the College was expressed in a letter to the Men's Bible Class of the Brick Church in New York, of which he was the beloved pastor. The class had helped to send him on his visit to the Near East in 1901, and until almost the day of his sad death from disease near the conclusion of his tour, Dr. Babcock wrote to them regularly his impressions of the places he visited. His letter about the S.P.C. was dated Sidon, April 18, 1901: "The College," he wrote, "commands the admiration of friend and foe. The buildings thrilled me not alone because I belong to the Presbyterian Church but because I belong to Brick Church, for these noble moulds and matrixes of a new civilization are made of the blood of men I know and love, and are here today because of the past gifts and the present care of Dr. Stuart Dodge and Mr. W. E. and Madame Dodge and Mr. Jesup and Mr. Maitland, and Dr. Dennis, and other devoted men. In the fine chapel I preached to the students Sunday morning (this was Dr. Babcock's last sermon), and my heart was excited with hope as I thought of the part these men from Egypt, Algeria, and Persia, and who can say where else, are

[13] Minutes, January 21, 1895.

to play in the years to come. No one can see the kind of work they are doing, the new bodies physical exercise is giving them, the new standards, the mental training they are getting, and wide horizons and Christian motives, and doubt for a moment that they are to be the leaders of their day and generation. From the little handful of a dozen beginners in some rented room the college, in less than forty years, has grown to its noble proportions. No one can forecast its future, for it is growing not merely in numbers but in percentage of increase, and in ever-widening fame and deepening respect. No college I know of offers a more encouraging outlook for investment of money for the Kingdom than this one. . . . The need and the promise of the Beyrout College are far and away beyond those of any of our well-known home colleges today, for from this beacon and from Robert College, this Eastern world must find its way out of darkness.

"The Medical College gives men an unparalleled opportunity—not only because of the distinction of the faculty, but because the students practically become interns two years earlier than in America, working in the hospital, and being junior assistants in all kinds of operations. A dozen of them were with Dr. Post yesterday morning when he literally dissected a young woman's forearm, removing a colloid tumor that was woven among the muscles and tendons and had eaten into the bone. I do not believe there is a man living who from first to last could have operated more swiftly and skilfully than Dr. Post. A little longer and it would have been necessary to amputate the arm and that would have meant celibacy and poverty and obscurity for the poor girl. Then I saw Dr. Webster remove a cataract from a blind man's eye. When the doctor moved his fingers afterwards before the man's face and he said he could see, the thought came instantly, "Lord, that I might receive my sight." Is not such Christian work, multiplied all over the world, work of minds and hearts and hands that owe their impulse and skill to the life and love of Jesus Christ, the fulfilment of our Lord's words, "and greater works than these shall ye do"? Only from Christian roots are such fruits growing. Men sometimes think, when they see the vast temples of the elder days and the Cathedrals of the middle ages, that religion must have lost much power because she builds so few shrines today that can compare with them. But let them learn what the word means, "I will have Mercy and not sacrifice." And add to the buildings today where men worship those equally sacred structures where the sick are healed, the orphans are trained, the blind and deaf and dumb, the aged and insane and recreant are ministered unto, and they will see how intrusive and extrusive has been the growth of intelligent Christian devotion, how close to the ways of Christ His people have been coming."[14]

[14] Babcock, Maltbie D., Letters from Egypt and Palestine (Scribners, 1902), pp. 126-31.

V. GROWTH

1. ENROLLMENT

THE TABLE of student enrollment covering the years 1866-1902 shows graphically the way in which the College increased in size as it became known and as its equipment was enlarged to provide accommodations for additional students. A glance at the chart enables one to guess when a new building was provided, for a sharp increase in numbers followed immediately. Thus in 1872-73 the new campus was occupied. In 1881-82 the expanded Preparatory Building was completed, while in 1885 the Ada Dodge Memorial Hall became available. Its effect was not as immediately felt because the increasing number of high schools in the area somewhat diminished the number of applicants for preparatory school work. The increase began again very soon however with the appearance of larger numbers of students from Egypt and Cyprus. This was almost coincidental with the completion of the Chapel in 1891, and the sharp rise following the cholera year of 1892 coincided with the enlargement of the observatory, the erection of a chemistry laboratory and the completion of the so-called "Annex" for medical students, situated across the street from the main gate. The acquisition of Jesup Hall in 1897-98 was followed in rapid succession by the construction in 1900 of Bliss Hall, a new wing to Dodge Hall, and one wing of Pliny Fisk Hall. The new science building, Post Hall, was still under construction in 1902 when the attendance reached the 600 mark.

The numbers of students and buildings were, however, only the evidences of an internal development in the College which was of greater importance. To be sure, they were concomitant, for the expansion of curriculum was dependent upon an increased student body, which in turn required a larger faculty and greater physical facilities. These in turn were reflected in further gains in attendance. But the development of the curriculum and the faculty were more important to the strength of the institution than were the numbers of students. A college should be judged by what it

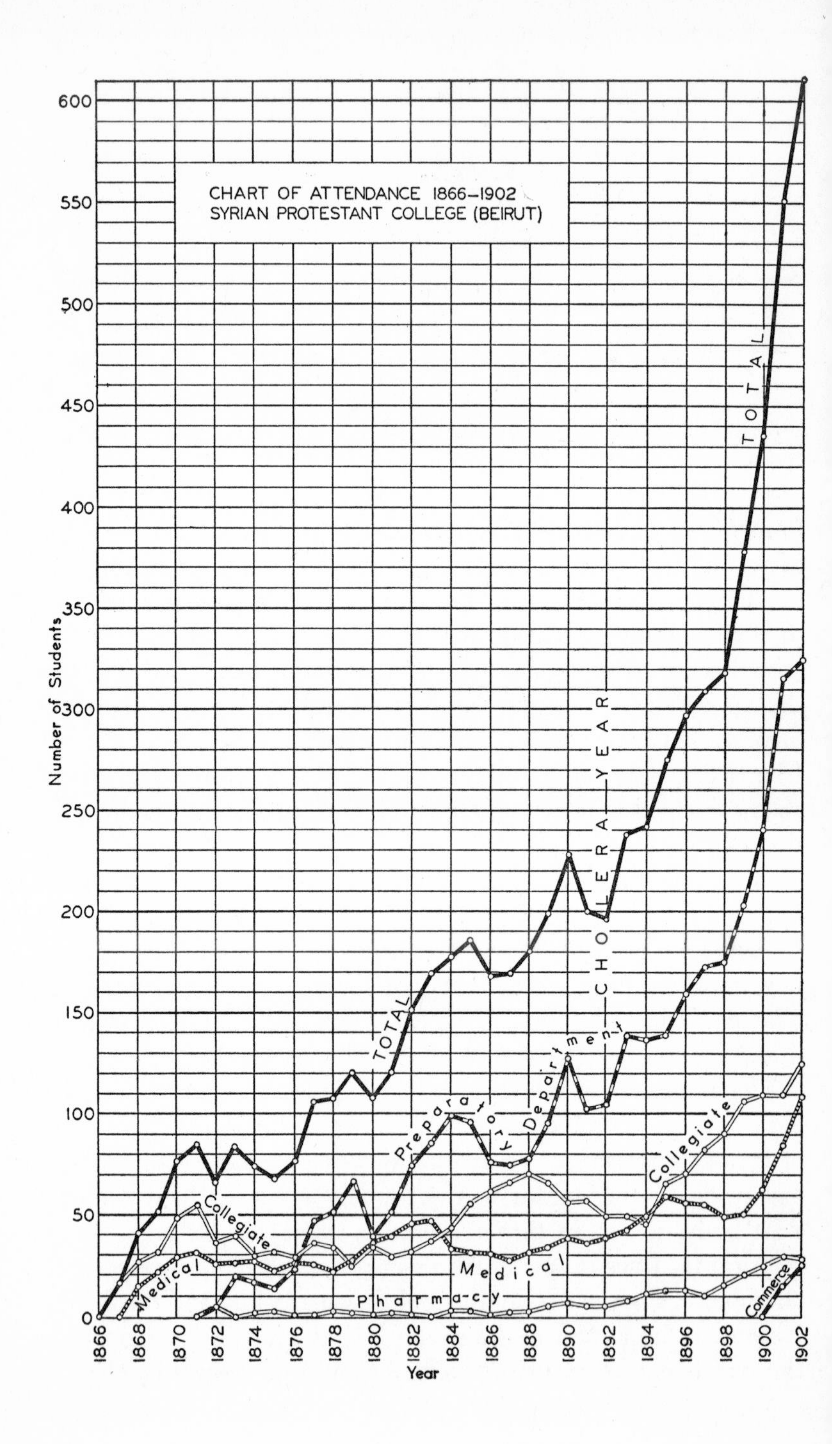

ALLEGHENY COLLEGE LIBRARY

teaches and how it teaches rather than by the quantity of human material which it attempts to digest.

2. FACULTY

The S.P.C. was exceedingly fortunate in the quality of the men who made up the faculty, both in the literary and in the medical departments. The original faculty of Bliss, Dodge, Van Dyck, Wortabet, Porter and Lewis, with their local assistants, were able to handle all the work until 1874, when Professor Isaac H. Hall was sent out as teacher of English in place of D. S. Dodge who had had to return to America. Professor Hall, who remained but one year, was chiefly noteworthy for his discovery in the College library of an ancient Syriac manuscript of the New Testament which he brought back to America with him by permission. The "Beirut Codex" as it came to be known proved to be of immense value to Biblical scholars and was later deposited in the new library of Union Theological Seminary.

The Lewis affair in 1882 precipitated a series of faculty changes and brought to the staff professors who, for the first time, were neither ministers nor missionaries. Professor Porter had been a layman when he arrived in 1870, but in 1880 he returned to America and was ordained by a Congregational Council in Westfield, Massachusetts. Doctors Dight, Kay, and Neal, however, were medical men without theological training, and after their appointment in 1884 the greater proportion of new appointees were laymen, the only religious requirement made of them being that they sign the detailed "Declaration of Principles."

The arrangement for short term instructors, hitherto described in the case of Mr. Crane, was continued with great success, bringing to the staff of the College a number of fine men. (Appendix J.) The appointments were staggered in such a way that there was never a total turnover of the staff in any one year and some experienced teachers were always left to help break in the new men.

A few of these "staffites" either stayed on by invitation after their term had expired or were asked to return to Beirut after further graduate study in America. Robert Haldane West was one of the most outstanding men in the first group. His memory will forever be perpetuated at Beirut in the magnificent building which was erected in his memory in 1913-14. He was appointed in 1883, just after his graduation from Princeton, as instructor of English in place of Frank E. Packard who had resigned because of ill health. When Mr. Packard found he could remain, West became instructor in mathematics and astronomy and director of the observatory. Through the years he served successively as instructor (1884-87), professor (1887), principal of the Preparatory Department (1899-1903), director of the Observatory, Treasurer of the College and Dean of the College faculty (1905) until at his death in 1906 he was one of the most influential and beloved members of the faculty.

"The mere mention of the offices he filled indicates his ability to serve and his willingness to serve. He feared no labor, however arduous; he spent himself freely, without stint, without anxious thought; he put the very best qualities of his mind and heart into routine duties and drudgery and distasteful work, far removed from the natural aptitudes of his studious and scholarly traits. He possessed a rare power of insight; he could see through the manifest complexities of a problem, whether in his own department of science, or in finance, or administration, or discipline, or a student's individual character; and with almost unerring skill he could bring to light the few outstanding simple factors out of which he organized a solution of difficulties which to many might seem insoluble.—Great was his service to the Institution: but still greater was his service to many a boy and young man whose complexity of emotions, ambitions, temptations were simplified by the insight of this teacher; whose character was moulded and strengthened and purified by contact with this strong personality."[1] This description, by Dr. Franklin T. Moore, one of Professor West's great colleagues, speaks volumes for the affectionate respect and regard in which this remarkable man was universally held.

Another of the great professors who came from the ranks of the "staffites" was Alfred E. Day, who was appointed tutor in the natural sciences in 1889. Before his term was up it was reported to the Trustees that "the services of Mr. Day . . . were felt to be per-

[1] Al-Kulliyah, V, 5:128. Article on West Hall by Dr. Franklin T. Moore.

THE MEDICAL FACULTY IN 1898

Standing, L. to R.: Webster, Moore, Day, Adams. Seated: Post, President Bliss, Graham

THE COLLEGE FACULTY AND STAFF

(About 1902)

Seated, L. to R.: Graham, Post, Bliss, Porter, West. 1st row standing: Chamorel, Swain, Day, Nicely, Adams, Moore, Dumit, Jureidini. 2nd row: ———, F. Jessup, J. B. Brown, Wisner, Badr, Webster, Khuri (now Faris Bey Khuri, Damascus). Back row: Hall, ———, S. Maluf, Khauli

ALLEGHENY COLLEGE LIBRARY

DANIEL BLISS HALL

POST HALL

ALLEGHENY COLLEGE LIBRARY

manently necessary," and he was appointed professor of Natural Sciences, to begin his service in that capacity in the fall of 1892. He served with great distinction in that position and later as Professor West's successor as Dean of the Faculty of Arts and Sciences. He was then professor of Biology and he occupied the latter post until his death in 1930. Few colleges have been blessed with a more able teacher of the biological sciences or a more perfect Christian gentleman than Professor Day.

Of those who returned to the faculty after an absence for advanced study, the most outstanding in this early period was Dr. Franklin T. Moore. Mr. Moore went to Beirut as a tutor of English immediately after his graduation from Princeton in 1891. Returning to America in 1894, he took up the study of medicine at Jefferson Medical College in Philadelphia and after receiving his degree was appointed in 1897 professor of Physiology and Diseases of Women at Beirut. He also taught Hygiene and Legal Medicine, particularly difficult subjects because there were no English textbooks which covered the peculiar conditions to be found in the Near East. Under Dr. Moore the Department of Gynecology and Obstetrics developed so markedly that he was at length forced to give up the teaching of Physiology. When Professor West was made Principal of the Preparatory School, Dr. Moore became secretary of the General Faculty as well as of the Medical Faculty. He was also a member of the Beirut Executive Committee of the Lebanon Hospital for Mental Diseases, and during the last five years of his life was secretary of that committee.

When Dr. Moore died at Beirut in 1915, the faculty of the College adopted a minute in his honor which records the high esteem in which he was held by faculty, students and public. In part the minute reads: "As a teacher he possessed special gifts of clear, forcible presentation of the subjects belonging to his chair and a masterful grasp of the principles which underlie the wide range of Medical Science.

"As a surgeon in his own specialty he carried his professional skill to a high degree of proficiency, proving himself an expert operator of marked skill, ingenuity, resourcefulness, thoroughness and conscientiousness. His work in the women's pavilion, the pavilion which he himself designed and which he regarded as the jewel of his life work, will be a perpetual memorial to his name, not only of good works, of high surgical achievements and of an honorable professional career, but also of a great hearted Christian physician."[2]

Another Princeton man called back to a professorship was Frank S. Woodruff, who came first to Beirut in 1885 as tutor of English and was made head of the English Department in 1891 after his graduation from Princeton Theological Seminary. Unfortunately Professor Woodruff's health forced him to withdraw early in 1893 and he died in America in May of that year, shortly after his return from Beirut. He was succeeded by yet another Princeton man, John W. Nicely, whose elevation to the professorship in 1896 coincided with a pledge from John Wanamaker to provide $1,500 annually for its maintenance. Professor Nicely was also the first official College Treasurer. From 1896 to 1903, when to the deep regret of all his associates he resigned, he accomplished amazing results in systematizing the local business affairs of the College. He was a fine teacher, as well as having one of the most powerful Christian influences on the campus.

The most extensive faculty developments took place in the medical school, where a succession of able men joined Dr. Post in building up the curriculum and improving the capacity of the school for first-rate instruction. Dr. Charles F. Dight (1883-89) of the University of Michigan, professor of Anatomy, Physiology and Hygiene; Dr. Thomas W. Kay (1883-88) of Baltimore Medical School, professor of Materia Medica, Zoology and Botany; and Dr. Robert J. Neal (1883-84) of the University of Michigan, have already been mentioned. The following year they were joined by Dr. John C. Fisher (1884-90) of Princeton and Long Island Medical College, professor of Gynecology, Dermatology, Pediatrics and Legal Medicine. In 1885 Dr. Samuel P. Glover (1885-89) of the University of Pennsylvania was appointed and in 1886 he was made professor of Anatomy and Histology, and Lecturer on Diseases of the Skin, Physics and Geology. Dr. Franklin C. Wells was ap-

[2] Al-Kulliyah, Special Number, 1915, pp. 25-26. The minute is preceded by a striking article on Dr. Moore by Dr. Walter B. Adams.

pointed in 1888 for a three-year term as Lecturer on Obstetrics "and other branches."

It seems incredible that teachers could be expected to carry successfully such a complex load of subjects, but it was done for a time. Relief was given through new appointments as rapidly as they could be financially supported. Until that time the work was handled by requiring all professors to teach fifteen hours a week. In 1884 Dr. Post wrote to the Trustees concerning the offerings of the College: "We have added within two years, Toxicology, Diseases of Children, Diseases of the Skin, Zoology, Geology (in *fact* now), Mineralogy, Gynecology (a meagre course was before given in alternate years by Dr. Brigstocke), Gynecological clinique, Histology and Embryology. It is almost beyond belief that we could add so much, but it illustrates the advantage of insisting upon the three hours system for daily teaching by professors. It has increased our effective instruction by about 30%. The quality of the teaching is excellent. There are no slipped hours. Hospital roll is called and punctuality is now the rule."[3]

In 1890 and 1891 five new medical men came out to Beirut. Two of them stayed for only four years but are of particular interest because of their families. Dr. William Gray Schauffler (1890-95), grandson of the famous missionary of the American Board of Commissioners for Foreign Missions at Constantinople, and married to the granddaughter of David Hoadley, founding Trustee of the College, was appointed in 1891 as Lecturer in Anatomy, Hygiene, and Diseases of the Skin. In 1892, he was made professor of Physiology and Diseases of Women. Dr. Charles L. Bliss (1891-95), son of the veteran missionary in Turkey, Isaac G. Bliss, was first made Lecturer in Anatomy, Skin Diseases, Pharmacy and Hygiene, and in 1893 was appointed professor of Anatomy. It was in large measure due to Dr. Bliss' influence that the clinics at the hospital were differentiated into sections for the handling of specialties. Before his time all ailments had passed through a general clinic.

The other three men became a vital part of the great tradition of long, valuable and devoted service in the medical school which

[3] Trustees Minutes, January 23, 1885.

had been inaugurated by Van Dyck, Wortabet, and especially Post. With the latter, until his death in 1909, they formed the nucleus of the permanent faculty which really raised the medical school at Beirut to the high rank which it occupies today. They are names which will always be honored in Syria: Harris Graham, Franklin T. Moore[4] and Walter B. Adams. To them should be joined Charles A. Webster who was appointed in 1895 and still serves the institution as professor-emeritus of Ophthalmology. The combined period of service of these four men amounts to more than one hundred thirty years.

Dr. Graham and Dr. Webster were Canadians, both graduates of the University of Toronto. Dr. Graham took his medical work at Michigan and shortly after graduation was appointed by the American Board as professor in the medical school at Aintab, Turkey. The school was closed early in 1889 and Dr. Graham came to Aleppo to take up private practice, but was shortly thereafter appointed to the professorship of Pathology and Practice of Medicine at Beirut. He held this position until his sudden death in 1922. Dr. Webster spoke of him at that time as "the central, solid pillar of our Medical School."

So great was his industry and all-round ability that it was necessary at his death to ask the Trustees to provide two men to take his place. A remarkable administrator and teacher, he was an even more skillful diagnostician. His experience and keen intelligence served him nearly as well as X-rays do modern practitioners. "It is a cause of great regret . . . that he did not write . . . the results of his experiences. At the time of his death no one knew more about the causes and treatment of dengué fever, and yet his knowledge died with him. Called in consultation on the day he was stricken, a very skilled physician from the city said: 'I cannot help him. He knew more than I about the strange disease he has.' "[5]

Within three years of his appointment to Beirut, Dr. Graham had so won the confidence of the Turkish authorities that they sent him to the Huleh district in Palestine to report on the cholera

[4] Moore as has been seen was only a tutor in 1891. He joined the medical faculty in 1897.

[5] Al-Kulliyah Review, II, 12:5 (April 13, 1935).

epidemic there. Later in the same year they asked him to study the spread of typhus, the cause of which was then unknown, among the pilgrims on the way to Mecca. He successfully performed both these tasks, which involved no little risk to himself from a variety of causes (he nearly died as a result of typhus infection acquired during his investigation). It was because of such services as these that both Dr. Graham and Dr. Webster, though technically enemies of Turkey, being Canadians, were permitted to practice freely in Beirut during the Great War. Both were called frequently to minister to high officials and their families.

Dr. Adams, a graduate of New York University Medical School, was first appointed in 1890 as Lecturer in Chemistry, Pharmacy and Electrotherapeutics. Of his work at that time he later wrote: "I taught chemistry, general, inorganic and organic, analytical and physiological chemistry, practice of pharmacy and laboratory pharmacy, anatomy, and served as demonstrator in the dissecting room. . . . I had no assistant except in chemistry and it was easier to do things myself than trust him to do them. He was sure to do them wrong."[6]

Two years later Dr. Adams was made professor of Chemistry and Materia Medica. He gave up the Chemistry in 1902 when Therapeutics was assigned to him. In 1899 he took over the department of Dermatology when, according to Professor Webster who had directed it, it amounted to very little, and built it up into the largest clinical practice in the Hospital Clinics. He himself became one of the foremost dermatologists of the world.

Dr. Adams suffered a stroke in 1924 and a year later was retired as professor-emeritus. Until his death in the summer of 1928 he maintained an active interest in the work of the College, and his genial, humorous spirit continued to enrich the experience of medical students and faculty alike. He was universally beloved and admired.

Dr. Charles A. Webster was appointed to the chair of Anatomy and Pharmacy, with Diseases of the Eye and Ear added for good measure and because of his special training. He fell heir to Dermatology also but succeeded in passing that on to Dr. Adams. Al-

[6] Al-Kulliyah, XIV, 5:119 (March 1928).

though for thirty years he was professor of Anatomy, his greatest interest and most valuable medical skill lay in the field of Ophthalmology, which chair he occupied for thirty-one years before his retirement in 1928 as professor-emeritus. In a land where eye disease is one of the major afflictions of mankind, such rare ability as Dr. Webster's was as manna from heaven. As it was joined with the gentle kindliness and spirituality of his nature, it is not hard to understand what deep affection for him developed among all who knew him.

On Dr. Webster's retirement, the Faculty adopted a minute in his honor which indicates some of his other values to the community: "Dr. Webster from the first and for many years took his place as a leader in the religious thought and life of the Institution. His message from the college pulpit was delivered with eloquence and inspiration." (For this reason he was usually called upon to prepare memorial addresses when elder statesmen of the faculty passed on.) "For many years he was chairman of the Athletic Committee, at a time when interest in athletics was being aroused, and principles of good sportsmanship were being established. Dr. and Mrs. Webster together made their home a center of hospitality to many succeeding generations of students."[7] The same may be said of their graciousness to generations of staff members, some of whose warmest recollections of Beirut center around the Webster home. Dr. Webster still maintains his active interest in the institution and still makes Beirut his home. In 1939 he was decorated with the silver Order of Merit of the Republic of Lebanon for his services to the country.

One other professorial appointment should be mentioned here though much more will be said of Professor Edward F. Nickoley somewhat later. When the Trustees decided in 1900 to establish a department of Commerce for the more adequate business training of the many students who wished to take up that type of work, Mr. Nickoley was secured as "principal." A graduate of the University of Illinois in 1898, Mr. Nickoley had had but two years of teaching experience before going to Beirut. His success, however, was immediate, and a year later official comment was made to the

[7] Al-Kulliyah, XIV, 9:250 (July 1928).

Trustees of "the increasing success and popularity of the School of Commerce." It was therefore voted to make Mr. Nickoley a full professor, beginning October 1, 1902, and to establish the School of Commerce with a full three year course of study.

It is unnecessary here to trace Professor Nickoley's highly successful and devoted career as professor of economics, acting president, and Dean of the College of Arts and Sciences until his death in March 1937. Suffice it to say that his was one more of the great figures which made the American University of Beirut what it is today.

As early as 1882 steps were taken to strengthen the faculty by creating a new professorial rank between instructor and full professor. The idea behind this move was to make it possible to promote qualified native teachers without at once putting them on the same level as the American professors, both in rank and salary. Two "Adjunct professorships" were established at that time in Chemistry and Physics, and Higher Mathematics, though it was understood that they were not to be occupied until 1885.

The two chairs were planned for those two remarkable graduates, Yaqub Sarruf, 1870, and Faris Nimr, 1874, both of whom were then employed in the College, the former teaching Arabic, the latter Mathematics and Latin. Strangely enough, when the time came for the appointments to take effect, the Trustees voted, on recommendation of the Board of Managers, "to terminate the connection with the College of the native tutors, Sarruf and Nimr, and to rescind the proposition to make them Adjunct Professors . . . at the same time commending them for their ability and assiduity during their long term of service."[8]

This mysterious action seems, in the light of recent studies, to have been based on well-founded suspicion that the two young men were playing too active a part in dangerous politics. There is now no question but that both were leaders in a secret Arab society which attempted to foment rebellion against the Turks, and which quite certainly was the effective beginning of the Arab Nationalist movement of the present day. The identity of the members of the society was so well hidden that none was ever detained by the

[8] Minutes, January 23, 1885.

Turkish authorities, but their publications caused great furor and even resulted in the unfortunate recall of the liberal governor, Midhat Pasha.[9] The faculty of the S.P.C. probably had only very shrewd suspicions about Sarruf's and Nimr's part in the society, but to have them remain on the staff was too dangerous for the College. That no hard feelings were held is shown by the fact that both Sarruf and Nimr were given honorary Ph.D. degrees in 1890, the first honorary degrees awarded by the College.

It thus happened that the first adjunct professors were actually appointed in 1895, when Monsieur A. Chamorel, French instructor, and Jabr Dumit, '76, head of the Arabic department, were given that rank. Little information is now available about the former, but the latter became one of the great figures on the faculty. In 1909 he was raised to a full professorship, one of the first Syrians to attain that rank. He remained head of the Arabic department until 1922 when he retired as professor-emeritus. Until his death in 1930 he kept up his writing and teaching, both of which had contributed greatly to the reawakening of an interest in Arabic literature and to the uplift of the people of Syria.

Three other adjunct professors were appointed during Daniel Bliss' administration, though their appointments were not confirmed by the faculty until a much later date: Messrs. Labib Jureidini, '90, Shukri Ma'luf, '91, and Bulus Khauli, '97. The first and last taught in the Preparatory Department at the time of their advancement in 1901 while Ma'luf, who had been assistant librarian since 1891 was given the rank of adjunct professor in 1899 with the title of permanent assistant librarian. He served in that position until 1902. Jureidini gave up teaching for newspaper work in 1905, but Khauli, after completing graduate work at Columbia University, became head of the department of Education and in 1910 received the rank of full professor. He is scheduled to retire in 1941 after forty-four years of active service.

[9] Antonius, The Arab Awakening, ch. V, p. 79: "The first organized effort in the Arab National Movement can be traced back to the year 1875 . . . when five young men who had been educated at the S.P.C. in Beirut formed a secret society." Antonius later attributes much of his information about this society to Dr. Faris Nimr Pasha, one of the founders.

3. ENDOWMENT

With all the additions to the faculty which occurred between 1882 and 1902, it is obvious that the income of the College must have been enlarged considerably, even taking into account the increase in the number of students. Rare is the college which can support itself on student fees, and at Beirut, where for economic reasons fees could not be high, no exception was to be found. The total endowment in 1882 of $179,100, which included the Post hospital fund, was far from being sufficient to produce enough income for the expansion which was foreseen as desirable.

The most notable endowment increase to start the period of expansion was occasioned by the gift of $10,000 by the Rev. Gerald F. Dale, Jr., of Zahleh, Syria, to whom the fund had been left by his late sister-in-law for aid in the missionary work in Syria. Mr. Dale, son-in-law of President Bliss, gave the money to be used as a scholarship fund, on condition that $20,000 additional be secured during the next twelve months. The conditional gift was accepted, and Dr. Henry H. Jessup of the Mission went to America to aid in raising the funds necessary to meet the condition. Announcement of the complete success of his efforts was made in January 1884. Of the additional amount raised, $10,500 had come from the Marquand estate through the generosity of Mr. E. B. Monroe. At the same time it was announced that William E. Dodge, long treasurer of the Board, who had died in March 1883, had left in his will an additional $20,000 for scholarship purposes.

In the fall of 1887, Dr. George E. Post was sent to America to raise a fund of $100,000 for the endowment (a) of a professorship of Mathematics and Astronomy ($30,000), (b) of the Library ($30,000), (c) of additional scholarships ($30,000) and (d) of the scientific and archaeological collections ($10,000). Dr. Post presented his plan to the Trustees at a meeting in December and Morris Jesup immediately pledged $10,000. Dr. Post had to return to Beirut in the summer of 1888 with but $57,492 raised, but the professorship, occupied by Professor West, was assured and a respectable amount was left over.

More or less constant effort was thereafter made to increase the endowment funds but no further formal campaign for endowment may be said to have been made during Dr. Bliss' administration. The total of $326,962.50 which was the market value of the endowment funds at the close of his tenure was nevertheless a very respectable sum, considering the fact that he had begun from absolute scratch.

4. LAND AND BUILDINGS

Mention of the endowment leaves entirely out of account the investment in land and physical plant which took place over the same period and which reached the impressive total of $645,000. The construction of each new building involved a small campaign in itself or represented several large gifts. The following is a partial list of building acquisitions made since 1882:—

YEAR	BUILDING	COST	PRINCIPAL DONORS
1885	Ada Dodge Memorial	$20,000 exclusive of furnishings which were also given	D. S. Dodge
1891	Chapel	$30,000	E. B. Monroe
1893	Chemical Laboratory	$2,000	D. S. Dodge (chiefly)
1894	New Observatory	$9,500.12 (equipped)	25 donors, largest being D. S. Dodge and G. N. Laflin (Chicago), W. E. Dodge, J. S. Dennis
1895	Medical Annex	$2,000	Paid from income
1897	Jesup Hall	$20,000	Morris Jesup, A. L. & J. S. Dennis, Wm. E. & D. S. Dodge
1900	Daniel Bliss Hall	$37,430.88	Mrs. Melissa P. Dodge, W. E. Dodge, D. S. Dodge, M. K. Jesup
1900	Wing on Dodge Hall	$4,453	D. S. Dodge
1900-2	Pliny Fisk Hall	$20,000	Paid from Income

Year	Building	Cost	Donors
1902	Post Hall	$40,213.50	M. K. Jesup, Mrs. C. B. Wood, Mrs. C. N. McCormick, G. N. Laflin, W. E. Dodge, Mrs. M. P. Dodge, D. S. Dodge, Alexr. Maitland, Mrs. W. E. Dodge
1902-3	Gate House and Administration Offices	$5,000	D. S. Dodge
	Total	$170,597.50	

Of this total, somewhat more than $40,000 apiece is known to have come from D. Stuart Dodge and Morris K. Jesup. How much in addition Mr. Dodge secretly provided can only be guessed. He had the habit of supplying quietly, from his own pocket, funds which were needed but which were not in sight from the regular sources.

The construction of the dormitory buildings was made possible by the final acquisition in 1898 of several isolated pieces of land, including the famous "Fig Orchard" and a large section formerly owned by Midhat Pasha, which now contains Fisk Hall, Bliss Hall and the hockey field. The experience of negotiation for this plot was refreshingly different from that in connection with the "Fig Orchard" which required twenty-nine years of jockeying. President Bliss visited the heir of Midhat Pasha, then living in Smyrna, and asked the price of the land. "He mentioned a sum," said Dr. Bliss, "and, though it seemed high, the bargain was completed. On my going to him the next day with the cash, he said: 'Since you were here I have looked over my deeds and I find there is not so much land as I had thought. I shall reduce the price agreed upon by fifty pounds sterling.' "[10] The total cost of the plot was $6,580 and that of the much smaller "Fig Orchard" was approximately $2,000. President Bliss rather ruefully contrasted this price of a little more than one dollar per square yard with the original pur-

[10] Bliss, Reminiscences, p. 197.

chase of Ras Beirut property at the rate of seven cents per square yard. The campus, however, was for the first time a complete unit and could be enclosed by a wall,—a very great advantage from the standpoint of discipline.

The construction of the new buildings was required by the increasing popularity of the College and the necessity of raising the educational standards to a level comparable with those of similar institutions in America. The development of scientific work required additional and improved laboratory facilities, and the progress of astronomical studies demanded new equipment for the observatory. As the old building was not suitable for the installation of the desired 12½ inch telescope and other instruments, it seemed advisable to reconstruct it entirely on a new design approved by Professor Young of Princeton. The dome was built by Sir Arthur Grubb of Ireland. The telescope was built by Warner and Swasey of Cleveland, makers of the Yerkes 40-inch equatorial, and the spectroscope to go with the new telescope was constructed by Brashear of Allegheny, Pennsylvania.

The installation of the telescope was a difficult problem, for nothing of its size had before been seen in that part of the world. Thanks, however, to the ingenuity of Mr. von Heidenstam, engineer of the Beirut Water Company, a method of installation was devised which has been permanently satisfactory. It was hardly to be wondered at that the College did not look with favor upon the request of Professor David Todd of Amherst to permit the telescope to be taken to Sumatra for the observation of that summer's solar eclipse. Raymond S. Dugan, later a famous astronomy professor at Princeton, was then instructor in astronomy at Beirut and was to go to Sumatra with the telescope, the College of course being expected to pay all expenses. It need hardly be said that the expedition was not made.[11]

The scientific collections of the College had become so extensive by 1898 that a safe museum was required for their housing. At the time the valuable botanical, geological, and archaeological collec-

[11] It is interesting to note that Professor Dugan later gave to two asteroids which he discovered the distinctive names "Buklawy" and "Halawy." Dr. Adams reported that young Dugan was over-fond of these Arab sweetmeats, and occasionally required medical assistance because of them. Professor Dugan died in the summer of 1940.

tions were scattered in various parts of College Hall, while the zoological and mineralogical collections were badly displayed in the medical building. Additional laboratory and classroom space was also needed for physics and biology. The answer to the problem seemed to be a new science building, which it was decided should be placed between the chapel and the chemistry building.

It happened that during the summer of 1899 Dr. Post, on vacation in Europe, met Mr. and Mrs. Morris Jesup in Germany. Very shortly thereafter Mr. Jesup became seriously ill and was brought back to health by the devoted care of Dr. Post. On his return to America Mr. Jesup offered $20,000 for a science building on condition that a total of $40,000 be raised and that the building bear the name of George E. Post. The total was pledged by January 1900, and construction of the building, designed by Dr. Post himself, was at once begun. Under Post's supervision the work was completed in 1902.

Dr. C. A. Webster, writing of Post Hall in *Al-Kulliyah,* makes this interesting statement: "I had the privilege of reading a personal letter from Mr. Jesup to Dr. Post in which he made the request that a marble bust of Dr. Post should be made and placed in front of Post Hall upon the completion of the building. Dr. Post, for personal reasons, was unable to accede to this request. The bust which now stands at the entrance to the two main museums on the ground floor, was made after Dr. Post's death and was unveiled by the late Dr. Porter at a special memorial service."[12]

Post Hall was always the scene of the medical examinations given by the Imperial Examining Committee which, after 1903, tested the graduates' ability to qualify for a license to practice in Turkey. Dr. Webster's description is vivid: "Here in the presence of sarcophagi, busts and other memorials of the harmless past, they (the candidates) came face to face with the living and awe-inspiring personalities of Pashas, Beys, Professors and Doctors, the representatives of the Imperial Ottoman Medical School. . . . We still hear the soft, approving, comforting 'Peki'; the insinuating, pursuing, insatiable 'Bashka'; and the abrupt and annihilating 'Yok,' marking the favorable or unfavorable progress of the ex-

[12] Al-Kulliyah, XVI, 2:33 (December 1929).

amination. Post Hall has many pleasant memories; these are among the most memorable of all."[13]

Bliss Hall was completed in 1900 to house the preparatory department which had again outgrown its quarters. It had originally been planned to erect it and Pliny Fisk Hall on the Midhat Pasha lot where the hockey field now is, but Dr. Post and Dr. Webster thought otherwise. Interested in the crying need for a good athletic field, they organized a dramatic student parade before the faculty, which thereafter voted to preserve the field for athletics. The two buildings were put up along the sides of the field.

Dr. Webster incidentally should be known as the father of athletics in Syria for it was he who in 1896 organized the first College Field Day, or track meet, and who introduced soccer football to the campus. A makeshift football field was constructed in 1897 between the chapel, College Hall and the street, and a year later an instructor of physical education was appointed to the faculty. Lieutenant Volmer Krohn was a Swede and emphasized the Swedish system of physical drill rather than competitive games. He was succeeded in 1902 by Joseph A. Goodhue who had had several years' experience in physical education work with the Young Men's Christian Association.

5. CURRICULUM

The striking development in the work offered by the College in the last twenty of the thirty-six years of Daniel Bliss' administration can be most clearly shown by a comparison of the catalogues of 1882 and 1903. These indicate that the faculty had grown in size from fifteen to fifty-three:

	PROF.	ADJ. PROF.	LECTURERS	TUTORS OR INSTRS.	ADMIN. STAFF
1882	6		2	7	
1903	12	6	1	25	9

In 1882 there were three departments in the College, preparatory, collegiate, and medical (including pharmacy). Twenty years later there were six schools, preparatory, collegiate, medicine, pharmacy, commerce and Biblical Archaeology and Philology (the latter having been established for theological graduate students in

[13] Ibid., p. 34.

1887). The Library had grown from 1,800 European books and 500 Arabic to 13,800 European books and 1,000 Arabic and Turkish, with 4,100 additional volumes in special collections or alcoves.

The admission requirements to the various schools had been increased noticeably except in the case of the preparatory, where the age of admission alone had been changed from ten years to twelve. In the college, entrance examinations in English, and Arabic, French or Turkish had been added. Whereas in 1882 Arabic had been the language of instruction in the medical school, in 1903 entrance examinations in English were required together with either French or Turkish. Examinations in geography and physiology had been added while Arabic was dropped. S.P.C. students could enter the medical school without examination if they had finished Sophomore year but they could only qualify for the M.D. degree accepted by New York State if they had completed Junior Year.

In the preparatory, collegiate, and commercial schools, at least three years of either French or Turkish was required for graduation. Physical education was compulsory for all students in 1903, while in the earlier catalogue it was not mentioned.

In the college in 1903, there were six departments, while in 1882 there was no such division. Courses had been given in most of the fields, but the offering had been greatly broadened by departments of religion, philosophy, history and economics, physical and natural sciences, mathematics, and languages. Of course the three-year school of commerce was entirely new with its offering of business courses, bookkeeping, commercial law, typewriting, industrial chemistry and physics. It is interesting to note that in 1882 the typewriter was as yet unknown.

At the earlier date, medical students were required to spend some time each year in "hospital attendance." Before 1903 six separate clinics had been established, in surgery, eye and ear diseases, internal medicine, children's diseases, skin diseases, and women's diseases. In comparison to the rather limited number of medical courses offered in 1882, there were, by the turn of the century, twelve medical departments, including zoology, chemistry, histology and pathology, anatomy, physiology and hygiene, materia medica and therapeutics, dermatology, children's diseases, eye and ear, obstetrics and gynecology, surgery, pathology and practice of medicine. To the work in pharmacy had been added special courses in business methods, first aid, pharmaceutical physics, pharmaceutical microscopy, zoology, practice of pharmacy and dispensing. Many of these had probably been included in the blanket terms "pharmacy" and "materia medica" found in profusion in the second year schedule for 1882. Incidentally, the second year was then the last of the course. Twenty years later an additional intervening year of practical dispensing experience was required of all pharmacy graduates.

About the only things which had not changed in the twenty years were the fees. In spite of the tremendously increased facilities the only difference in the charges on students was that they were reckoned in pounds sterling instead of Turkish liras. But tuitions in preparatory and college were still £5 ($25.00) in 1903 and £10 annually in pharmacy and medicine. Room and board were still £12–£25 for the year, dependent upon whether the student ate at a special table or restricted himself to the ordinary food. In 1903 it was possible to secure a private room at an extra charge of £3–£5 a year and that opportunity was noticeably lacking at the earlier date. It was, however, still true that the college student could get his entire year of education at a total minimum cost to himself of £17 ($85.00) *including* his keep. Medical students needed to pay but $110 a year exclusive of certain laboratory fees.

6. TRUSTEES

The development of such an institution as the S.P.C. had become in 1902 speaks volumes for the administrative ability of Daniel Bliss and for the devotion and loyalty of the faculty. To their self-sacrificing interest should be added that of the local Board of Managers and particularly that of the Board of Trustees. This story of the amazing growth of the College should not be closed without a tribute to the great men in America who gave so freely of their energies, their thought, and their money to the ideal embodied in far-away Beirut. The few changes in the Board's personnel were largely caused by death alone. If in 1903 none of the

DANIEL BLISS, PRESIDENT, 1864-1902

ALLEGHENY COLLEGE LIBRARY

HOWARD SWEETSER BLISS, PRESIDENT, 1902-1920

ALLEGHENY COLLEGE LIBRARY

original Board was listed in the catalogue it was solely because the College had outlived them.

Below is the list of men who, until 1902, served as Trustees, with the dates of their service. It constitutes a record which few educational institutions anywhere could equal or surpass. Endowed with a missionary zeal as great as that of any servant of Christ on the field, they gave their hearts to the S.P.C., which gained as much thereby as by the money which they had to offer.

Name		Years	Remarks
William A. Booth, President		1863-1895	Died in Office
William E. Dodge, Sr., Treasurer		1863-1883	Died in Office
David Hoadley		1863-1873	Died in Office
Simeon B. Chittenden		1863-1883	Resigned, ill health
Abner Kingman		1863-1878	Resigned, ill health
Joseph S. Ropes		1863-1873	Resigned, living in Boston, could not get to New York for meetings
Alfred C. Post, M.D.		1873-1886	Died in Office
Alfred L. Dennis		1873-1890	Died in Office
D. Stuart Dodge, D.D.,	Serving in 1903	1882-	Secy, 1882 & Treas. 1883
William E. Dodge, Jr.	"	1883-1903	Died in Office
Morris K. Jesup	"	1884-	President 1896
Elbert B. Monroe		1887-1894	Died in Office
Samuel S. Dennis	"	1892-	
Alexander Maitland	"	1895-	
V. Everit Macy	"	1897-	

During this period of trusteeship the By-laws were twice altered. The first change was made in 1882 in order to bring the Constitution "into more exact conformity with the statutes of the State of New York regulating such organizations." It constituted the "Society" as distinct from the Trustees of the Society of the Syrian Protestant College, and provided a classification of the Trustees with staggered six-year terms. Thus Dr. Alfred Post's term was to expire in 1883, Mr. Chittenden's in 1884, that of A. L. Dennis in 1885, etc. Reelections were thenceforward to be made for six-year terms. In case a vacancy should occur in the Board, it was to be filled for the remainder of its term, preserving the annual succession. Thus though Mr. Monroe was elected in 1887, he filled the vacancy caused by the death of Dr. Post and so came up for re-election in 1889.

In 1897 the name of the "Society" was changed to the "Corporation," in conformity with provisions of the "Membership Corporation Law" which took effect on the first of January of that year. This form of organization persisted until the reorganization of the institution and the amendment of the charter in 1920, when the American University of Beirut was established.

The number of Trustees, however, was increased from six to twelve in 1906, as a direct result of the astonishing growth of the previous years. The Trustees felt that their child had grown to such proportions as to need a larger number of guardians.

VI. IN THE FULNESS OF YEARS

I. RESIGNATION OF DANIEL BLISS

Daniel Bliss tendered his resignation from the presidency of the College at the close of the year 1901, to take effect in June 1902. He was in the seventy-ninth year of his life and though still in excellent mental and physical condition, felt it to be the part of wisdom to retire.

The Trustees accepted the resignation with regret, tempered by the consolation that a worthy successor was at hand in the person of Dr. Bliss' son Howard, then pastor of the Union Congregational Church of Upper Montclair, New Jersey. At their meeting on January 30, 1902, the following resolution was passed by unanimous consent:

"The Board of Trustees receive the resignation of Dr. Bliss with mingled sorrow and congratulation.

"We deplore the sundering of official relations, which have been so prolonged and so gratifying.

"We rejoice with him in having been a chief agent in the initiation and expansion of an enterprise which has few, if any, parallels in the history of missions.

"From the time, more than forty years ago, when the first conception of this College was formulated by Rev. William M. Thomson, D.D., . . . and the Syria Mission set aside one of its members, Rev. Daniel Bliss, to go to America and endeavor to interest the Christian Public in the effort to establish a literary institution, which should promote Protestant Missions and Christian civilization in Syria and the adjacent countries, the retiring President has given his undivided, unbroken and unselfish service to this one great object.

"He repeatedly urged its claims both in the United States and Great Britain and rarely failed to win the confidence and the gifts of enlightened friends of Missions; while the kindness, the patience, the firmness and the wisdom of his administration in the College itself, secured for him the respect and affection of his associates, the veneration of the students and the wide approval of the natives.

"His clear vision of the needs and possibilities of the future led him to lay broad foundations and to plan for growth on vital and permanent lines; and in no advance did he lose sight of the supreme aim of the College to foster Christian Missions and disseminate evangelical truth.

"His executive ability, business training and sound judgment have been largely exercised in securing adequate premises and erecting substantial and commodious buildings.

"His name will always be associated with the noble site, the broad campus, and the impressive array of structures now enjoyed by 600 students.

"In reluctantly accepting his resignation, we cordially and unitedly congratulate him upon the marvelous success in which he has had so prominent a part, and as he now lays down the onerous burden of official duty, while still in the happy vigor of advanced age, we take pleasure in the anticipation that the cause, to which he has devoted the energies of a lifetime, may yet for years enjoy the blessing of his frequent presence and his ripened counsel."

At the same meeting the Trustees elected Dr. Bliss President-Emeritus and voted him permanently the full salary of a professor, i.e., $1,500 a year. As long as he was able he insisted on earning it by continuing his courses in Bible and Ethics. He attended faculty meetings regularly until 1912.

After nearly forty years of such service as that of Daniel Bliss it was only to be expected that many honors would be paid him. In June of 1902 a service was held in the chapel at which gifts were presented to him and to Mrs. Bliss by students, alumni and friends. The alumni in Egypt and the Sudan withheld their gift until the spring of 1904 when it could be completed—a life-size marble statue of President Bliss, carved in Italy. This memorial was presented to the College as a permanent testimony to the love and affection of these former students, many of them leaders in the life of their respective countries.

Dr. Bliss himself spoke at the service of presentation, and because his remarks underline the philosophy of education which was the pattern of his administration they deserve extended repetition:

"A few months since, this statue was a part of a mountain in Northern Italy. Strong men, by means of drills, wedges, sledge-hammers and levers, broke out from the mountain a large block of marble. This block by some mechanical device was placed upon a wagon with high wheels; and then was drawn by four large white oxen with branching horns, down to the workshop on the plain, where the marble block was unloaded before the artist's door. In the meantime, or before, the artist had received measurements of the person represented by the statue, his height, length of limb, breadth of shoulder, width of forehead, size of nose, mouth and chin, and a photograph of the person. Having erected a wooden frame, the artist then from these measurements and the photograph covered the frame with plastic clay until it assumed a certain size, form and look.

"The workmen commenced with hammer, chisel, gouge, bit, auger, rasp, file and calipers to break off and cut away all of that block of marble except this statue which stands before you: it alone remains.

"The success of the artist is measured by the resemblance of the statue to the living model.

"Back of all the labour and the tools connected with the making of the statue were the loving thought, the thorough purpose and the liberal gifts of the Alumni of Egypt and the Sudan, which set in motion all these instruments and agencies. Behind all things there is a mind and a purpose, human or divine, whether it be the formation of a statue, the creation of a world, the lifting of a hand, or the revolving of the celestial bodies in the starry heavens.

"The labour of making a College may, in general or in a remote way, be compared to the work of an artist. The word 'College' is an abstract word, suggesting much and varied labour, many and varied implements and forces. The buildings, the apparatus, the books, the teachers, the campus and even the location, enter into the conception of a College and conspire to build it up. Looking down upon the placid sea in calm weather and upon the boisterous wave in the storm, and looking up at the grand gray old Lebanon, has an effect upon the purpose for which our College was founded. As in the case of the statue, back of all buildings, books, and teachers, there was the loving thought, the firm purpose, the liberal gifts of men far beyond the sea and ocean, which set in motion all these agencies. . . .

"No block of marble was brought to us to be worked upon, but living boys and living men came to us from the East, from the West, from the North and from the South, to be influenced for good. They were all human and consequently imperfect; they were all human and consequently capable of perfection.

"God created man in His own image, therefore man partakes of the Divine Nature. 'But the creature (man) was made subject to vanity, not willingly, but by reason of Him who had subjected the same in hope'; and in view of this subjected hope the College was founded. God made men upright but they have sought out many inventions.

"As the workmen broke off from the block of marble all that surrounded this statue, so the College tries to break off from these young men, vanity and inventions and to leave standing the ideal man, made in the image of God.

"The artist worked from a pattern; he had at first a photograph and then the living model; we have a pattern in forming the character of our students: first photographs seen in our moral nature, in the Ten Commandments, in the Sermon on the Mount, and then the living Model, born in Bethlehem, living thirty-three years a perfect life, overcoming all vanities and inventions. We do not aim to make Maronites, or Greeks, or Catholics, or Protestants, or Jews, or Moslems, but we do aim to make perfect men, ideal men, God-like men, after the model of Jesus Christ, against whose moral character no man ever has said or can say aught. Opinions may differ about His origin, His nature, His death, His resurrection, His future and a thousand other questions that cluster about His great Name, but the Image of God in man, the breath of God in the soul, man's moral nature, must recognize in the moral life of Jesus Christ the perfect model of human conduct."[1]

[1] Bliss, Reminiscences, pp. 220-3.

In analyzing the causes of the remarkable growth and commanding position which the College attained during his administration, President Bliss outlined four factors which he felt were of vital influence. The Trustees and the Faculty were rightly included. In his own words, the other two factors were, first: "trust in God and faith in man as such, without regard to race, color or religion." The College opened its doors "to the members of the most advanced and the most backward of races. As for me, I would admit the Pigmies of Central Africa in the hope that after the lapse of a few thousand years some of them might become leaders in Church and State."

The remaining factor, and the most important in the eyes of the first president, was "the character, standing and influence of our graduates and others who were with us for a longer or shorter time. Without claiming for them superiority to or even equality with the graduates from Universities of the West, we know that they are far more honored and respected by the people of their own countries than Western graduates are by their own people."[2] This, of course, was the effect of the other three influences working together, but it nevertheless is the most important cause of the institution's continuing success. It is most assuredly true of all the American colleges in the Near East that by their fruits they are known.

2. ADMINISTRATION

It goes without need of saying that Daniel Bliss possessed in high degree the qualities essential to a successful college administrator. He was able to secure the cooperation of Trustees, faculty and students in developing the type of institution which he envisaged. He created respect by his ideals. He was tireless in devotion to his manifold duties, careless of personal glory or credit. He knew the psychology of students and of the people in the country he hoped they might serve. His educational goal was to make the College supply the needs of the country rather than to have it fit a preconceived educational formula. He was an accomplished diplomat able to steer a safe course in the dubious waters of Ottoman politics.

[2] Bliss, op. cit., pp. 212-13.

He could arouse enthusiasm and raise money, but he could also make it go far in a land where westerners are traditionally outclassed in business acumen. He possessed the patience of Job and a saving sense of humor, the lack of which is often more fatal to a college president than any other defect.

As a leader of the faculty, Daniel Bliss was usually content to exercise as little constraint as possible. He got things done by suggestion rather than command. He really seemed to feel that of all the crew of the college ship he had no more to do with its successful functioning than anyone else. And yet on occasion he could take strong command. Frederick Bliss tells the following story of his father: "At a Faculty meeting, held in the early days of the College, two motions were made involving radical changes of College policy which the President felt to be premature and hence unwise. After the first motion, he took up a little red book and said: 'On page so-and-so of this Constitution, you will find that the matter proposed is not within our province but belongs to the Trustees.' A similar reply was made to the maker of the second motion. Whereupon a third and younger member said: 'How is it that all these years we have been voting as we pleased and have never before been confronted with this little red book?' The President gravely replied: 'When the sky is clear and the sea is calm, the mariner steers by the sun and stars, but when the clouds are dark and the waves high he turns to his chart.' 'And who is to decide as to the state of the weather?' asked the young professor. Instantly the answer rang out: 'The Captain!' "[3]

To the ordinary duties of a college administrator President Bliss had to add those of diplomatic agent in a country which was not always too friendly. When the College was small and weak in its early life its diplomacy consisted in being as unobtrusive and agreeable as possible. When the school increased in size and importance it became necessary for the President to see that his charge was not crippled by restrictive political measures, hampered by official interference or smothered by preferences shown to rivals. Here was required all the patience, ingenuity, courtesy, determination, persistence and knowledge which an unusual man might

[3] Bliss, op. cit., pp. 219-20.

command. Dr. Bliss was such a man, and with the help of the faculty and the Trustees succeeded eventually in solving—at least temporarily—most of the problems with which he was faced.

The problem of official recognition for graduates of the medical school was not cleared up until after his resignation, but Daniel Bliss had directed many of the negotiations which led up to the final success. He had been hampered for years by the weakness of American diplomatic policy which seemed inevitably to remove from office its ministers in foreign capitals just as they had begun to acquire a certain amount of influence. America was very far away from Turkey and its representatives carried less weight with the Sublime Porte than did those of European powers. It must have been exasperating to the College administration to see favors granted, for example, to the French Jesuit College which were denied to the American institution. Indeed in numerous instances the College was dependent on British diplomatic intervention for its very continuance.[4] Time and again influential trustees went to Washington "to keep our own Government informed and to stimulate it to protect American interests in the Turkish Empire." They also sought to have the United States representative at Constantinople raised to the rank of Ambassador and to insure that the post was filled "by a person of diplomatic experience and authority." Fine men like Straus and Angell did their best but were not clothed with sufficient authority by their own government to secure major concessions readily granted to other powers. Likewise the rank of the American consulate at Beirut was not impressive. The College had long sought to have

[4] e.g. In the Minutes of January 28, 1897, William E. Dodge cited a letter from London, "stating that private advices from Constantinople made it evident that it was the intention of the Sublime Porte to close foreign schools; and that representations had been made to Lord Salisbury urging him to prevent, if possible, the issuing of such a proclamation."

Again, a year later, Turkish authorities forbade Egyptian students coming to the S.P.C. to land at Beirut. "At the request of the President, the English Consul-general made inquiries of the Governor of the City and the American Consul urged our Minister at Constantinople to interfere." In this case Dr. Angell was successful.

President McKinley told W. E. Dodge that he was "disposed to resort to coercive measures if necessary," but that the situation in Cuba required the presence of the fleet in home waters. This was in 1898. Many other American interests in Turkey were in jeopardy at the time.

it made a consulate-general, and renewed its effort in this direction in 1900, though the desired result was not obtained until 1905.

One evidence of the skill of an administrator is the success with which the aims of the college he heads are attained. The record of Daniel Bliss on this count was remarkable, as has been seen. In one respect at least it was astounding: in the determination engendered in the students to work in their own countries. Whereas previous experience had shown that a large proportion of the graduates of foreign institutions went abroad to reap the benefits of their education, a relatively small number from the S.P.C. did so. By the year 1903 only nine medical graduates from a total of 221 were away from the Near East. Eight pharmacy graduates out of 118 had gone abroad, and but forty-three B.A. men of the entire 237 were in foreign countries, many of them pursuing graduate studies. No record was available of the 577 Preparatory graduates but it is safe to assume that their showing was no worse. These figures refer, of course, only to actual graduates, for the total number of students who had had some connection with the College was nearly three times the number graduated.

3. TEACHER

In addition to his administrative duties the president was, of course, expected to teach full time. In this Daniel Bliss delighted, for he looked upon his classes in Bible and Ethics as his greatest opportunity to influence the students for good. He had a rare ability to reach his pupils' minds—those typical oriental minds which think in pictures and parables, which are devoted to colorful imagery rather than to bare abstractions. He was a past master at the apt illustration, the telling example, the story with its own moral. His was the teaching method of Jesus, which literal-minded westerners are prone to misunderstand. Bliss often called himself "professor of story-telling," but he taught his enthusiastic students with a success which has seldom been surpassed in its enduring quality.

To teach the Bible or Christian ethics to a mixed class of Protestants, Catholics, Maronites, Moslems and Greek Orthodox students without encouraging antagonisms already ripe was no simple matter, but it was simply and wisely done. Let Dr. Bliss himself tell how the awkward question of intercession was handled: "The question was asked: 'Is it wrong to ask the Saints and the Blessed Virgin to pray for us, to intercede for us?' Had the question been answered: 'Yes, it is wrong,' two-thirds of the class who were in the habit of calling on the Virgin and Saints, would have turned a deaf ear to all that might have been said afterwards. Had the question been answered: 'No, it is not wrong,' the Protestant boys would have reported to their parents and to the missionaries that the President of the College had turned Roman Catholic or Maronite.

"So I turned to the one asking the question and said: 'I thank you for asking that question. It is an important one and a most natural question.' (The Protestant boys sat in their seats with upright heads, expecting the others would be placed on the left hand with the goats.) 'A most natural question for you to ask, living in this country, for everything is done here through mediators or intercessors. If you wish a favour of me you do not come to me directly, but you go to some Tutor and ask him to ask me. You have been to my wife and besought her to induce me to give a holiday. I have bought several horses, rented several houses, bought various pieces of land, but always through a broker, that is, an intercessor. Not only in business matters but in political and social affairs also the intercessor must be appealed to. You cannot call on the Pasha of Beirut directly; you must first pass the guard, the doorkeeper, see his Secretary, and he will go and ask the Pasha to receive you. Not only in this country but in England and all over the world you must appeal to intercessors. I cannot call upon the King of England, directly, but must appeal to the Ambassador of the United States, who will intercede with I know not how many English officials, and then perhaps I might possibly see the King. Your question is a most natural one. You say: If I cannot visit the President of the College, the Pasha, the King, without intercession, how can I go direct to God,'—(the heads of the Protestant boys hung low); then I added:

'There is an infinite difference between the President of the College, the Pasha of Beirut and the King of England on the one hand, and the Lord Jesus Christ on the other. These never have invited you to call; He says: Come unto me all ye that labour and are heavy laden. We know little, He is all wise; we have little compassion, He is full of grace and truth and loves you more than all the Saints in Glory can possibly love you. So, whether it is right or whether it is wrong to ask the Saints to intercede for you, it is wholly unnecessary, it is useless, it is a loss of time,—'Before they call I will answer, saith the Almighty.' "[5]

The understanding of the student psychology, the sympathy for points of view which might be in error, the constant desire to enlighten without dogmatism, these were qualities of Daniel Bliss' teaching which are constantly found only in great teachers. Couple them, as in his case, with a love of subject and a mature understanding of it which comes only from devoted study and familiar thought, and one has a teacher whose students should rise up and call him blessed.

4. DISCIPLINARIAN

Further light on the peculiar fitness of Daniel Bliss for the position he held is shed by his activities as disciplinarian-in-chief of the College. Here he showed again the understanding of eastern psychology and the balanced judgment which were his greatest assets. Here again he was able to emphasize to his students the qualities of conduct which it was most important for them to recognize.

In the Near East, even now, the necessity for rather strict supervision over student life is greater than it is in America. Not only are serious temptations more numerous and more accessible, but the early training of young men does not produce in them as much facility for moral judgment as is found in the average American student. This is not the fault of the student so much as it is that of family and school background. There, discipline is apt to be rigid but merely for the sake of discipline, rather than for the cultivation of intelligent respect for sound principles of behavior. The result is that a Syrian boy for example, turned loose in the comparatively free atmosphere of an American college, may misuse

[5] Bliss, Reminiscences, pp. 207-9.

his freedom in reckless indulgence simply because he is unaccustomed to lack of restriction. The problem in the Syrian Protestant College was to bridge the gap between rigid surveillance and natural self-government, encouraging the development of independent self-control but keeping it rather strictly within bounds. The importance of being able to construct a wall around the campus was not to be exaggerated. It greatly facilitated a necessary check on the goings-out and the comings-in and permitted greater freedom within the campus.

In other Syrian schools of Daniel Bliss' time students were frequently encouraged to spy on one another and report to the authorities any infractions of the rules. This the S.P.C. utterly repudiated. As President Bliss put it: "I trusted the boys. Sometimes I treated one as if he was telling me the truth when I knew he was lying to me. I cannot explain the philosophy of it but trusting a boy makes him trustworthy."[6]

In minor matters of discipline the President frequently used what he himself called "the undignified and almost frivolous" way of disciplining students. It may be illustrated by three examples cited by his son:

"It was once reported to the President by a Professor that during the prayer at Evening Chapel a medical student had the habit of turning to the small boys on the seats behind and, by making faces, of setting them to giggling. In duty bound, though somewhat unwillingly, the President verified the story by keeping his eyes open during the prayer. As soon as the 'Amen' was said, he rose and asked the young man to remain (not an unusual thing when he wished to see a student). The President resumed his seat. The Faculty retired as usual, followed by the Seniors and other classes in their order. Then, without looking at the student, the President took his hat and went out, leaving the young man alone. (Prayers were then held in what is now the library on the second floor of College Hall.) He descended the stairway, passed along the corridor lined with curious, silent students, and went out into the open air. A moment later echoes of clapping and derisive laughter reached his ears. For the student, who had been

[6] Bliss, op. cit., p. 200.

thus abandoned, had, on coming out, to run the gauntlet of the boys, waiting for his emergence! 'If the President had taken me into a room alone and beaten me,' said this crestfallen humorist later, 'I should not have minded, but to set the students laughing at me—!' This was before the Mikado was composed and the young man had not heard of 'making the punishment fit the crime.' 'When did you decide on the plan?' one of us asked the President. 'I never planned it,' he replied; 'I intended to speak to the boy, but when the time came there seemed nothing to say, so I left.'

"There was a regulation against smoking in the rooms. 'One night in November,' a graduate relates, 'I was studying very late in my fourth-story room, and, supposing the authorities were all in bed, I was smoking a cigarette, which, when half finished, I chucked out of the window. In a few minutes came a knock at the door. 'Come in!' I called. The door slowly opened. Instead of some fellow-student, there stood the President! And the room full of smoke! 'Good evening,' he said, with his usual air of dignified politeness. 'Have you studied Astronomy?' 'Ye-e-es, sir,' I stammered. 'Then perhaps you can tell me whether this is one of the nights when we may expect meteors falling through the air?' 'I-I-I don't remember,' I said. 'Ah,' he said, 'I thought perhaps you could. Good-night.' That was all, but there was no more smoking in that room at least.

"In later years when no one was supposed to smoke anywhere on the campus, a student was enjoying a cigarette behind the Chapel. Presently he heard the firm step of the President advancing. He hastily thrust his right hand, burning cigarette and all, into his side coat-pocket. Instead of passing by with a salute, as usual, the President extended his hand. The student was obliged to extend his. 'How is your father in Damascus?' said Dr. Bliss. 'And your mother and (still shaking the hand) your dear old grandmother? Give them my salaams when you write.' At this juncture the cigarette dropped from the burnt pocket to the ground. The President saluted and passed on with no further word. Such stories were too good to be kept even by the victims and hence the regulation usually took care of itself."[7]

Dr. Bliss was by no means incapable of severity but he reserved it for occasions which warranted its use. In his own phrase, "we were patient in cases of small irregularities, but when a student endangered the morality of others, then we isolated him as in the case of smallpox or plague." As a single example of quick and drastic action, the following is perhaps typical: "I was told by one of the professors that a certain student had vile books in his possession, illustrated by obscene pictures. I went into his room and demanded that he open his trunk. He did so and I saw that the report of the professor was correct. I told him he could send for his trunk but that he must go immediately from the College. I had my cane in hand and used it not as a staff but as a rod. I kept in *touch* with him as far as the medical gate, out of which he went, not saying a word, not even thanking me for accompanying him thus far."[8]

From such experiences as these, it is easy to imagine what at least nine student generations must have thought of President Bliss as guide, philosopher and friend. His patriarchal appearance alone would have aroused respect among the later generations. It was, however, an unnecessary adjunct to the kindly but firm justice of his nature which of itself evoked the admiring esteem even of those upon whom his discipline had to fall.

The graduates of the College did not fail to realize their obligations both to Dr. Bliss and to Mrs. Bliss whom they loved as a mother. They did not hesitate frequently to express their feelings both in word and in deed like the presentation to the College of the marble statue. It is perhaps not fair to say that students in the Near East feel more deeply about such things than do westerners, but it is generally true that they are less shy at expressing themselves. One of the finest of these expressions was given utterance at the presentation of the statue in 1904. Nesim Birbari, '88, who had returned to Cairo after having recently been made Licencié

[7] Ibid., pp. 202-3.

[8] Al-Kulliyah, V, 3:74 (January 1914) Article: Recollections of a Long Life, by Daniel Bliss.

en Droit in France, and who in 1920 was given the title of Bey by the Egyptian Government, made the presentation address, in which he said: "As I stand today amid the favorite surroundings of my youth . . . memory carries me backward to my student days and the picture I have of Dr. Bliss is not that of the stern president who presided over the College and its destinies or of the public man who represented its interests before the world, but rather that of a wise counselor, a trusty friend and a kind father. It is in this light that I like to remember Dr. Bliss, not as he appeared to outsiders, but as he appeared to his large family of which we all formed a part. . . . He was to us a 'living epistle known and read of all men.' . . . Long after we have joined the mighty host that preceded us, and long after these buildings have given place to others, the immortal work of Dr. Bliss will remain impressed forever on the national character of the people of this country."[9]

[9] 38th Annual Report of S.P.C., pp. 21 and 22 (1903-04).

PART II

The Administration of Howard S. Bliss

1902-1920

VII. DEVELOPMENT

I. THE NEW PRESIDENT

"WITH THIS REPORT closes the first generation of College history. From a few rented rooms we have reached the threshold of a university career. May the great work that calls the second generation be achieved in the fear of God." Thus Daniel Bliss ended his last report as President of the Syrian Protestant College. For him the figure was particularly happy, for his successor was indeed of the second generation, being his own son, Howard Sweetser Bliss. Not until the end of the second generation would the College become a university in name, but the work of that generation was none the less great. The hope of the retiring father was abundantly fulfilled in the administration of his son.

Howard Bliss was born in Suq-al-Gharb on December 6, 1860, the year of the great massacres. His boyhood was spent in Beirut and he grew up, so to speak, on the campus of the college which was so nearly his own age. As the son of the president he naturally met the distinguished visitors who came to see the college, and during an extended visit of Mr. Theodore Roosevelt he and his older brother, Frederick, frequently rode through the cactus lanes on the same donkey with young Teddy. One cannot but wonder whether this early association had any bearing on the friendliness with which President Roosevelt in 1902-03 supported the claims of the College and the missions before the Turkish Government.

Mr. Bliss graduated from Amherst in 1882 and for two years thereafter taught at Washburn College in Topeka, Kansas. Returning to New York he entered Union Theological Seminary and graduated at the head of his class in 1887 with a fellowship which gave him a year at Oxford under Dr. Fairbairn and another year in Germany at the universities of Berlin and Goettingen.

After his return to America, Mr. Bliss spent five years as associate pastor in Dr. Lyman Abbot's Plymouth Church in Brooklyn. He then became the minister of the Christian Union Congregational Church in Upper Montclair, New Jersey, and was occupying that pulpit when he was called to the presidency of the Syrian Protestant College in 1902. He and his talented wife, the former Amy Blatchford of Chicago,[1] sailed that summer for Syria and reached Beirut on November 11 ready for their new duties. The formal inauguration of the new president took place from May 10-13, 1903.

2. BOARD OF MANAGERS

Among the important events which took place during the inauguration period not the least significant was the dissolution of the Board of Managers which, throughout the first generation of the college life, had supervised the operations of the institution with faithful devotion and singleness of purpose. When the College was first established, communication with America was slow and uncertain, making it impossible to get speedy action from the distant Board of Trustees. The faculty was very small and felt the need of constant advice from the experienced missionaries and laymen who made up the Board. The College itself, without precedent and reputation, needed a group of men well known for their intelligence and probity to give it weight in the country it hoped to serve.

How different was the situation when Howard Bliss became president! The College had arrived. It was far better and more widely known than any members of a Board of Managers. Its influence extended to Persia on the east, to the Sudan on the south, to North and South America on the west, and to Bulgaria and Turkey on the north. Instead of a faculty of three professors it had eighteen, with twenty-six other teachers. The problems of the College were now more internal than external, dealing more with teaching and administrative affairs than with the cultivation of influence outside the walls. Such problems the experienced faculty were better qualified to handle than were men without their professional training. And communications with America were

[1] Mrs. Bliss died in Jerusalem, June 27, 1941. She had been forced to leave her beloved Beirut by the approach of the war. Three of her daughters are wives of faculty members, and one son, Huntington Bliss, is professor of English at the American College of Sofia. Her other son, Daniel Bliss, is pastor of the Second Congregational Church of Greenwich, Conn., and a Trustee of International College.

now so relatively swift that major matters of policy could be submitted direct to the Trustees, whose local representatives the Board of Managers had always been. The work of the Board was, in short, no longer necessary and its continuance was thought to place an unessential burden upon an institution already become sufficiently complex in its internal structure.

The initiative in the dissolution of the Board came from the members themselves, who expressed the conviction in their meeting of July 9, 1902, that "the growth of the College and the consequent change of conditions rendered it no longer possible to discharge the functions of the Board as originally contemplated, and made it desirable to revise the Constitution and establish different relations for the executive control of the Institution." The Trustees voted to accept the Managers' request that they be formally dissolved but asked them to retain their organization until the official inauguration of the new president. At the same time they expressed their profound appreciation for the past services of the Board of Managers and their hope that they might expect the continued cooperation of the Managers as individuals "in promoting the interests of this Institution as part of the common missionary work, in which we are all engaged, thus perpetuating the fraternal sympathy and helpfulness which has been a marked and beneficent feature of our mutual relations during the forty years of the existence of the College."[2] They received the cordial promise of the retiring Board that their hope would not be disappointed.

3. NEEDS OF THE COLLEGE

In his last annual report to the Board of Managers, Daniel Bliss, in typical fashion, devoted a good deal more space to an analysis of the needs of the College and its weaknesses than he did to a résumé of its past successes. His clear vision enabled him to outline a course of development which the succeeding administration sought to bring to fruition. There was no conflict in aims or methods, no "dropping the pilot" in the sense that the new régime dispensed with the principles of the old. One of the striking features in the success of the College throughout its history has been the

[2] Trustees Minutes, January 21, 1903.

continuity of purpose and plan which has characterized its three administrations. They have all shared the educational and spiritual principles which were built into the foundation of the work.

The retiring president noted as the greatest weakness of the institution the lack of development of the collegiate department, "the very center of our system. . . . The Preparatory School leads up to it, the Schools of Medicine and Pharmacy branch out from it, the School of Commerce somewhat parallels it. Weakness here is weakness at the heart of the institution. . . . The Preparatory School cannot reach its proper standard of work until demands are made upon it from above. The Schools of Medicine and Pharmacy cannot advance as they should until there are higher ideals of thoroughness and higher attainments of scholarship in the preparation of their students. The presence of a weak sister department certainly cannot help the students of the School of Commerce to form high ideals of work and it is not strange if it has the opposite tendency."[3]

Daniel Bliss found three main flaws in the collegiate department: a paucity of permanent staff members; a curriculum not brought up-to-date; and *a course of study without definiteness of practical aim as its end.* With regard to the latter, the words of the octogenarian Dr. Bliss, in 1902, have a curiously modern ring and mark him as a man ahead of his time.

The collegiate department, he said, "needs more definiteness of adaptation to the needs of practical life as the aim of its higher courses of study. It has been a favorite educational theory that education and culture are in themselves sufficient spurs to urge students on to effort and it cannot be denied that they form the noblest aim. But for the mass of students even in America the ordinary college course, as an end in itself, is said to lead to ineffective work, that the best work is done by men who are using their college course as definite preparation for further and professional study. The same fact has been experienced here. The collegiate course, above the sophomore year which admits to the medical course, leads nowhere except to an academic degree; and

[3] Annual Report, 1901-02, p. 11.

in no other place in the whole institution is the work of the students themselves so desultory and unsatisfactory."[4]

One solution of this difficulty was proposed in the introduction of further professional courses, of which Dr. Bliss mentioned specifically law, engineering, technology and pedagogy. These, he felt, might be slowly attained through the development of existing departments, *"devising electives so that each man may choose according to his bent."* These were rather advanced words for that stage in the history of education, but it was not more than two years before a controlled system of electives was introduced in the Syrian Protestant College. Within one year, the first of Howard Bliss' administration, it was announced to the students that the M.A. degree was obtainable by those who could satisfy the conditions, namely: "one year's residence with courses of study, thesis and examination, or three years study outside the College."

Of course the strengthening of the collegiate department required first of all an increase in the staff, which in turn depended upon the acquisition of sufficient endowment to support additional chairs. Daniel Bliss reported the discouraging fact that in 1901-02, there were but four permanent faculty members who gave their full time to the department—the professors of History (Porter), English (Nicely), Arabic (Dumit) and French (Charbonnier). Professor Day, who occupied the chair of Natural Sciences, had a heavy schedule in the medical department where he taught both Zoology and Histology. Professor West, who had occupied the chair of Astronomy-Mathematics, was principal of the preparatory department which occupied all his time. Forty percent of the instruction of the collegiate section was in the hands of temporary tutors whose three-year terms hardly enabled them to reach their full efficiency as teachers before they had to be replaced by new men. Such a condition could not be permitted to continue if the department were to assume its proper place in the College organization.

The retiring president further called attention to the need for development in the medical school, faced as it was with the competition of the Jesuit school which had obtained the advantage

[4] Annual Report, 1901-02, p. 10.

long but unsuccessfully sought by the S.P.C. of having an Imperial Commission come to Beirut to examine its graduates. The Government Medical School in Cairo, too, was "no longer the moribund institution of a few years ago, but a live, aggressive school under the care of able Englishmen who are determined to make it a success." To meet this competition the American school would have to improve its equipment even though its staff was already first-class. The Johanniter Hospital's eighty-two beds were insufficient to handle the increasing number of patients and no facilities at all were provided for gynecology and obstetrics. As Dr. Adams once wrote: "When babies were once born into this world of tears, no nurses loved them more devotedly and nursed sick ones more tenderly than the German sisters; but they seemed to have an abhorrence of Dr. Moore's work, especially the helping of the little ones into this world."[5] A separate hospital for women, to be operated by the College seemed the only solution to this problem and to it the Order of St. John had given its approval. More space was also needed for children's diseases, and eye and ear work. A chair of Children's Diseases was urgently indicated.

In the preparatory department the greatest weakness apparent was the lack of segregation of the small boys from the large. Only some 15 percent of the preparatory students were under fourteen years of age but that small group was a continual source of trouble and worry. Even with Fisk and Bliss Halls completed, it was not possible to segregate the primary students so that they could be subjected to special discipline, and be given separate classes and different teaching methods. They could not be eliminated, for there existed elsewhere no suitable boarding or day school in which they might be prepared. The logical answer was the establishment of a distinct Primary School, preferably with separate campus as well as its own buildings.

All of these developments required money, either for endowment or for new buildings or both. It was obvious that one of the first tasks of the new administration would be the securing of new funds. When Howard Bliss was elected he had urged the Trustees not to expect him "to devote his energies to the raising of funds,"

[5] Al-Kulliyah IX, 5:75 (March 1923).

but to permit him "to apply himself chiefly and continuously to the direct and absorbing work of such an office."[6] *Sic transit spes praesidis.* His own father had outlined a plan which would inevitably plunge the son into the sea of financial responsibility. He was to find himself blessed, however, with a Board of Trustees who would take the initiative in money raising and relieve him of a great part of what is frequently the most onerous burden of a college president.

4. THE MEDICAL IRADÉ

The problem whose solution would do most immediately to inspire the whole College was that of securing the official recognition of the medical school which had been so long and so fruitlessly sought. The matter was more important than it might seem, for it had become intimately associated with the entire question of the relations between the Ottoman Government and all American institutions in Turkey, and stood as a symbol of the Turkish refusal to grant to America the "concessions" freely given to European powers.[7] In spite of numerous representations to the Sublime Porte by the American Minister in Constantinople, no satisfaction had been obtained as late as the fall of 1902.

Feeling that more emphatic action must be taken at once, the faculty earnestly requested Dr. Post to go to the United States as part of a deputation from Turkey to urge the importance of the matter upon the President. The deputation consisted of the Rev. Wm. K. Eddy, representing the Syria Mission, and Dr. W. W. Peet, representing the American Board, in addition to Dr. Post of the Syrian Protestant College. In America these men proceeded to form a committee representing all the American missions and institutions operating in the Turkish Empire. The enlarged committee, numbering twenty-three men and including Morris K. Jesup as chairman and D. Stuart Dodge, met in Washington and

[6] Trustees Minutes, January 30, 1902.

[7] According to President Washburn of Robert College these concessions had first been gained by France "as a result of its naval demonstration and occupation of the island of Mitylene." They were then extended to English, German and Russian institutions but not to American. Cf. Washburn, 50 Years in Constantinople (Houghton, Mifflin 1911), pp. 285-86.

called upon President Roosevelt on December 11, 1902. The following day the delegates from Turkey called upon Secretaries Hay and Foster and other officials, "and were informed that emphatic instructions were to be given to the Minister at Constantinople to insist upon the rights of this country."[8] This was undoubtedly the result of the promise cordially given to the main committee by President Roosevelt, who had willingly agreed to take a personal interest in the matter.

It is of interest to see the case which the committee presented, as embodied in a memorial letter to the President prepared at that time. It summarizes the entire situation and gives evidence of at least one effort already made by Mr. Roosevelt on behalf of the College. This was certainly not the first occasion when Turkish affairs had been brought to his notice for he had had at his own request during the preceding summer a long conversation with President George Washburn of Robert College. The letter follows:

To the PRESIDENT OF THE UNITED STATES OF AMERICA

Sir: American Missions in Turkey date back to 1819, eleven years before the first Treaty between the United States and the Ottoman Porte. They were organized by Americans, and permitted by the Ottoman Government, in the same manner and with the same privileges as the pre-existing missions of other countries. In Turkey such a recognition and permission carry the force of law. Under it the Missions acquired property, established institutions, carried on commerce in the products of their printing presses and industrial institutions, imported the articles necessary for their maintenance and for their work, free of duty, and obtained other immunities similar to those of the other nationalities. Under the Treaties of 1830 and 1862, American citizens were placed on the same footing in Turkey as those of the most privileged nations. This included their missionary immunities and privileges, as has been in numerous instances maintained by the United States, and admitted by the Ottoman Porte. Similar principles have been reaffirmed in the Hatti Humayun of 1856, the Treaty of Berlin of 1878, the laws of 1864 and of 1868, the notes to the United States Legation of 1875 and 1889 and 1892, and Secretary Bayard's letter to Minister Strauss in 1887 and a letter from Mr. Foster to Mr. Thompson, November 29th, 1892.

Of late years these privileges have been abridged by regulations and arbitrary executive acts of the Turkish Government. In many instances they have been submitted to by American missionaries, and those of other nations, in

[8] Trustees Minutes, January 21, 1903.

the hope that compliance would conciliate the Turkish Government, and put a stop to further encroachment on the rights secured by treaty and immemorial usage. These concessions only produce demands, which, if complied with, would result in the crippling of all missionary work, and imperiling pecuniary investments amounting in the aggregate to $6,000,000 belonging to citizens of the United States.

In view of the progressive obstruction and encroachments of the Turkish Government on missionary work of all nationalities, the French Embassy at Constantinople, in November, 1901, obtained the following settlement:

> "By a letter written in virtue of an Imperial Iradé mentioned in that letter, the Ottoman Minister for Foreign Affairs declares that the Porte, after having acceded to our first demands, accepts the new demands of France, viz:
>
> "(1) Recognizes the legal status of our existing schools, and grants them the Customs immunities stipulated in the Treaties and Conventions in force;
>
> "(2) Recognizes the legal status of our present charitable and religious establishments, and grants them exemption from the Land Tax, and the Customs immunities stipulated in the Treaties and Conventions in force;
>
> "(3) Authorizes the construction, repair, or enlargement of the scholastic, charitable, or religious establishments damaged or destroyed during the events of 1894, 1895 and 1896, in Asiatic Turkey and at Constantinople;
>
> "(4) Undertakes to regard as fully and legally authorized the foundations, enlargements, constructions, and repairs we may desire in the future to effect, if, after being warned of our intention, the Imperial Government has not raised objections within the delay of six months; and
>
> "(5) Sanctions the election of the Chaldean Patriarch.
>
> "Moreover, the documents proving that the decisions enumerated above are put into execution have been communicated to the French Embassy in Constantinople."

A similar settlement, except that relating to the Chaldean Patriarch, has been obtained by the Governments of Russia, Germany, and Italy for similar institutions belonging to their subjects. The United States Legation, at the request of the American missionaries, has filed an application for a similar settlement of American missionary rights, but up to the present time no notice has been taken of this demand.

Furthermore, anterior to the above settlement, the Turkish Government conceded five years ago to the French Medical School of Beirut the recognition of the right to issue a French diploma of Doctor of Medicine and Master of Pharmacy to graduates in those departments. His Majesty the Sultan also issued an Iradé, directing the Imperial Faculty of Medicine at Constantinople to send, each year, a Commission to participate in the examinations in Medicine and Pharmacy in the French School of Medicine at Beirut. Successful candidates receive from the Imperial Faculty the diploma of Doctor of Medicine and Surgery and of Master of Pharmacy without further examination.

The Syrian Protestant College applied, through the United States Legation, for similar privileges for its Medical Department, which has been much longer in existence than the French School. After years of fruitless negotiations, the Rev. Howard S. Bliss, D.D., President of the Syrian Protestant College, appealed directly to you on this subject. In a dispatch, sent in August last to the American Minister in Constantinople, you drew the attention of His Majesty the Sultan to the invidious distinction made in favor of the French School, and requested His Majesty to grant the petition of the Syrian Protestant College and to place its Medical Department in every respect on a footing of equality with the French Medical School. To the present time, His Majesty has taken no notice of this communication, and it is possible that it has never been given to him by the Grand Vizier. The attitude of the Ottoman Porte on these two questions needs no comment.

We therefore beg you to take the necessary steps;

(1) To secure for the American Missions and Institutions in Turkey the prompt and full confirmation of their pre-existing rights, and a settlement similar to that accorded to Missions and Institutions belonging to French, Russian, German and Italian subjects; and

(2) To secure the appointment of an annual Commission by the Imperial School of Medicine at Constantinople to cooperate in the Syrian Protestant College at Beirut in the examinations in Medicine and Pharmacy of graduates of the Medical Department of the same, and the award by the Imperial Faculty of Medicine, to successful candidates, of the diploma of Doctor of Medicine and of Master of Pharmacy, without further examination.

(signed)

Morris K. Jesup	Chairman
	Representative of—
Samuel B. Capen	The American Board of Commissioners for Foreign Missions
Hon. Darwin R. James	The Board of Foreign Missions of the Presbyterian Church in the U.S.
Andrew Alexander	The Reformed Presbyterian Church of North America
D. Stuart Dodge	The Syrian Protestant College at Beirut
John S. Kennedy Rev. Edward B. Coe Hon. John R. Foster	Robert College at Constantinople The American Bible House at Constantinople The American Bible Society

Rev. Judson Smith	The Euphrates College at Harput
Rev. James L. Barton	The Central Turkey College at Aintab The Anatolia College at Marsovan
Henry M. MacCracken Frederick A. Booth, Treas.	St. Paul's Institute at Tarsus
James M. Speers	The American Hospital at Cesarea

Dr. Post set out for Beirut shortly after the Trustees' meeting in January 1903, stopping at Constantinople by request of the Trustees, "to counsel with the American Minister (Mr. Leishman) and others, in connection with the question of the 'Concessions' from the Sultan." It is not at present possible to determine exactly what happened there, but the results were soon apparent. The long sought Iradé was granted by the Sultan in the spring, and the first Imperial Commission of medical examiners arrived in Beirut on June 22, accompanied by Dr. Post. Whether the latter had stayed all spring in Constantinople does not appear, but one gets the impression that Dr. Post was unwilling to permit the cherished Commission to escape from his sight. Certainly he and Minister Leishman deserve all the credit which could be given them for their skill and persistence.

The first Commission, composed of Mahmoud Pasha, Kheiriddin Pasha and Rifaat Bey—all professors in the Imperial Medical School—made an excellent impression on the American faculty and in turn were favorably impressed themselves, for one of them expressed a desire to send his son to the Preparatory Department and later to the medical school. The fact that all seniors in both medicine and pharmacy passed the numerous examinations, "the majority in a most creditable manner," according to President Bliss, could hardly have failed to excite the approval of the visitors.

Until the World War put an end to the annual visits of the Commission, they appear uniformly to have been occasions which were thoroughly enjoyed by all, except, perhaps, the students being examined. President Bliss described the second visit in 1904 as being "as delightful as the first. The Commissioners—Zoeros Pasha, Houloussi Rashid Bey and Hickmet Emin Bey—expressed themselves as much pleased with all that they saw of the College. Two public addresses were made by the President of the Commission,

Zoeros Pasha—one on the occasion of Afternoon Prayers and one when the oath of office was administered to those who had successfully passed the examinations. On the latter occasion, as a mark of the feeling of appreciation and regard which he felt for the venerable President-Emeritus, the Pasha, in the presence of the large assembly gathered to view the impressive ceremony, kissed the hand of Dr. Daniel Bliss."[9]

The granting of all the concessions sought by Americans was not secured until 1907 when, through the constant efforts of Mr. Leishman, by then Ambassador, an Imperial Firman was issued, formally according to all American institutions the same standing as those of other nations. Along with it was given an order granting permission to the College to erect a hospital for women, and officially recognizing the whole Medical Department. At long last, the brakes were off the progress of medical work in Syria.

5. MEDICAL EXPANSION

The development of the medical school was given a mighty impetus by the Imperial blessing which it had at last received, but the course for it was already prepared. The plans outlined by Daniel Bliss in his final report had been carried further during the summer of 1902 by the purchase of the Nino-Adham property lying south and east of the medical gate. Added to a small adjacent plot already owned, it provided an area of three acres for future hospital buildings. It contained one large house, the palatial residence of the Adham (Azm) family, which was suitable for remodelling into a hospital pavilion or nurses' training school and which actually served an infinite variety of purposes before its final destruction by fire on December 30, 1939.

The purchase and enclosure of this property at a total cost of over $25,000 was made possible by contributions from J. P. Morgan and John T. Terry and through the establishment by Morris K. Jesup, president of the Board of Trustees, of the Maria C. DeWitt Jesup Foundation, to provide hospital facilities for women's and children's diseases and a nurses' training school. This foundation, named in honor of Mrs. Jesup, contemplated the immediate con-

[9] Annual Report, 1903-04, pp. 14-15.

struction of the Woman's Pavilion, already authorized by the Johanniter Order, and the later construction of buildings for the other two services. In 1904 Mr. Jesup provided $10,000 for the Woman's Pavilion and set up the Maria DeWitt Jesup Trust Fund of $100,000 to endow the Foundation. This endowment was later increased by $400,000 through the terms of Mrs. Jesup's will in 1916-17.

For more than four years after the money was on hand, official permission to build the Woman's Pavilion was delayed, and the remodelled Adham house had to accommodate all the work when it was begun early in 1905. Dr. Adams recalled, many years later, that it served as "administration building, the superintendent's and head nurse's home, the pupil nurses' home, the kitchen, and wards for gynecology and obstetrics, children's diseases, and even two beds were allotted to dermatology and Dr. Adams abandoned his 'cow-house ward' of two beds, where he had hitherto accommodated his patients at the Johanniter Hospital."[10]

Dr. Adams' last remark gives a hint that relations with the Johanniter Order was not wholly satisfactory. The hospital possessed but eighty-two beds for all branches of medical service. The Knights of St. John were willing to give up the women's work but they strenuously opposed the separation of children's diseases, eye diseases and skin diseases, all of which branches had developed so materially in recent years that they were seriously hampered by lack of space. The Order declined to enlarge the hospital but looked upon the proposal of the College to provide its own pavilions for these specialties as being exceedingly ungracious.

Friction finally became so great that in the summer of 1906 the Order gave notice that they wished to terminate the cooperative agreement which had stood for thirty-five years. The ever-reliable Dr. Post was dispatched at once to Berlin to confer with the officials of the Order, but in spite of his best efforts, he failed to get anything but an assurance that the relation might be continued until October 1908. He then proceeded to New York to present the matter to the Trustees.

[10] Al-Kulliyah, IX, 5:75 (March 1923).

Before the Trustees met in December 1906, a letter arrived from Count Zilten Schwerin, executive of the Noble Order of St. John, asking a postponement of any decision to build a general hospital until the end of January. This was followed by a cable asking Dr. Post to return to Berlin as the authorized agent of the Board of Trustees. To this the latter agreed and gave Dr. Post his instructions. These were: to accept any proposal of the Order involving its construction of an eye and ear pavilion to be supported by the Order, or, alternatively, permission for the College to build its own pavilion; also to require the assignment of all the wards of the present Johanniter Hospital to medicine and surgery. Further since skin diseases lay outside the province of the Order, it should permit the College to make its own provision for that service. If this arrangement should not be acceptable, and further adjustment should prove impossible, Dr. Post was to report that "The Board will feel under obligation to revert to the necessity of providing a general hospital of its own."[11] In this the Board was acting in perfect good faith, for Mr. Jesup had agreed to erect a suitable building, a preliminary sketch of which had already been submitted by Dr. Post. The Board, however, would sincerely have regretted a separation from the Order. Upon further consideration, the Order too decided that the prospect of divorce was unbearable, and submitted to the conditions. The way was clear for the new construction required by the College.

The Woman's Pavilion was ready for occupancy in the fall of 1908, and construction of the Eye and Ear Pavilion was begun in the summer of the same year through a gift of $15,000 by Marcellus Hartley Dodge, newly elected trustee. The treatment of skin diseases was accommodated in a remodelled house near the Woman's Pavilion, and provision was generously made by Mr. Jesup for a Children's Pavilion, which opened in October 1910, a Mortuary, a Hospital Gate House and Waiting Rooms. All the new buildings were designed in large part by the doctors in charge of each,—i.e., the Woman's Pavilion by Dr. Moore, Eye and Ear by Dr. Webster, Children's by Dr. Dorman. With the completion

[11] Trustees Minutes, December 11, 1906.

of these facilities, the medical school had approximately two hundred beds available for its clinical instruction.

Proper provision for the teaching of pediatrics had been made during President Howard Bliss' first year by the establishment of a chair of Children's Diseases and the appointment of Dr. Harry G. Dorman as Lecturer. Dr. Dorman, a graduate of Harvard and the College of Physicians and Surgeons, had worked for two years in the Presbyterian Hospital in New York and had spent eight months in additional study of his specialty in New York and Paris. During his first year in Beirut, he was married to Mary Bliss Dale, daughter of the late Rev. Gerald F. Dale, Jr., and granddaughter of the President-emeritus. Dr. Dorman became Professor of Children's Diseases and Physiology in 1905 and has remained a prominent member of the faculty to the present day. His valuable service to the College will come to an end with his retirement in 1941.

The establishment of the College hospitals and the nurses' training school required the engagement of a superintendent of hospitals and a supervisor of nurses. In both appointments the College was marvelously fortunate. Mrs. Gerald F. Dale, Jr., eldest daughter of Daniel Bliss, who was then working with the American Mission, was wonderfully qualified for the superintendency. She had the administrative ability of her father and could speak and write Arabic, French, Turkish and German. From 1905 to 1923, she was in charge of the hospitals, and daily conducted the morning worship and Bible reading in the wards. Of her, Dr. Adams wrote: "Early and late her hand was on every pulse, so to speak, and her eyes everywhere, no detail escaping her observation, so that when she resigned . . . her resignation to take effect when her successor should be found, it was felt that never could it take effect."[12] Mrs. Dale died in Beirut in 1930 at the age of seventy-three.

The new Head Nurse and Superintendent of the Nurses' Training School was found in America by D. S. Dodge. Miss Jane Elizabeth Van Zandt, a graduate of the training school of the New York Postgraduate Hospital and a nurse of valuable experi-

[12] Al-Kulliyah, IX, 5:76.

ence, reached Beirut on April 25, 1905. She found no nurses and no pupils, but on May 30 she opened the training school with two of the latter. Starting thus from absolute scratch, Miss Van Zandt built up the School of Nursing to the excellent institution which it is today, with its graduates forming foci of healing service all over the Near East. Until her retirement in June of 1940 Miss Van Zandt exercised a quiet but potent influence over the development of this new field for women's service in lands where women were traditionally valueless except as bearers of children. Her part in the demonstration to a sceptical world of the dignity and worth of the native woman's potentialities can never be over-emphasized.

Among the sceptics were to be numbered some of the American doctors and all of the Kaiserswerth sisters. They had little faith in the Nurses' Training School until one of the probationers opened their eyes. This was Hosanna, the fourth student to enter the school. According to Dr. Adams, she appeared one day with her baggage, announcing simply, "I'm Hosanna. I've come. I'm going to be a nurse." She had no home to return to in summer so she volunteered to serve in the Johanniter Hospital. "In the middle of the night," wrote Dr. Adams, "Hosanna heard in the surgical ward, drip, drip, drip. She peered under one bed after another, hearing this drip, drip, drip. 'Here it is,' she said to herself, as she saw a pool of blood on the marble growing larger with each dripping drop. Off came the covers, a bandage was quickly slipped around the thigh of the amputated leg, and a tourniquet applied. Then she aroused the servant, who summoned Dr. Post. But all this took time, though the doctor came with his usual promptitude. Entering the ward, he asked what was wrong. 'This amputation patient, Doctor, had a secondary hemorrhage.' 'Had!' said Dr. Post. 'Yes, sir, it is stopped now.' 'Who put on this tourniquet?' 'I did, sir.' 'Why didn't you send for me to do it?' 'If I had done that, sir, you would be putting it on a corpse. I put on the tourniquet first and then sent for you.' 'Hosanna,' said Dr. Post raising both hands above his head with great solemnity, 'Hosanna, blessed art thou among women! You will become an ideal nurse

—and she did."[13] Thereafter the scepticism regarding the value of the Nurses' Training School diminished markedly.

6. PHARMACY

The expansion of the medical work was preceded by an improvement in the pharmacy department. This was made possible by a generous gift from D. S. Dodge in 1902 for the remodelling and enlargement of the chemistry laboratory, and by the appointment of James A. Patch as professor of Chemistry. The enlargement made room for a model dispensary which provided for many of the needs of the medical department. The appointment of Mr. Patch as professor enabled this very able and well-trained man to devote all of his time to the work of chemistry and pharmacy. A graduate of Boston Tech., Mr. Patch had come to Beirut in 1900 as instructor in chemistry and physics. He had served in that capacity for two years and as lecturer in those subjects for one, demonstrating an ability which was to make him one of the very valuable permanent members of the faculty. His retirement in 1921 to enter pharmaceutical manufacturing was a great loss to the College.

An interesting sidelight on the condition of the pharmacy department in 1903 is given in a report made to the Maryland Pharmaceutical Association by one of its members who had visited Beirut by chance. Mr. A. R. L. Dohme, now of Sharpe and Dohme, Baltimore, took a Mediterranean cruise on which he interested himself in observing the condition of pharmacy in Europe and the Near East. On his return he reported extemporaneously to his state association and his remarks were published in its Proceedings. In part they run as follows:

". . . We passed from here (Greece and Constantinople) into various other parts of Turkey, first to Smyrna, which is worse, of course, by far than Constantinople, and as we progress down the coast it gets worse and worse with few exceptions. We next came to Beyrout, in Syria, which is not much better than the others, although it is quite a port. The conditions here are of the same general character—filth, backwardness, everything behind the

[13] Al-Kulliyah, IX, 5:76-77.

times. You can scarcely understand how human beings can continue to live under the sanitary conditions we found here. If there is anything in antiseptics or the rules of hygiene these people ought to have been dead long ago. There was, however, one very bright oasis in that desert and that was the American College at Beyrout. I cannot speak in too high praise of this wonderful institution. I did not know it was there and none of the rest of our party knew it and it came as a great surprise to us. It has had a wonderful influence in the Orient. I remember well the day we drove up there. There were 425 of us in carriages and as we drove along, of course, it made a great cavalcade. We drove up this beautiful avenue and were going along when we came to a large wall, a beautiful wall with flowers on top, and the first thing we saw was the American flag on a flagstaff. Of course, we all wondered at this and at first sight it looked like a large private residence. And as we went on further up we saw one fine building after another and all of them beautifully located. And as we got closer we saw several young men playing baseball and we began to feel that we were nearing home. There are four thousand (sic) students at this college, with departments of law, medicine, theology, philosophy, etc. We also learned that all the faculty there were American graduates of our various colleges. We met most of them from the President down—the President is Professor Bliss. The Johns Hopkins had a representative there and all the larger colleges. Of course, they were all glad to see so many Americans there and we all had a great time. Another thing that came as a surprise to me was that there was a professor of Pharmacy there, the son of Professor Patch of Boston, a well-known member of the American Pharmaceutical Association. He showed me all through the pharmaceutical laboratory and I must say it is not behind and perhaps ahead of the Maryland, New York, or Philadelphia College of Pharmacy. It is right up-to-date, and they have spared no expense to provide it with the most modern equipment. They have a regular pharmacist in their pharmaceutical department and prescriptions are regularly compounded there and the students have a practical four years' course, the same as in Medicine.

"We went into one of their quizzes. One in nervous histology, one in pathology and one in chemistry but all were in the English language. Here were all those Turks, each one with his Fez on, because a Turk never takes his Fez off, sitting around the amphitheatre and the professor would ask them the most intricate, scientific questions, and they would answer just as quickly and in just as good English as we could use. There are four thousand of them from Greece, Syria, Abysinnia, Egypt, Persia, Arabia and other countries, and the influence of this college is extending further and further each year. They are speaking English, incidentally of their own free will adopting Christianity and they are being educated up to the limit of modern science.

". . . The work that a single man or woman, for instance Mrs. Stone, might do in that benighted country is not a circumstance compared to what this school is doing for that part of the world. When we were as far away as Egypt we ran across some drug stores and we asked the pharmacists where they had studied, and they were all from the American College at Beyrout. And in many other places the answer was the same. In all the Orient there is no other institution of this kind. The English have none and the Germans have none."[14]

Mr. Dohme was in error concerning the number of students in the College, but the total effect upon him of this unknown institution must have been well nigh overpowering. His absolutely unbiased views bear excellent witness to the type of work which the department of pharmacy was doing.

7. THE SCHOOL OF DENTISTRY

Among the professional courses listed by Daniel Bliss in his final report as desirable, dentistry was not included, possibly because it was presupposed in the development of the medical school. The question of the desirability of establishing a dental department had been, however, under consideration for some time before it was brought before the faculty for definite action in 1904-05. During that year the Medical Faculty made a report to the General Faculty, which adopted it unanimously, recommending the establish-

[14] Proceedings, Maryland Pharmaceutical Assn. 1903, p. 28.

ment of a Dental School, "it being understood that the project should not take precedence over projects already approved by the Trustees, but not yet realized." At the time there was not a single dental school in the Turkish Empire, and nothing adequate was to be found even in neighboring lands such as Greece. It was believed that an original outlay of $1,000 would provide sufficient equipment for a beginning to be made, leaving only an additional $1,500 for salary to be raised. The school could rely for much of its work upon the departments of pharmacy and medicine.

The Trustees approved the recommendation at their meeting in January 1906 but specified that the funds must first be raised. The actual appeal for such funds was not made before 1909 and the necessary appropriation was voted a year later. Arthur R. Dray, M.D., D.D.S., was appointed Professor of Dental Surgery in the fall of 1910 when the school began operations. Since the first year of the three-year course was practically identical with first year medicine, it was possible to begin work with the three students who qualified before the arrival in April 1911 of Dr. Dray, who brought with him the special equipment. It was installed in four rooms of a building across the street from the medical gate and was ready for the use of the students the following fall.

By 1912 the enrollment had risen to ten and the four rooms were no longer adequate. The dental work was then moved to the house in which Dr. Post had lived until his death in 1909. There it flourished and though the war temporarily crippled it, the department became one of the great factors in the contribution which the College has made to the welfare of the Near East.

8. ENDOWMENT AND PLANT

The problem of raising a sufficient endowment for the expanding work of the College had been emphasized in the Board of Trustees during the administration of Daniel Bliss, but not until the visit of Dr. Post in 1903 did a campaign particularly for endowment get under way. Then at the request of Mr. Jesup, Dr. Post prepared a printed "Appeal to the Christian Public" asking for $500,000, four-fifths of which was for endowment purposes. Within the first year over $58,000 had been received, more than half of it from D. S. Dodge. Caroline Phelps Stokes, with a gift for the nursing school, John D. Rockefeller and the Dennis brothers were also major contributors. The following year the Jesup Foundation was endowed, and large gifts were made by D. Willis James, the estate of Wm. E. Dodge, and the remaining members of the Board of Trustees. The total endowment of the institution was then $586,000, but so much of this was allocated for special services like hospitals, nursing, museums, library, etc., that a deficit in general operations was still unavoidable. This was true in spite of the fact that 68 percent of the running expenses were provided by field income. To be sure, the Trustees followed the extremely pleasant practice of covering yearly deficits from their own pockets, but they realized that balancing the budget was a wiser policy.

An interesting fact in the College financing was the relatively small number of contributors who supported the work. In spite of so-called general appeals it was still the Trustees who as late as 1906 provided most of the money. In the light of that fact it is hardly surprising, though slightly pathetic, that the Board should feel it necessary to enlarge its membership in that year from six to twelve. To that end they applied for a charter revision, which was granted June 8, 1906. (Appendix E.)

Acquisitions of property and buildings by the College were not always made at the expense of the Trustees, though in this respect again they were extremely generous. In addition to the gifts of Morris Jesup and D. S. Dodge already mentioned, the latter, in 1903, also provided the land for a suitable athletic field, now used by the preparatory department. But the first building for the preparatory school, erected adjacent to this field, was provided by a gift of $50,000 secured from Mrs. Russell Sage through the good offices of Dr. Post. Sage Hall, completed in 1911, was soon joined by the principal's residence, a house remodelled by funds provided through a legacy from a Mrs. Martin of Vermont. Then three other fine buildings, Rockefeller Hall, Thomson Hall (named in honor of Dr. Wm. H. Thomson, originator of the idea of the S.P.C.) and the Refectory, were added to the preparatory school plant through the generosity of John D. Rockefeller. These buildings, largely planned by William H. Hall, principal of the school since 1903, provided magnificent facilities for the separate maintenance of the preparatory and primary departments which had been advocated by Daniel Bliss in his final report. They were ready for occupancy in the fall of 1913.

Yet another great building deserves extended mention, for its beauty and its influence in many ways still dominate the campus at Beirut. This is Robert H. West Hall, the idea of which was launched in 1906 by a group of Syrian and American staffites in the interests of the College Young Men's Christian Association and those "extra curriculum activities which form so large a part of the ideal College life." These young men, one cold and stormy night that winter, "built in fancy a mighty house for the happiness of students. They placed it near the refectory where men could dry off and wait in comfort for the last final rush for food! They made provision for game rooms and 'quiet' rooms for writing and study. They added a few bedrooms for old alumni to use when they revisit the academic home of their youth. They made a great 'common' room, with fireplaces and comfortable chairs; a room to be used by all in common—by *all*—by medical men, and college men, and commerce men; by men hailing from many countries, speaking many languages, observing many widely divergent formulae to express their inner faith. . . . They added also an auditorium capable of accommodating the Shakespearian efforts of the Student's Union, the public and routine meetings of literary and debating societies; and aware of the social force of simple religion, of religion free from metaphysical distinctions, they made this 'castle in Spain' the home of the religious organization of the College."[15] They decided that such a building should most suitably be a memorial to Robert H. West, the honored and respected dean of the College who had died a few months before.

Unlike many such grandiose schemes, this one was not permitted to die a-borning. The staff group expanded into a committee which canvassed all former staff members in the hope of raising the necessary funds. But though a great many students and alumni joined the Staff in responding as best they could, the sum raised after several years was still insufficient to provide for the accom-

[15] Al-Kulliyah, V, 5:129 (March 1914). Article by Dr. Franklin T. Moore.

plishment of the plan. Then in April 1910 an angel in the guise of Cleveland H. Dodge,[16] president of the Board of Trustees of Robert College, visited the campus and "authorized" the construction of the building. When the announcement of the gift was made at a chapel service where Mr. Dodge was to speak, the student body rose to its feet and cheered itself hoarse. Mr. Dodge, greatly moved, had difficulty in beginning his address.

The original estimate of cost by the committee had been £6000, but as time went on the first attractive plans, sketched by Staffite Carl L. Fox (1904-07) were seen to be inadequate. At the time of Mr. Dodge's visit the preliminary estimate had been nearly doubled. Mr. Dodge, with a gift of over $53,000, made possible the construction of the building on very generous lines, following closely the plans drawn by Professor Patch, who later also supervised the construction. The beautiful white stone structure which would be an ornament to any campus in the world, was dedicated on February 24, 1914. At the dedication ceremonies tribute was paid to Cleveland H. Dodge, Robert H. West, and James A. Patch, the three men whose names should always be remembered in connection with West Hall. Mr. Bayard Dodge, son of Cleveland Dodge, was present in his capacity as Director of West Hall, the position which first brought him officially into connection with the College.

9. FACULTY DEVELOPMENT

The growth of the Syrian Protestant College prior to and immediately after the inauguration of Howard Bliss had been so rapid that administrative and educational problems multiplied incredibly. It became apparent that to bring before the General Faculty all the problems of each department was not only a waste of time but was highly inefficient. During the year 1903-04 President Bliss sought to establish a more suitable organization and set up a committee system for the handling of specific problems, such as Finance, Scholarships, Library, Athletics, Entrance Examinations, etc., etc. In addition the various departments or faculties were encouraged to organize and meet at regular times to deal with ques-

[16] Cleveland H. Dodge, grandson of Wm. E. Dodge, founding Trustee, was the nephew of D. Stuart Dodge, then president of the Beirut Board.

tions particularly affecting Medicine, Pharmacy, College and Preparatory School work. In the General Faculty meetings only those holding the rank of full professor were entitled to vote. There was a real danger that instructors and adjunct professors might feel no sense of responsibility for the conduct of College affairs. Being represented in the departmental faculties, they were more apt to take a personal interest in the work of their colleagues, and to develop a keener devotion to the purposes of the institution as a whole.

The situation was made the more difficult by the paucity of full professors, all of whom were Americans, and the large dependence for instruction upon adjunct professors and instructors, many of whom were members of other nationalities. Writing of the success of the new plan in 1906, when the Collegiate Department had been organized under Dean West and the Preparatory under Principal Hall, President Bliss said: "Not only has the adoption of this plan already brought relief to the General Faculty and secured a better informed consideration of matters relating to the individual departments, but it is doing much to obliterate the irritating distinction between the Anglo-Saxon teachers and our fellow instructors of other races, while still safeguarding the important responsibilities committed by the Trustees to the General Faculty. If this general scheme shall eventually bring every teacher of the Institution into stated and responsible face-to-face contact with certain phases of College problems—intellectual, disciplinary and moral—it cannot but serve to develop a spirit of solidarity of the utmost benefit to any college, and especially to an institution like ours composed of men of such a variety of race, religion and antecedents."[17]

The enlargement of the collegiate department faculty recommended by Daniel Bliss was very slow in coming, because concentration upon the development of the medical work was accompanied by no increase in general endowment. To be sure, in 1903, Professor West returned to the college from the preparatory principalship, his place being taken by William H. Hall, associate principal, who was to fill the position with great success until his death in 1927. Rev. J. Stewart Crawford of Damascus, another out-

[17] Annual Report, 1905-06, p. 7.

standing acquisition, replaced Mr. Hall as associate principal. Professor Patch took over the department of chemistry in 1902 and Professor Day was to some extent relieved of his work in the medical school the following year, so that he was able to give more time to the teaching of the natural sciences. But in June of 1903 Professor Nicely resigned, leaving the teaching of English wholly in the hands of young instructors. Professor Porter was obliged to carry History, Psychology, Sociology, Economics, Logic and Philosophy, in addition to being Librarian. It was apparent that some relief must be gained.

The plan was followed of raising to permanent status the exceptional members of the Syrian staff who, though denied voting status on the General Faculty, were considered regular members of the departmental faculty. Da'ud Kurban and Bulus Khauli were appointed adjunct professors of Arabic and Education respectively in 1905. They were followed by Mansur Jurdak as adjunct professor of Mathematics in 1906. With adjunct professors Dumit, Charbonnier and Ladakis (the latter appointed to Pharmacy in 1904) there resulted a total of six adjunct professors, and in 1907 the Board of Trustees expressed its apprehension at the large number of such appointments. They even requested that the faculty consider the question of reducing enrollment in order to limit the number of teachers.

The fine work which was done by these appointees, however, and the obvious fact that an enrollment of 200 in the collegiate department was not too large, brought about a changed point of view. But still the needed professorial appointments were not achieved. The retirement from teaching of the President-emeritus in June 1906 and the death of Professor West in December of the same year weakened the faculty yet further, leaving four professorships, long authorized, unoccupied. The English department had been headless for five years; professorships in Physics (authorized in 1901) and in Philosophy and Psychology (authorized in 1905) had never been filled; and Professor West's death left vacant the chair of Astronomy and Mathematics. President Bliss was obviously concerned when he wrote of the crippling effect of Professor West's death: "We do not expect to duplicate his strong personality, but the point is that no Department should be so slenderly equipped with full professors, in the forty-second year of its existence, as to feel so seriously the loss of a single professor, however brilliant and capable he may have been."[18]

The situation was relieved in 1908 by the appointment of Harold H. Nelson as professor of English and that of J. Stewart Crawford as professor of Bible and Ethics, his place as associate principal of the Preparatory being filled by the promotion of Harry N. Irwin from the staff. Two years later Robert B. Reed, another former staffite, was made professor of Social Sciences, relieving Professor Porter of a considerable part of his burden, and Julius Arthur Brown was appointed professor of Physics, permitting Dean Day to limit his teaching to the biological sciences. In 1911 Alfred H. Joy, a staffite who had come out in 1904 and had become acting director of the observatory, was appointed professor of Astronomy and director of the observatory. Each of these men made a valuable contribution to the life of the College, though Professor Brown, now Dean of the School of Arts and Sciences, is the only one at present remaining on the faculty. Professor Crawford retired on account of ill health in 1935 and died in 1939.

During the year 1909 it was decided by the Trustees, on recommendation of the faculty, to establish a new category of full professors without vote in the General Faculty, to be composed of native department heads. They were to have full responsibility in the departmental faculties but were to be kept from voting power in the General Faculty, which had the final authority, under the Trustees, in the determining of College policy. Probably this decision was made with a view to a time when there might be a majority of Syrian professors who might not care to cooperate with the Trustees. Possibly it was done as an experiment to determine the efficiency and reliability of Syrian professors as administrators before giving them equal standing with the Americans. At any rate, the distinction between non-voting and voting professors was definitely eliminated when the institution was reorganized in 1920 as the American University of Beirut.

[18] Annual Report, 1906-07, p. 14.

The first Syrian to be made full professor under the non-voting classification was Jebr Dumit, famous teacher of Arabic, who was promoted in 1910. The following year he was joined in his new rank by Khauli (Pedagogy), Ladakis (Pharmacy), Jurdak (Mathematics) and Kurban (Arabic). Every one of these men had a distinguished record and they fully justified the confidence which had been placed in their ability.

Two major losses to the faculty occurred in the years just before the World War. Dr. George E. Post and Professor Harvey Porter resigned, the first in the fall of 1908 after forty-one years of unbroken service, the latter in 1913 when he had completed forty years at Beirut. Both men resigned as a matter of policy rather than necessity, feeling that their advanced years might prove a hindrance to their colleagues. Dr. Post explained his action in the following remarkable letter to the faculty:

Beirut, October 13, 1908

The Faculty of the Syrian Protestant College

Dear Brethren:

I have never had more difficulty in nerving myself to the performance of any duty than in asking you to forward to the Trustees the enclosed letter of resignation of my Chair of Surgery in the College.

The very blessings of health and of unimpaired enthusiasm for my work, which assure me that I might pursue it awhile longer, make it more difficult to lay it aside now. But it has been and still is my earnest desire to hand back the trust committed to me forty-one years ago in as good a shape as possible. I am glad to report to you that, during the academic year which has just closed, I have had more, and more important, operative work than ever before. I have not lost an hour of teaching, nor asked excuse from other academic duties, during this period. I have also been able to carry more extra work, in the way of planning and building, than I ever undertook before during a single year. I might possibly be able to present as good a record again, but I could not exceed it. It seems to me, therefore, at my age, that this is precisely the ideal period for retiring. I hand you back my scalpel rather than let it drop from my hand. I hand you back my classes before I have failed to hold their attention and arouse their enthusiasm. But the chief difficulty I had and have is the inexpressible trial of withdrawing from my connection with a body of men with whom I have so long labored, who have borne with my shortcomings, and shown a confidence and affection which I would fain have deserved. The only consolation I can extract from the situation is my assurance that you will pursue, unembarrassed by my failing years, the high and holy work committed to you, and that I can watch with unchanging faith the growth and consolidation of the Institution to which I have given nearly all my active life. Praying for God's blessing upon you and your work,

Your affectionate colleague,

(signed) GEORGE E. POST

The resignation was accepted with the greatest regret, and the unanimous recommendation was made that Dr. Wilfred M. Post, son of Dr. Post, be appointed to succeed his father in the chair of Surgery, while the latter should be made professor-emeritus. Dr. Wilfred Post, then serving as a missionary of the American Board in Caesarea, did not feel able to accept the appointment and it was subsequently given to Dr. Edwin St. John Ward, who had been serving with the American Board at Dyarbekir. Dr. Ward took up his work in Beirut in the fall of 1911.

Too little has been said thus far of Professor Porter, who continued to serve the College as professor-emeritus and curator of museums until the year before his death in January 1923 at the age of seventy-eight. Fifty-two years of devoted service he gave to the Syrian Protestant College.

Harvey Porter enlisted at the age of seventeen and fought with the North in the Civil War from 1862-64. Belatedly he then took up the studies which brought him his degree from Amherst in 1870. He intended at once to enter the ministry, but in New York, when he was about to begin study at Union Theological Seminary, he happened to meet Rev. D. S. Dodge, then a professor in the S.P.C. As a result he went instead to Beirut, beginning his career there in November 1870. Still devoted to the ministry, he pursued his theological studies privately, and was publicly ordained on a summer visit to America in 1880. In 1892 he received an honorary Ph.D. from Amherst and in 1920 was given the Doctorate of Divinity by the American University of Beirut. Three times he served as acting president and it was to his initiative, skill and tireless industry that the fine library and archaeological museum were due.

An interesting glimpse of Mr. Porter at the time of his arrival in Beirut is given in a summary of letters from Daniel Bliss to D. S.

Dodge, recorded in the latter's notes. Under date of December 8, 1870, Bliss wrote that "Porter is a fine scholar and takes hold well." By December 30 he noted that "Porter is already taking over the accounts from Elias (?) and talks considerable bad Arabic." On January 16 Mr. Porter's clear knowledge of mental philosophy had impressed the president as well as the fact that he was hard at work on Arabic. He was then teaching the Seniors in Latin and giving one class in English, sandwiching Arabic lessons in between recitations and taking long walks with his teacher in the afternoons. In March Dr. Bliss again commented that "Porter is getting Arabic very well." It was characteristic of the man that he devoted himself to mastering the language, and it was hardly surprising that within a year or so he was able to help Dr. Wortabet with his English-Arabic dictionary—hardly an occupation for a novice in that very difficult language.

At the time of Dr. Porter's death many sincere and moving tributes were paid him by Dr. Webster, Professor Hall, Professor Khauli, who spoke in Arabic, and by Acting-president Nickoley. In conclusion, Professor Nickoley spoke of Dr. Porter as follows: "As a linguist he not only mastered the Arabic language, but also had a wide grasp of other languages, ancient and modern. More might be said of him as an administrator; he was the founder and organizer of the library and the museum and was frequently called upon for other administrative duties. More might be said of him as a builder, for several of the buildings on the campus were planned by him and constructed under his direction. As an author he has written much in addition to the books that have been mentioned. Especially as a philanthropist . . . much might be said, for many alumni and former students could not have completed their education without the financial help that he gave them. This I have learned, not from Dr. Porter himself but from those who were aided by him. How much he did in this way will never be known.

"The work of his hands will pass away with the passing of time, but his spirit and the influence of his life will not pass away. These are built for all eternity into the lives of those who lived and worked with him. . . . Others may have been more prominent, may have made a more brilliant showing before the public, but in conscientious, consecrated devotion to duty, in preaching the Kingdom of God in deed and in word, in building and shaping the lives of men for eternity, he stands unexcelled. He has completed his work but his influence is always with us."[19]

The place of Dr. Porter as professor of history was filled at once by the appointment of Professor Nelson, who had until then been head of the English department, but who had in 1912 received his Ph.D. in history at the University of Chicago. A replacement for Dr. Nelson had been appointed in America when the World War broke out, preventing his departure for Beirut. From then until the war's end the faculty had to accept its losses without hope of relief.

10. THE BOARD OF TRUSTEES

Mention has been made of the enlargement of the Board of Trustees which took place after 1906, but one important change occurred before that time. William E. Dodge, Jr., son of the original treasurer of the Board, died in August 1903. Mr. Dodge had been a member for just over twenty years, during which time he had been sincerely devoted to the interests of the College. His colleagues recorded in a memorial minute that "he believed in such an institution in that part of the world as an outpost of our Lord's Kingdom in its destined conquest of those historic lands. . . . We esteem it a privilege and an honor to have been associated with one whose whole life was so estimable, whose career was so distinguished for public services and philanthropic benefactions and whose devotion to this especial enterprise, which we all love, was so hearty and unwearied."[20]

Mr. Dodge's place was filled by the election of Cornelius C. Cuyler, who, like the majority of his fellow members, served with sacrifice and real interest until his death, which occurred in 1909. Mr. Cuyler was a nephew of Morris Jesup, and after his uncle's death, when D. S. Dodge became president of the Board, Mr. Cuyler was elected treasurer.

At the first meeting of the Board following the charter revision of June 1906, an immediate start was made toward the expansion

[19] Al-Kulliyah, IX, 4:60-61.

[20] Trustees Minutes, January 20, 1904.

THE EYE PAVILION

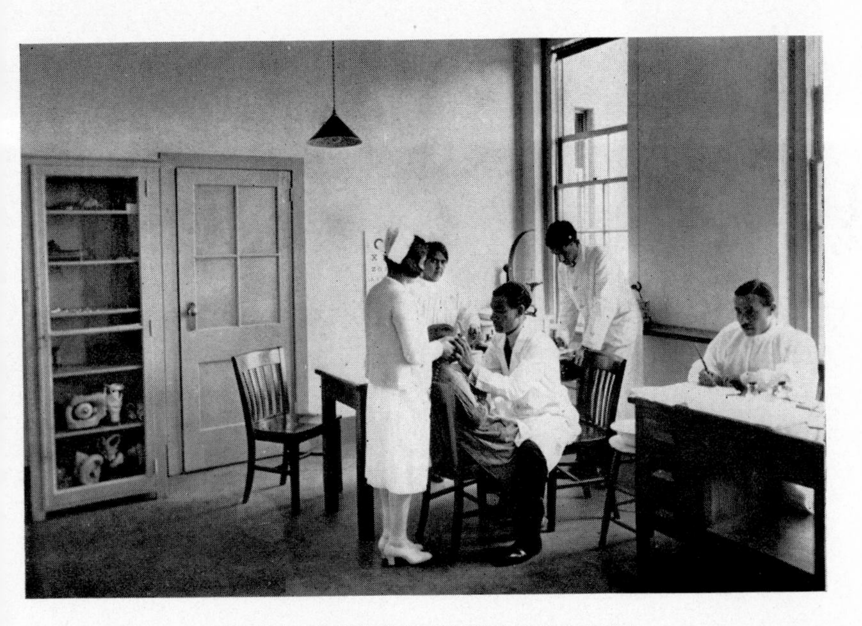

MEDICAL STUDENTS IN THE EYE CLINIC

ALLEGHENY COLLEGE LIBRARY

L. to R.: THOMSON HALL, ROCKEFELLER HALL, SAGE HALL (Preparatory School)

ROBERT H. WEST HALL

ALLEGHENY COLLEGE LIBRARY

of the membership to the permitted twelve. Arthur Curtiss James, William M. Kingsley and Marcellus Hartley Dodge were elected on December 11, 1906. They were followed in January 1908 by Alfred E. Marling, William Fellowes Morgan and the Rev. James S. Dennis.

These additions brought the Board to its full membership but the deaths early in 1908 of Morris K. Jesup and Alexander Maitland again decreased its numbers. The roll was further reduced by the death of Mr. Cuyler in 1909. These gaps were filled by the election in 1912 of Mrs. Morris K. Jesup and Dr. Francis Brown, President of Union Theological Seminary and father of Professor J. A. Brown of the College. Their election was followed in 1913 by that of Edwin B. Cragin, M.D. Miss Eleanor de Graff Cuyler, sister of C. C. Cuyler, was elected in 1915 to succeed Mrs. Jesup who died the year before.

Following the death of Mr. Jesup, D. S. Dodge was elected president of the Board, and his place as secretary-treasurer was filled by the election of C. C. Cuyler as treasurer and the Rev. James S. Dennis as secretary. When Mr. Cuyler died after but one year of service, William M. Kingsley was elected his successor. Dr. Dennis, who died in 1914, was succeeded as secretary by his brother, Samuel S. Dennis.

The enlargement of the Board was accompanied in 1908 by a reorganization of the membership into four classes of three members each, their terms overlapping so that one entire class would come up for re-election each year. Each trustee was, of course, elected to serve for at least four years.

Several of the Board members were able to visit Beirut before the war put an end to such travels. All of them took a keen interest in the work of the institution, to the advantage of which they gave a great deal of money, time and thought. The S.P.C. continued to be richly blessed in its Trustees.

II. THE ALUMNI

Howard Bliss, like his father, was as keenly interested in his students after they had left the College as when they were undergraduates. He tried to keep in touch with them, to follow their work and to promote their interests. Occasionally he made trips through the Near East to seek them out, to find out how they were doing and what their associates thought of them. Like the father of a very large family he was devoted to the interests of his sons, and they, quite naturally, were devoted to him.

He was particularly pleased with the fact that so large a proportion of the alumni settled in the Near East. The very effective answer to criticisms sometimes directed at the College, to the effect that it de-nationalized or Americanized its students, was a presentation of the facts. The following table for the year 1910 is revealing.

	Living Medical Grads. 1871–1910	Living Pharmacy Grads. 1875–1910	Living College Grads. 1870–1910	Living Commerce Grads. 1902–1910	Combined Percent-ages
Residing in Syria	161	56	153	No	46.3%
Egypt & Sudan	90	81	92	figures	27.4%
Other parts of				given	
Turkish Empire	96	46	6		16. %
U.S.	8	8	47		6.6%
Europe and elsewhere	9	4	22		3.7%
TOTAL—964—	364	195	320	85	100%
% in Turkish Empire	95.3%	96%	78%	90%	89.7%
% Outside	4.7%	4%	22%	10%	10.3%

As early as 1902 an effort had been initiated to organize the alumni into a permanent association, but not until 1910 was this accomplished. Then, at Commencement, the large and enthusiastic body of alumni present voted to set up a central association in Beirut with branches in towns all over the Near East. Within the first year branches were established in Alexandria, Cairo and Jerusalem. Khartoum, in the Sudan, soon followed, and before very long there were strong groups in Syria, Turkey, North and South America. More will be said of them later.

Great impetus to the organization of the alumni was given by the establishment in February 1910 of a College magazine, *Al*

Kulliyah. This was a serious journal, published in English and Arabic, with the definite purpose of keeping its subscribers informed of events at the College and interpreting to them the institution's policies and performance. *Al Kulliyah* was scheduled to appear eight times yearly, and during its long history it brought to the attention of alumni an immense amount of fascinating news about the College which they would inevitably have missed without it. It served ideally as a center around which the interests of alumni could crystallize and it aided immeasurably in binding them in a useful way to their alma mater.

For *Al Kulliyah* was not only a record of College events. Under the careful editorship of Professors Nelson, Khauli and Crawford, it became a medium for the publication of articles of real value in many fields, medicine, education, history, literature, archaeology. Graduates in out-of-the-way places could find mental and moral stimulation in its pages. There can be no question but that *Al Kulliyah* made a very considerable contribution to the expanding influence of the College by keeping alive in the alumni the cultural traditions with which they had become imbued while on the campus. In the isolated Near East this was a far more important matter than it might have been in the average American college.

To the historian of the College, *Al Kulliyah* is a rich mine of information to which constant reference must be made. It is a matter of regret that it was not begun earlier. One can easily appreciate the disappointment of the alumni when publication was of necessity suspended during the World War, and their satisfaction when it was resumed in January 1920. Tribute is owed to those successive faithful editors who shouldered the heavy extra-curricular burden of producing a magazine of such consistently high quality.

VIII. RELIGIOUS PROBLEMS

I. A COLLEGE CHURCH

REFERENCE HAS BEEN MADE to the relatively small proportion of non-Christian students who came to the College during the administration of Daniel Bliss. In his later years and throughout the first decade of the next administration, the number of Moslems, for example, increased respectably. In 1905, out of 750 students there were 98 Moslems, or 13 percent of the student body; in 1908 there were 128 out of a total of 876 students, only a slightly larger percentage but a considerable absolute increase. Over the same period the total number of non-Christian students, including Jews, Druzes and Bahai's as well as Moslems, rose from 154 to 242.

These increases took place in spite of the fact that all students were still required to attend daily chapel and take the regular courses in Bible, which were not listed among electives. It may perhaps be considered a concession that in 1905 the Y.M.C.A. established a new category of memberships for non-Christians, but the pledge which they were required to take diluted in no way the Christian principles for which the campus organization consistently stood: "In becoming a Fellowship Member in this Association, you desire to testify to the help you have received in your daily life from the teachings and life of Jesus, and you desire to associate yourself with those who are learning from Him. You promise that you will attend regularly the weekly meeting of the Association (the mid-week prayer meeting), and one of the Association Bible Classes, and that you will make it a special object of your prayers and endeavors to help your fellow students—particularly in the advancement of the spiritual life among them. Do you promise this"?[1]

In spite of the remarkable spiritual influence which the College unquestionably exerted upon all its students, a rather disappointingly small number of the Moslems became Christians. What many devout supporters of missions in the Near East fail to understand,

[1] Annual Report, 1905-06, p. 20.

however, is that this is by no means evidence of a failure to produce a spiritual awakening among the followers of the Prophet. The disappointment in the small number of conversions is evidence of a lack of appreciation of the Moslem world.

Primarily, for a Moslem to become Christian in name was similar to having him change his nationality. In the early days of the College a question on the registration card, "What is your nationality"? was almost invariably answered, "Moslem," rather than Syrian, Arabian or Palestinian. Moslem society constituted a unit stronger than national groups. To some extent it does so today even though nationalism has become greatly intensified in recent years.

For a Mohammedan to become a Christian in the Near East also practically meant that "he went on relief," a phrase sufficiently pregnant with meaning in America today. He became an outcast from his family and tribe and at the same time could *not* become a member of any typical native Christian group. Intense mutual suspicion between Christian groups and Moslem groups prevented the convert's acceptance into the Christian societies without a strong feeling of distrust and aversion. He was therefore practically doomed to a chronic inability to earn a livelihood for himself or his dependents.

Furthermore, the Moslem world had, with some reason, a strong aversion to the native Christians whose internal divisions and antagonisms, none the less bitter for the minor nature of their grounds, evoked little but disgust in the mind of the spectator. Protestantism is bad enough with its various sects; add to them the other Christian groups, Maronite, Greek Orthodox, Nestorian, Jacobite, Copt, Chaldaean, Gregorian, Greek Catholic, Roman Catholic, and the Moslem observer could with some justice question both the meaning and the desirability of the Christian faith.

Theological distinctions insisted upon by some of the Christian sects had no appeal to the practical minded Mohammedan. Even today it is extremely difficult, for example, to persuade him that Christians are not tritheists. Then too, the spectacle of supposedly Christian nations in the West greedily cutting each other's throats for personal gain was not calculated to inspire great respect. "The principles of Jesus," the thoughtful Moslem might well say, "are noble and worthy of my sincere appreciation and practice, but may Allah preserve me from becoming a Christian!"

This was the problem which the Syrian Protestant College had to face in its desire to bring the "Light that shineth evermore" back to the Near East. It is not surprising that in the first year of Howard Bliss' administration a proposal for the establishment of a College Church should have been advanced.

"While we believe," wrote President Bliss, "that the past year has witnessed the growth in the student body of true spiritual religion, we also believe that not a little loss in the good effects of the Christian services and atmosphere of the College has been experienced by failure on our part to offer a concrete opportunity to those who have experienced a change of heart to commit themselves openly to the new course of life. In a word, the establishment of the 'Church of Christ in the Syrian Protestant College' would seem to be a necessity in the near future. Such a church," he continued, "would of course be absolutely undenominational—absolutely Christian and in its conditions for membership absolutely religious rather than theological; practical rather than metaphysical. It must seek to include all who are seeking to lead their lives as children of God, in the spirit of Jesus Christ. It must exclude all others."[2]

The proposal was not immediately taken up, but in 1907 the Trustees requested the faculty "to open communication with other Missions and native Protestant ecclesiastical bodies, to aid in determining what conditions would seem to be desirable in establishing an independent, undenominational, evangelical College Church, whose members would be cordially recognized and received into fellowship by the Missions and native Protestant Churches in the countries where the students reside."[3] This was a logical extension of the principle involved in Dr. Bliss' suggestion but it proved the stumbling block over which the plan came to grief. The ideal cooperation involved was simply not possible of attainment at the time. The Trustees Minutes for February 24, 1908 say no more than that "it was voted to concur in the judgment

[2] Annual Report, 1902-03, pp. 7-8.

[3] Trustees Minutes, May 16, 1907.

of the Faculty that the time was not yet ripe for such an organization," but a world of tragic meaning may be perceived behind those words. The matter of a College Church was not brought up again.

Whether or not the Church was actually established, the College nevertheless did produce in part the same effect as if it had been done. Frederick Bliss cites as typical the case of a student who had been some years in the College and was re-registering one autumn. In response to the question "What is your religion?" he replied, "The religion of the S.P.C." The boy was a Moslem.[4]

At Commencement in 1914 the President of the Senior class, a Moslem Tartar, spoke at the Alumni Banquet. He spoke of "singing his own song," the song of the Senior class. "My song," he said, "is our Ideal. I want to measure my life in the wide world school of life by the standard of love. I want to choose in each case what is best, to accept cheerfully the incidental evils involved, to put my whole self into all that I do, to see present and future as one and to worship God in all that is good and true and beautiful." The College Church may never come into being; this Moslem boy may never have called himself a Christian; but such a spirit as he showed tempers our feeling of regret.

2. INSURRECTION

The opposition to the tyranny of Sultan 'Abdul Hamid, with which, in its early stages, students of the S.P.C. had considerable to do, eventuated in a military revolution the result of which was the granting on July 24, 1908 of a constitution for Turkey. Censorship was abolished, political prisoners released, the army of spies disbanded. To Turkey it seemed that the Young Turks had succeeded in bringing the millennium. But in April of 1909 'Abdul Hamid tried once more to assert himself and much blood was shed before he was again overcome and forced to abdicate, with his brother, Reshad, proclaimed as Sultan Mehemed V.

The Young Turks were destined to produce a tyranny worse than that of Hamid,[5] but at its beginning the new régime was sin-

[4] Bliss, Reminiscences, p. 218.

[5] For detailed discussion see Antonius, "The Arab Awakening," ch. 6.

cerely hailed for the hope of a dawn of liberty which it brought. "Throughout the length and breadth of the land," wrote President Bliss, "men and women and children have been stirred as never before with elemental feelings; they have learned a new and noble vocabulary the meaning of which they cannot yet understand; they are conscious of new and mighty forces whose nature they have not fathomed; they are filled with aspirations and intentions which they cannot easily define.... A long, arduous journey awaits this people—much longer than the mass of people imagine—with many bitter disappointments, many unsuspected dangers, many disheartening defeats. But none of us believes that this *annus mirabilis* with all its drawbacks and mistakes and crimes has not brought with it permanent blessing to the mighty Empire and to the cause of Righteousness."[6]

The Constitution itself was anachronistic,[7] ill suited to the needs of the day as well as being internally inconsistent. It proclaimed Islam as the religion of the state and at the same time announced that there was to be universal religious liberty; all schools were to be under the surveillance of the state but there was to be perfect freedom. In the excitement, confusion, and awakened hope of the people, false ideas were certain to be followed. It was not surprising that schools and colleges which had long striven for such an awakening should find themselves in some danger from the abnormal reaction, the sometimes misguided insistence on freedom from restraint.

At Beirut trouble came to the College first in the form of opposition on the part of Moslem students to the regulations requiring attendance at Bible classes and religious exercises. On January 8, 1909, the majority of these students absented themselves from chapel and Bible classes, and many of them bound themselves by oath not to attend these exercises and to refuse to leave the grounds in case they should be expelled by the faculty. They claimed that their consciences did not permit them to attend, but in all other questions of college discipline they declared that they intended to

[6] Annual Report, 1908-09, pp. 3-4.

[7] It was the Constitution drawn up by Midhat Pasha in 1876 which was established without revision in 1908.

show a spirit of complete obedience. On the 12th of January, 98 of the 128 Moslem students presented a petition to the faculty respectfully requesting the withdrawal of the regulations requiring attendance at religious services and instruction.

To the average American, unfamiliar both with the heterogeneous national and religious make-up of the student body at Beirut and the peculiar conditions of that particular period in Turkish development, the explosive possibilities of this demand are not apparent. Fortunately the faculty did perceive trouble ahead and sought to avoid it by a gentle but none the less firm statement of principle, which ran as follows:

"Inasmuch as we have recently received several requests to define the position of the College in matters of religious instruction, and inasmuch as we have found that many misconceptions exist in the minds of those making these requests, the Faculty desires to make the following statement:

"1. The aim and purpose of the College is to develop character, that is, it seeks to develop in its students the love of truth and the desire to do right, and it believes that this should be the aim and the result of all true education.

"2. The College believes that the highest type of character cannot be developed, or for any length of time maintained, without the aid of religion, and for that reason, we say to every student that he has no right to neglect his religious life, whatever the form of religion his conscience leads him to adopt. Thus we seek to make him a conscientious and God-fearing man.

"3. The College accustoms its students to respect the religious belief of others, and its students learn to discuss freely and with mutual respect and consideration the points upon which they differ. Thus they learn to understand the intellectual and moral principles which underlie all religious thought and progress.

"We believe this to be especially valuable in a land where many religions are represented, and where the desire has become so strong to unite as far as possible on common ground. The College feels that in order to be true to its ideals it must teach religion. It is self-evident that the College, as a Christian College, believes that the Christian religion can do more for character than any other form of religious faith. It is also clear that the influence of the Bible and of the Christian religion has produced this College which represents the modern type of education.

"4. This is a Christian College and was established with the money of Christian people, the land was purchased, the buildings were erected, the hospitals were established and the equipment was supplied by them, and without their constant support the institution could not be maintained. All this was done for the purpose of providing an education in which the Bible should be taught, and the claims and benefits of the Christian religion should be presented to every student.

"We accordingly as faithful servants of those who appointed us, are in honor bound to present to every student the truth of the Christian religion, leaving him entirely free to accept it or reject it. Our students know that they are left wholly free in this respect, and our students also know that those who frankly disagree with us in religious matters suffer no disadvantage in their relation to the College or to their teachers. This we consider true religious liberty.

"The College believes that in requiring its students to attend religious services and instruction it is not trenching upon the religious liberty of its patrons. It publishes in full, in its annual Catalogue, its rules and requirements in this respect, so that no man who sends his son to the College, need be under any misapprehension as to what will be required of him. These regulations have been in force since the foundation of the College, and have been found most useful in securing our purpose to give all our students an equal opportunity to learn our principles, and to create no special privileges for any one class or sect.

"For these reasons, we believe that our regulations are fair to all concerned, and that they serve to promote the highest type of education."[8]

This reply to the student petition was not satisfactory and the petitioning group, joined later by others and by all the Jewish students to the number of 88, renewed the oath of non-attendance at compulsory religious exercises and of refusal to leave the campus if expelled. They were strengthened in their attitude by several factors in addition to the refusal of the faculty to grant their request. A petition for the establishment of a society for the study of Islamic culture had earlier been turned down. An address delivered during the regular Week of Prayer "was grossly misunderstood and misinterpreted as being an attack upon the Moslems." Added fuel was piled on the flames by the active encouragement received from Moslem and Jewish friends in the city and in Egypt. "A number of newspapers vehemently expressed their sympathy with the students, and vociferously challenged the right of the College to impose such regulations upon the students." With only two or three exceptions the entire press of Syria and Egypt either attacked the College or failed to give it any support.

[8] Annual Report, 1908-09, pp. 7-8.

The situation would have been more dangerous had not the rebellious students, throughout the whole affair, been scrupulously careful to observe all other College rules and to offer no opportunity for criticism of their behavior on other grounds. At one time it looked as if a mob from the city might attack the College property, but it did not materialize. Throughout the whole controversy the students expressed their warm admiration for the College and insisted that their country needed just such an institution. They pointed out the unrivalled opportunity that the College would have, if the regulations were amended, to reach the Moslem world and thus become the greatest force in moulding the citizens of the new empire. A visitor to the campus would never have realized that a "strike" was in progress.

Dr. Bliss was in America on furlough when the news was cabled to him and the Trustees. They met together at once and affirmed their support of the faculty's position that the regulations could not be suspended, but urged the faculty to continue to apply to the situation "methods that, while firmly maintaining the principles of the College, shall not, if possible, arouse antagonism or dissension."[9] This the faculty was able to do through personal interviews with the individual students in which they were able to make clear the reasons behind their decision, and to emphasize the fact that they fully appreciated the conscientious objector's belief in the necessity for religious liberty.

President Bliss and Dr. Dodge called at once on President Roosevelt and Secretary of State Robert Bacon, and then Dr. Bliss returned post-haste to Beirut, stopping only to visit the Foreign Office in London and the American and British Ambassadors in Constantinople. After his return, a temporary settlement was reached through the following letter which was sent to the parents or guardians of all the students involved:

March 18, 1909

To ....

After paying the duties of respect I beg to state that you have undoubtedly learned of the strike engaged in by most of the Moslem and Jewish students in our College. You are also aware that the Faculty of the College has not

[9] Trustees Minutes, January 26, 1909.

been hasty in reaching a decision in reference to the matter but have considered the subject wisely and carefully. Since this question is of utmost importance, and since the College seeks to advance the best interests of the students and their development, we have done our best to solve the difficulty and with the help of Almighty God (may He be exalted) we have reached the following decision.

(1) The Faculty will treat the striking students in the spirit of indulgence, and will thus excuse them from attendance during the times of worship, and will occupy them during those times with something useful to them. This exemption comprehends the present academic year only.

(2) If desired, the Faculty will offer the students a study in the science of religion which will not take the place of the Bible study but will be in addition to it.

(3) The Faculty will take up this question which has been the cause of the present difficulty, will consider it and will then submit it to the Board of Trustees in New York for their final decision. They cannot, however, make any promise or hold out any hopes as to the outcome.

As to the students, they will be required:

(1) To disclaim everything that suggests the spirit of disloyalty or disobedience or conspiracy against the authority of the College.

(2) To undertake in a special manner a strict observance of the regulations of the College as a sign of the above mentioned disavowal and their sincerity in making it.

(3) To resume attendance at the regular Bible classes.

We send you this letter that you may know clearly what has happened. It remains for us to say that beginning with Monday, March 22nd, this decision will go into effect. If there is any parent, however, who would prefer to withdraw his son from the College he can do so and the College will make the necessary settlement with regard to the second instalment of fees he has recently paid.

Accept abundant respect, and may your existence be prolonged.

For the Faculty of the College

HOWARD S. BLISS, *President*

On March 22 the faculty's decision went into effect. Eight students quietly withdrew from the College, but the rest agreed to accept the terms of settlement outlined in the letter. Before the succeeding year opened, great care was taken to make clear to entering students what responsibilities they were undertaking, as well as the fact that the Syrian Protestant College was a Christian missionary college. No student was admitted who could not give satisfactory assurance that he fully understood the rules and regulations and intended to obey them so long as he remained a student. The danger was safely passed.

In order that the position of the faculty and the Board may be clearly understood it will be of value to make public the admirable analysis presented by D. S. Dodge at the special meeting of the Board held on May 25, 1909. It presents seven cogent reasons for not relaxing the maintenance of the principles involved directly and indirectly in the whole dispute.

"1st: The College was not established merely for higher secular education, or the inculcation of morality. One of its chief objects is to teach the great truths of Scripture; to be a centre of Christian light and influence; and to lead its students to understand and accept a pure Christianity, and go out to profess and commend it in every walk of life.

"In attaining this end no agency can take the place of common religious exercises and the regular study of the Bible.

"The private counsel and personal influence of instructors will be an indispensable auxiliary, and always of inestimable value; it is part of the willing missionary service each one expects to render when he joins the teaching staff; but such efforts alone would be largely ineffective, if not futile.

"The public religious gatherings, attended by all the students, are essential to prepare the way for personal influence. They impart instruction, and exert a power not to be gained elsewhere. They impress upon the minds of the students the true design of the College; and, at the same time, they proclaim to the people at large its positive Christian and missionary character. There has never been any intention or desire to force students to adopt our religious views; but we have always held it to be a duty to use every legitimate and hopeful instrumentality to enlighten and win them to the Christian faith.

"2nd: It is manifestly unjust, as well as impracticable, to attempt discrimination on the basis of nationality or sect.

"All must attend, or liberty be granted to all; no class legislation can be allowed.

"This is emphatically necessary in the light of the present violent disorders which have wrought such indescribable misery and loss in the very regions from which some of our students come.

"The College was founded to reach, by every proper and kindly method of influence, the great Moslem population, as well as the Christian; but we need to guard against anything that might be construed as favoritism toward the dominant race.

"3rd: No one will be excluded who can meet the educational and other requirements for admission; but all who are received bind themselves by the very act to obey the College rules; and one of the most important is to be present at the regular religious exercises.

"4th: The assembling together for a common religious service tends, perhaps even more than contact in the classes, halls, and sports, to create and encourage the unity of feeling and obligation we desire to cultivate, and to dissipate the unhappy alienations and irreconcilable differences which so generally separate the people of the East, and hinder cooperation in social, industrial, or national movements.

"5th: It has been suggested that the system of voluntary attendance might relieve the difficulty.

"In the United States, few institutions except those supported by public funds have introduced this policy; but even in these the majority of the students, if not practically all, have had a greater or less degree of religious training before entering; a large number are already church members.

"It is found, however, that in many instances the appeal to attend the Chapel services receives only a limited and unsatisfactory response. Most of these institutions are classed as secular, not religious, and under no circumstances as *"missionary."*

"In such an institution as ours, and in such a land as Syria, with our students belonging to many distinct and antagonistic faiths and nationalities, and taught from childhood to look upon Protestantism with contempt, is it to be expected that any considerable number would find their way to Chapel, or if a few desired to enter, would they be apt to risk the hatred of the majority?

"Or, is it probable that students who demand exemption from such College duties would not, in time, make objection to other requirements?

"Moslems and other non-Christians would certainly ask soon to be released from any study of the Bible; and members of the Oriental Churches might refuse to listen to our interpretation of Scripture. Concessions such as these, if granted, would go far to neutralize any positive witness for Christ and evangelical Christianity which we might hope to maintain.

"Other regular studies in the curriculum, and certain other College restrictions, might become distasteful; possibly, members of the staff would be declared unpopular, and a request come to have them removed, with the threat of absence from classes, in case of refusal.

"It is not an imaginary conclusion that ultimately the control of the College would practically pass into the hands of the students, or their parents and advisers.

"6th: There is danger of interference by local authorities, or by the general Government, on the plea of religious toleration, or the right to impose State regulations in all educational institutions.

"Our defense must be that we are entitled to regulate our own internal affairs as an American missionary enterprise, supported by private and foreign funds, and possessing certain privileges under the protection of our own Government, and the official recognition of the Turkish Government.

"In such a controversy, it would prove a distinct disadvantage to have it pointed out that we had already granted important concessions, and could yield others. Such an argument, if successful, might easily be used as applicable also to other departments of missionary effort.

"7th: We commend the views of the Faculty in reference to our responsibility toward other educational institutions, and the entire missionary work in the Turkish Empire.

"By adhering for nearly half a century to the educational and religious principles originally proposed, the College has gained a position of influence and leadership, which makes any action on our part, especially in a matter of serious moment, inevitably affect other similar bodies.

"We desire to be true to this obligation, and to work in the closest harmony with all who are also endeavoring to enlighten, civilize, and Christianize the people of the Nearer East.

"In view of these considerations, and of all those presented in the communication from the Faculty,

"Be it resolved: that the Board reaffirms its position that the regulations requiring attendance at Chapel, and at the religious exercises, and the regular Bible Classes, shall be maintained."

As may be seen from this statement, the Trustees and faculty were moved by considerations of deeper import than the actual situation at first sight presented. They were concerned for the future, not only of the College but of other missionary activity as well. Nothing could show more clearly the sincerity of Christian purpose which has, throughout the history of the institution, motivated those responsible for its direction.

Though the difficulty was thus satisfactorily arranged it must not be supposed that the administration dismissed it lightly and without serious self-analysis. It clearly recognized that such regulations as that of compulsory attendance at religious exercises, while excellent in principle, were subordinate to the primary aims of the College, being simply means to an end. "Where the end," wrote President Bliss, "is not wisely apprehended and worthily utilized, the means becomes burdensome and mischievous. . . . The regulation is a wise one provided the opportunity presented is so used as to develop the habit of devotion, to evoke the spirit of prayer and praise, to enlighten the conscience, to strengthen the will and to reveal the sources of divine wisdom and strength." If not so used, it "will become a positive evil, developing irreverence, stereotyping devotion, prejudicing and embittering the unwilling student against all religion. . . . After all, compulsion has a high and noble meaning only when we put back of it and beneath it the compelling power of reason, of sympathy, of friendship, of love, of service, of personal effort. Thus and only thus will men of the Twentieth Century be compelled to come into the Kingdom and

PRESIDENT HOWARD BLISS
(After the War)

ALLEGHENY COLLEGE LIBRARY

ALBERT W. STAUB
Director, Near East College Association

ALLEGHENY COLLEGE LIBRARY

thus and only thus will compulsory Chapel become in the Syrian Protestant College a divine and eternal force in the lives of our students."[10]

3. REGULATION

No further trouble on religious grounds was experienced from students during the Bliss administration, but they were not the only possible source of distress. The Ottoman Government stood always like a cloud on the horizon, but through the remarkable diplomatic facility of Howard Bliss, who equalled if he did not surpass his father in that capacity, repeated threats of deluge were averted. The great respect in which the College was universally held, together with the active cooperation it received both from American and British diplomatic and consular officials, succeeded in preserving it inviolate from hampering official regulation. But to the Turkish cloud was added the menacing thunderhead of war, and in the fall of 1914 the rains came.

They first took the form of a new Educational Law, growing out of the abolition of the Capitulations and thus affecting all foreign institutions. Among other restrictive provisions the S.P.C. was forbidden to give religious instruction to any students except those of the Protestant denomination, or to permit the attendance of any but Protestants at any religious exercises. Ambassador Henry Morgenthau succeeded in obtaining a postponement of the application of the law until September 1915, by which time it was hoped that the provisions might be modified. Dr. Bliss spent part of the summer of 1915 in Constantinople conferring with the Minister of Public Instruction, Shukri Bey, and other officials. As a result the restrictions of the educational law were eased to permit the College to maintain its religious regulations for all Christian students, but attendance at religious services by non-Christians had to be made voluntary.

In order to avoid the total relaxation of control which purely voluntary attendance would entail, the faculty arranged that every required religious exercise should be paralleled by a non-religious exercise. Students were permitted to choose which they would

[10] Annual Report, 1908-09, pp. 14-16.

attend, but they were still required to attend one or the other. The institution of "Alternative Exercises" satisfied the requirements of the law but permitted a maintenance of the College regulations. The practice proved so successful that it has been maintained to the present day. Of course the Alternative Exercises, while strictly non-religious, were of a nature calculated to improve the minds and morals of the students who elected to attend them.

Because the division of these exercises made impossible the continuance of a service in which the whole student body could unite, a College Assembly, attendance required for all, was instituted on Friday afternoons at the close of class work. All religious observances were there omitted but opportunity was given for the development of the spirit of campus unity which had been threatened and which was so valuable a part of the moulding influence of the College.

Early in 1916 additional demands were made on the College, to the effect that Moslem religious services be established and courses in Moslem ethics be introduced into the curriculum. In short, the question was raised as to whether the Syrian Protestant College should remain a distinctively Christian institution. Whether the Turks actually expected capitulation on this point or whether they were simply testing the temper of the administration will never be known. At any rate the demands were transmitted in due course to the Trustees, who respectfully replied in the following letter to the faculty which, it was understood, would reach the Governor of Syria and the officials of the department of education:

"99 John St., New York, June, 1916

REPLY TO THE INQUIRIES OF THE FACULTY

"The object in establishing this College was to provide for the young men of Syria and adjacent countries a Christian Institution of higher learning, providing courses of literary, scientific and professional education enjoyed in American Colleges.

"It was hoped that such advantages would help to raise up an intelligent and thoroughly trained body of capable men who would be of special value in promoting among their own people the best features of modern civilization.

"For more than fifty years this aim has been steadily pursued. Graduates of the Institution have gone out into all parts of the Near East and to other lands, and, with few exceptions, have occupied positions of usefulness and influence, many of them being in public service. A large number are practicing medicine and some of them have gained distinction in this and other professions or occupations.

"During these years the College has received numerous evidences of appreciation from the Central Government. Several official documents of high importance confirm this recognition.

"The Institution is an independent organization, non-sectarian, and wholly free from political motives or affiliations. It aims to teach its students to lead upright lives, to love their country, to be loyal to the established authorities, tolerant toward the convictions of others of whatever origin or creed; to respect each other's rights, cultivate the habit of living in mutual harmony, to share each other's studies, sports and daily duties, without prejudices or friction, and to carry back these qualities to their own communities and countries.

"We believe that such training is of supreme necessity in any land having a population of diverse nationalities and religions. The College endeavors not only to impart secular knowledge but above all other considerations to implant enduring and fundamental principles of moral character.

"As a Christian Institution, the instruction given is based upon the teachings of the Book, which Christians hold is intended and adapted to be the standard for the conduct of life in all its relations and among all classes, races, and conditions of men; but in doing this we have never attempted to force our views upon any of the students.

"We frankly present the reasons for our Faith, and every one is left entirely free to accept or reject them. No religion has ever been denounced or its adherents treated with disrespect by the Instructors of the College, and acrimonious discussion of religious questions among the students is not allowed. All possible concessions have been made to meet the wishes and customs of our students. They are permitted to attend their own places of Worship on suitable occasions and under proper escort.

"Our own religious exercises are largely voluntary. We state publicly in our catalogues and circulars the requirements for entrance. Applicants come with the full understanding of the character of the Institution, and, if received, are naturally expected to observe its regulations.

"In respect to the official propositions now presented we are ready to see that every Ottoman student shall study Turkish, and that Ottoman History and Geography shall be taught in Arabic or Turkish by an Ottoman. We could also arrange to have Moslem students attend more frequently at the Mosque, where they are accustomed to go at present, but we cannot believe it would be consistent with the principles of a Christian College to establish

Moslem worship in the midst of the Institution or to have Moslem ethics made a part of its course of instruction.

"The College has on its roll representatives of at least ten different sects and nationalities. If special privileges are granted to one religion, they cannot be denied to others. This would subvert the foundations of the College and destroy any orderly continuance of its regular exercises.

"If Moslem parents for any reason feel it would be undesirable to have their sons attend this College, they can happily now find Institutions designed for Moslems exclusively. We understand that the system of education contemplated by the Government includes schools of all grades even to the highest. It would be a pleasure for us to cooperate with such Institutions at all times in efforts to improve the character of advanced instruction, to secure better teaching and larger equipment and to adapt the courses of study to the increasing wants of the country.

"In the midst of such a large population, with so many Faiths and races, schools for each would be almost indispensable, but all can unite in promoting the interests of National education and the creation or introduction of a literature vital to the development of an enlightened and progressive people.

"Where such opportunities are wanting, the most promising young men are apt to seek in other countries the higher training they ought to enjoy at home. This College desires to do its share in providing these facilities, and it feels assured the Government will appreciate its character and services, and render it the official assistance needed to make its efforts increasingly successful as an effective agency in promoting the best interests of the Empire.

D. STUART DODGE."

This was a mild, conciliatory, and courteous reply, well calculated to turn away wrath, but perfectly inflexible in its intention. It opened the way for further negotiation and doubtless helped to save the College. At any rate, no further requirements of a religious nature were made thereafter, though, as will be seen, this fact was a relatively small oasis in the desert of difficulty.

IX. WAR YEARS

I. ITALIAN BOMBARDMENT

TO CONDUCT THE WORK of a college in a foreign country when that country is threatened by or involved in war, is never an easy task. As Dr. Bliss once wrote, "however unreasoning it may seem to be, the fact remains that at such a time all foreigners are looked upon by the ignorant portions of the public as in some sort of league with each other against Turkey; fanatical feelings are easily aroused: the atmosphere is charged with combustible elements." When one recalls that in at least ten of Howard Bliss' eighteen years of administration Turkey was perturbed by wars or rumors of war, the magnitude of his accomplishment in preserving the integrity of the institution becomes the more apparent.

The effect of the internal revolution of 1908 and the period of adjustment which followed it has already been described. It was not over and the first wild enthusiasms had not yet been supplanted by discouraged resignation before Turkey was embroiled in foreign difficulties. The loss of Bosnia and Herzegovina to Austria-Hungary in 1908 was followed in 1911 by Italian aggression in Libya and the First Balkan War of 1912. The Ottoman Empire was, within five years, stripped of all its European provinces except eastern Thrace, of its Libyan territories, of Tripoli and Benghazi, of its island possessions including Crete and the Dodecanese. And only a year or so later came the final holocaust of the First World War.

The Italo-Turkish imbroglio concerning North African Tripoli, over which war was unjustly declared by Italy in the fall of 1911, brought the first taste of battle to the shores of Syria. On the 24th of February 1912, two Italian warships, accompanied by a transport, bombarded Beirut with resulting civilian casualties of 120, forty of them fatal.

Two small Turkish ships, a gunboat and a torpedo boat were at anchor in the inner harbor and these were the object of the attack.

The former was sunk by shellfire to which it could not reply and by a torpedo fired at close range. This occurred shortly after 9:00 a.m. The Italian ships then moved off, but returned at 2:00 p.m. and sank the torpedo boat, which had escaped much injury in the morning. In both attacks some shells went wild, exploding in the city near the port, and at least two went clear over the town, bursting in the sands near the Municipal Hospital.

Excitement in Beirut was intense, partly because it was believed that the Italians meant to occupy the city. Credence was given to this idea by the presence of the large transport with the warships. It was reported that arms were being distributed to the entire population, particularly the Moslems. Actually arms were being distributed to reserve policemen when an excited mob rushed up and either looted the arsenal or seized the arms being passed out. Several Italians and supposed Italians were attacked in the streets. Mrs. Nickoley, who happened to be in the city when the firing commenced, saw at least two persons fall, one of them a Russian Jew, mistakenly supposed to be an Italian.

The College, flying the American flag from each of its buildings, became a place of refuge. Mrs. Nickoley reported that in the indescribable confusion of the market place, the one word she could understand was "Al Kulliyah, Ras Beirut," repeated again and again—"not in anger but in gratitude that there was such a place in the city where refuge might be had." Hundreds entered the gates of the College and hospital compounds; and five or six recitation rooms in College Hall, several in Daniel Bliss Hall and one or two in Fisk Hall were used as dormitories that night by people afraid to return home even though the warships had departed. For several days thereafter the city was under martial law, but at length the excitement died down.

As an actual fact, the Syrian Protestant College gained greatly in prestige as a result of the attack. Its willing helpfulness, typified not only by its taking in the refugees, but by the volunteering of doctors and medical students for service in the city, was widely appreciated, as was the calm good behavior of the students. Graduates in the neighborhood showed to good advantage, particularly one nursing graduate who was superintendent of the Municipal Hospital. As the first shell burst near the hospital, the servants and staff simply evanesced, leaving her alone. She reported at the College but bravely returned at once to her post, being reassured and strengthened by Mrs. Dale in the recognition of her duty. Dr. Salibi, the assistant College physician, a medical graduate of the previous year, volunteered to go with her and help in any way he could.

It became clear, moreover, that the American community, far from being sympathetic to the western power, was heartily outraged by the unprovoked attack and awarded its sympathies without hesitation to the Turks. Perhaps, too, the fact that Prof. Nickoley was released by the faculty for some days to take charge of the American consulate-general during the sickness of the ranking official helped to emphasize the standing of the College. At any rate, when the normal tenor of events had been resumed, the general attitude toward the institution was greatly improved. The way seemed clear for that further healthy growth which brought the enrollment in 1913-14 within thirty of the one thousand mark.

Actual warfare did not return to Beirut for some years, and though during 1912-13 Turkey's armies were almost continuously in the field, Turkey's youth sought education in almost unprecedented numbers. Until the new preparatory school buildings were ready for occupancy it was necessary to turn away a number of applicants for admission. The prospects of widening influence and increasing service were reflected in Dr. Bliss' annual reports to the Trustees. Then, at the end of the glowing report of 1913-14, written in July and August, appeared an ominous paragraph: "This report of the past happy and successful year is written in darkening days when war and rumors of wars are hourly reported. Whether the clouds will break before the College opens in October, the future alone can disclose. They will break some day. Meanwhile, it remains our duty to realize as never before that the College's chief function is to teach its teachers and students how to do justly and to love mercy and to walk humbly with their God." How soon the time of testing was to come even Howard Bliss could not know.

2. 1914-1915

The war in Europe began early in August, but Turkey was not technically involved until the last of October. Actually, she had concluded a secret alliance with Germany as early as August 2nd when a general mobilization order was issued, and her intentions were hardly in doubt thereafter.[1] By the end of October it was apparent that a considerable decrease in enrollment at the College was certain, the reduction being due to "the wild and unfounded reports regarding the conditions of safety in Syria and especially in Beirut, and the enrollment of not a few students as soldiers in the Army or as assistants in the military Hospitals."[2] The clouds had already broken, but only to let loose the storm of war.

An immediate effect of the declaration of war was the closing and confiscation of the properties of French and British schools. It occasioned considerable surprise in some quarters that the American College should at once offer and give shelter to numbers of the Jesuit fathers, "Christian brothers" and "Sisters of Charity" made homeless by this action. The religious orders were sincerely grateful, and that one event succeeded in breaking down barriers of prejudice which had long resisted normal efforts at friendliness. As a result, some sixty former students in the French schools were encouraged by their teachers to enroll in the Syrian Protestant College.

Memories of the Italian bombardment of 1912 caused a panic of fear in the city that it would be immediately repeated. The abolition of the Capitulations increased the terror of reprisal. Dr. Frederick Bliss, who was then visiting Beirut, wrote to America that "the College grounds were looked to by all classes and conditions as the only place of refuge. The Consul appointed Howard (Bliss) a United States Marshal, with power to appoint deputies. A circular was sent out to members of the teaching and administrative forces, detailing the function and duties of the various members, according to an organized plan covering such items as 'admission to grounds and public security,' 'assignment of sleeping places by

[1] For a concise survey of the factors influencing Turkey, see "Turkey at the Straits," by Shotwell and Deák (Macmillan 1940), ch. 9 and 10.

[2] Annual Report, 1913-14. Addendum dated October 29, 1914, p. 28.

buildings,' 'night patrol of grounds,' 'commissary and providing beds,' etc., etc., etc." As the bombardment failed to materialize, after a time people gradually returned home.

Another cause for fear among the Christian population was the attempt of the Turkish Government, backed by the Germans, to stimulate a "jihad," or holy war, in order to bring to their side the Arab world, which was anything but heartily in sympathy with them. Early in November a "fetwa" from the Sheikh-ul-Islam proclaimed the jihad as "a religious obligation on all proclaimers of the Divine Unity, and it has become their duty to make haste to devote to the cause their life and wealth."[3] This was followed on the 11th of November by the Sultan's proclamation of jihad to the army and the fleet. Finally on the 23rd an Imperial Manifesto, signed by the Sheikh-ul-Islam and twenty-eight other religious dignitaries, reiterated the proclamation of the earlier fetwa. In spite of all possible pressure, however, the jihad failed to spark and later backfired because of the refusal of Husain, King of the Hedjaz and Grand Sharif of Mecca, to endorse it.[4] Nevertheless many Christians anticipated a general massacre until reassured by prominent Moslems. It all added to the confusion which disturbed the academic calm within the College walls.

With the declaration of war the British had made Egypt a protectorate, deposing the Khedive Abbas II and ending Turkish domination. That frightened the Egyptian students in Beirut, for it made them technically enemy aliens. Three of them left the College but the rest eventually decided to remain. Later they were unable to leave, for in December the authorities agreed to regard all the students who were subjects of states at war with Turkey as prisoners of war in the custody of the College, to be allowed to remain inside the College grounds. It was a remarkable evidence of the favor in which the College was held, but it was an expensive privilege. Before peace came the care of these students cost a total of nearly $80,000.

[3] Translation sent to the Trustees by Dr. Howard Bliss.

[4] For full details, see "Antonius, The Arab Awakening," ch. 7. During the revolution in 'Iraq in May 1941, the Germans again attempted to inspire a jihad. There was less chance of success in 1941 than in 1914.

The promulgation of the new educational law previously mentioned had many threatening implications for the S.P.C. other than those concerning its religious regulations. The official Firman of the College had to be presented for reregistration; the institution must be ready at any time for official inspection by the departments of Education and Health; it must submit to a new basis of tax assessments; instruction in the Turkish language was made compulsory on all students; no additions could be made to land or buildings. The application of the law was postponed and eventually its provisions were somewhat modified, but its existence required constant adjustment with officials and constituted an overhanging threat to the continued existence of the school which placed the administration under a heavy strain. The American faculty were threatened with application of the "Femettua," or income tax, from which they had previously been exempt. As this was a 3 percent tax on any income above $75 a year, it would bear heavily on men already struggling along on small salaries.

There were numberless minor regulations which required President Bliss to be in constant contact with various officials. Rules pertaining to registration, military service, permits to travel from Beirut, blacking-out all windows facing the sea, disuse of all telegraph and wireless apparatus, limitations on purchase of foodstuffs, etc., etc., were a constant source of worry, annoyance and danger. The burden on Dr. Bliss and George B. Stewart, the Treasurer, as Commissary General, was increased by shortage of supplies and rising prices. Fortunately fairly large stores had been laid in before war broke, and others were made available through the friendliness of the Mayor. Gas had to be cut off for lack of coal, but there was at first plenty of oil, and West Hall, the Library and the dining-room in Dodge Hall had electric light—the only buildings so equipped.

In December orders came from Damascus that all members of British and French communities were to be deported inland. This affected many friends as well as Drs. Dray, Graham and Webster. As many as could do so took refuge on the campus, while Dr. Bliss, the American consul, the Johanniter Order and others did their best to get the order rescinded or an exception made for the doctors. After what seemed an endless wait word came from Ambassador Morgenthau that the Minister of Interior had cancelled the order for deportation. This was followed, however, by stringent orders from Damascus for the deportation of all without exception. As Frederick Bliss wrote: "It is impossible to follow in detail the shifting policy pursued in regard to possible exemption of our doctors. Not till late at night, through efforts in which Sister Anna (of the Hospital), the Austrian and German consuls, Howard, etc., were involved, did the assurance come that the doctors could remain till the next night train. . . . This a.m. the Consul has received word that the doctors are to be exempted from deportation. I understand that this is from the Ambassador, but whether this is to be permitted by the military authorities at Damascus or not, has not yet transpired. An hour ago they had gone to the Consulate and, if necessary, were to go to the Police office to find out."[5]

The three doctors actually were exempted until April, but up to the time when they were suddenly arrested and shipped off to Damascus, the fear of losing them was a daily menace. Then, on the day the menace became a reality, Ahmed Djemal Pasha, Minister of Marine, Commander of the Fourth Army and supreme Turkish authority in Syria, made a visit of inspection to the College. He was tremendously impressed by the work being done, and three days later the missing medicos were returned to Beirut. Not only were they permitted to keep up their teaching work, but they were allowed to practice privately. In a great many cases they were called by Turkish officials and army officers, who trusted them and their skill far more than they did the ministrations of their own physicians. This, naturally, did the College no harm.

Soon after the outbreak of war, the faculty considered what the College might do in the way of war relief. The government was informed that any wounded soldiers sent to the College hospitals would be cared for free of charge. Dr. Bliss and Dr. Ward visited the Governor-General and through him tendered to Djemal Pasha the offer of a medical mission to southern Palestine on behalf of the soldiers of the Ottoman army. The offer was made possible

[5] Private letter, dated December 13, 1914.

through the activity of the Beirut chapter of the Red Cross which had received a considerable grant from America and had turned over to the faculty, as a committee of the Red Cross, the work of fitting out and conducting such a mission. Djemal Pasha accepted the offer. Dr. Ward was made Director and was sent to Damascus and Jerusalem to confer with Turkish authorities on details. The Rev. George C. Doolittle, of the American Mission, was appointed Associate Director. On January 17, 1915, the party, consisting of Dr. Ward, Mr. Doolittle, four German Sisters, fifteen seniors in medicine, pharmacy and dentistry, and three servants, left in a special train provided by the government. Tents, bedding, medicines and some provisions were supplied by the Red Cross. Transportation, hospital tents and general provisions were provided by the government.

The medical mission reached its station at Haffir-el-Anjeh just in time to assist in caring for the wounded brought back from the first unsuccessful attack on the Suez Canal. It remained in southern Palestine until the end of March when its services seemed no longer to be needed. The story of its adventures merits a chapter of its own, but it must here suffice to say that its service, direct and indirect, was very great. Particularly were Moslems astounded to see foreign Christians going into danger to serve the soldiers of an unfriendly army. Many Moslems who had for years been suspicious of the aims of the College, gave up their long held antagonism. Out of the horror of war may come an end to strife.

Early in May an urgent call came from the Red Cross chapter in Constantinople for surgeons and nurses from Beirut. Dr. Ward and Miss Van Zandt were released at once, and accompanied by three American nurses, two graduates of the Nurses' Training School and a medical student aide for Dr. Ward, sailed on the U.S.S. Vulcan, a collier, on May 27. The services of this mission as well as the other were sincerely appreciated by the Turkish Government, which learned not a little of the spirit in which a missionary enterprise is conceived. Dr. Ward was given the Turkish Military Medal with Red Ribbon in recognition of the mission's exceptional value.

Professors and students were not exempt from relief activity of another kind—the aid of suffering non-combatants in Beirut and the vicinity. Professor Patch, vice-president of the Red Cross chapter, organized the work. Professor Reed was in charge of an employment bureau to provide work relief. "The city was carefully districted and every family applying for aid was visited by members of the district committees. Professor Reed interested the Municipality in using these Red Cross employees for cleaning the city streets. A friend of the College has made it possible to use many of the Red Cross workers in laying out terraces on the College campus. Volunteers from the student body have rendered valuable assistance in dealing with applicants. A note of reality has been given to the many exhortations heard by the students to make *service* the fundamental principle of Christian living."[6]

With all these activities involving faculty and students, the regular work of the College was somewhat hampered. It was further hindered by the absence on furlough of Professors Adams, Brown, Nickoley and Joy and Dr. Khairallah. Two instructors, Philip Hitti and Byron Smith, were away for a year of study. Dr. Adams succeeded in returning in March but the others were destined to have a difficult time before they finally again reached Beirut.

Medical teaching was further weakened by the sudden death on January 13, 1915, of Dr. Franklin T. Moore, beloved professor of Woman's Diseases, who was only forty-four years of age. His death was referred to by Dr. Bliss as "the irreparable disaster of the year. . . . He belonged to the race of strong men." Dr. Dorman was shifted to Dr. Moore's chair, and the other vacant places were filled by the appointment to the staff of Dr. William T. Van Dyck, absent from the faculty since 1882, Dr. Charles C. Piper, a British missionary from Aleppo who shared the experience of the other British doctors, and Dr. Henry Watson Smith, formerly of the Lebanon Hospital for the Insane. Dr. Sami Haddad was unexpectedly available, and this "first-class man in every particular" became a permanent member of the faculty of the College from which he had graduated in 1913.

[6] Annual Report, 1914-15, pp. 19-20.

In view of the uncertainties of the year, it is surprising that the enrollment was as high as it was. The total of 817 students was not discouragingly below the 970 of the previous year, and actually the number in Arts and Sciences, Pharmacy and Nursing was higher than it had been in the spring of 1914. The decrease appeared in the Preparatory, when younger students did not return, and in Medicine and Commerce, whence several of the seniors were called to arms, all being given the unusual privilege of entering officers' training camps. President Bliss wrote to Dr. Dodge in November 1914 that "a few, but only a few, of our students have sought to escape military duty. Most of them dread it but hold up bravely in the face of it. Our policy of perfectly frank dealing with the government in this matter of military service has made our relations in all these calls for men, cordial and mutually helpful." He did not speak of his own part in heartening the men who were called, encouraging them to see their opportunity for real service. It did not ease the strain on the President to see his boys called to war.

With student life under constant strain and confined almost wholly to the campus, West Hall proved itself even more of a blessing than had been imagined by its creators. As the only main building with electric light it became the place of universal congregation in the long evenings. From the start of the year the Director, Bayard Dodge, outdid himself in organizing entertainments and opportunities for community recreation. Every Saturday night some program was arranged for the diversion, instruction or amusement of students and members of the American community. These began with an athletic rally, a band concert by sailors from a U.S. warship, a lecture on archaeology by Frederick Bliss, and were followed throughout the year by skating parties in the West Hall rink, playlets, motion pictures, concerts and lectures. The game rooms, billiard rooms and bowling alley were heavily patronized. The great common-room served constantly as a place of study and friendly gathering, helping materially to foster new friendships and compose troubled spirits. To West Hall Dr. Bliss attributed in greatest measure the preservation of the normality of student life in the midst of constant alarms and excitement.

Athletics played their part in providing normal outlet for pent up emotions and restricted energies. To the development of competitive sports in addition to physical drills, accomplished under successive physical directors Goodhue and Munro, had been added a still greater concentration on intramural sports by Mr. Smurthwaite in 1912. Every student in the preparatory and college departments had a chance to play soccer, basketball, hockey, cricket, or tennis, or to take part in boxing or wrestling or track meets. In 1914-15 a succession of visits by American men-of-war provided exciting outside competition in many sports and introduced baseball. Games in this last had to be played between sailors' teams, for the students lacked the specialized ability required, but these events were of great interest and were a source of satisfaction not only to the participants and observers but to the fleet officers and the College administration. A very fine spirit of sportsmanship was engendered and the war could be temporarily forgotten.[7]

But such forgetfulness was very temporary for the College officers. Students' problems, financial difficulties caused by exchange regulations, the question of food supply, were ever-present sources of worry. The last was made particularly difficult by "the confused and ever-changing plans for bringing to Beirut a sufficient amount of flour from the abundantly supplied interior" as well as by the fact that for months nothing reached the city from abroad. The feeding of a family of one thousand is not an easy matter in time of war. It was to become a problem of terrible urgency before this war was over.

Commencement was held on June 15 without any unusual occurrence except the absence of the Imperial medical commission, which was unable to come. Numerous high officials were present and Djemal Pasha himself wired his regret that circumstances prevented his appearance. At the end of June permission was granted for the opening of the Summer School at Schweir in the mountains, which had been inaugurated the preceding summer. It was largely attended, in part, because students unable to return home

[7] Naval units visiting Beirut in 1914-15 were: U.S.S. North Carolina, Capt. J. W. Oman; U.S.S. Tennessee, Capt. B. C. Decker; U.S.S. Des Moines, Commdr. J. R. Y. Blakeley; U.S.S. Chester, Commdr. F. N. Schofield; also the colliers Jason, Vulcan and Caesar.

took advantage of the opportunity to make good use of their vacation. Students interned on the campus were not allowed to go to the Summer School, but the library was kept open for them and they were given some supervision in study.

1915-1917

The next year opened with apparently little change except for a further reduction of the student body to 786, and a shortage of instructors. Several American staffites had been called home and replacements were difficult, if not impossible, to get. Many of the Syrian staff had been mobilized, and several returning staff members had trouble in getting back to the campus.

The provisions of the new educational law were now in effect and the study of Turkish was required for all Turkish subjects. To make matters more difficult the government insisted that Turkish should be as well taught as any other language, but they promptly mobilized all qualified instructors. No excuse for unsatisfactory compliance with the law, however, was acceptable and a source of dangerous friction was inescapable.

Shortly after the term opened, instruction in Turkish geography and history was added to the requirements, and more grief was the result. Suspicious inspectors, sniffing through the text books used in teaching geography to preparatory classes came across some passages which they regarded as derogatory to the Turkish Government. This was called to the attention of the authorities and they demanded the immediate dismissal of the teacher responsible for the use of the book. Professor Hall, as head of the department, assumed the responsibility, and the faculty had to accede to the demands of the government that he withdraw from Turkey. The Trustees approved of the faculty action in this regard, but noted concerning it that "our own understanding, however, would be that Prof. Hall should return to this country on furlough and go back to his post as soon as conditions in the Near East are more favorable."[8] For years were to pass before that happy day would arrive.

[8] Trustees Minutes, June 15, 1916.

The war period was naturally a time when suspicions on the part of the authorities were easily aroused. This was particularly true during the second and third years of the war when local officials, familiar with the College, had all been supplanted by men from some other section who knew neither Syria nor the College. To such men the S.P.C., as an institution supported chiefly by foreign funds and controlled by foreign authority, was an object of suspicion. They found it difficult to believe that there was no political significance in this educational work. They were inclined to see evil where none existed and to hunt for it even if it were not apparent. The Hall incident was a case in point, but it confirmed the suspicions of some officials and made them even keener to ferret out the subversive influences which they felt sure were emanating from the halls of learning.

To add to the general misery of the situation, economic conditions grew steadily worse. Supplies which had seemed sufficient at the outbreak of the war dwindled rapidly. The breakdown of transportation facilities, the blockade, the partial cessation of remittances from abroad, the depreciation of paper currency, the difficulty of communicating with America, all wrought their hardships on the College. In the country at large conditions were of course much worse, and particularly so after the Arab revolt in June of 1916. Actual starvation began to make its appearance. Before the British occupation in October 1918, more than 300,000 people in Syria alone were to die of starvation and disease.[9]

The College continued its efforts at civilian relief through the Red Cross, but in the early summer of 1916 the government forbade further foreign help. It apparently reasoned that Syria was Arab country: the Arabs of the Hedjaz had revolted and might be stopped if reprisals on their kinsmen were severe enough. But in spite of government prohibitions, a free dispensary was maintained at the College pharmacy to which students contributed liberally. Dr. Dray was able to maintain a relief station at Brummana in the Lebanon with the aid of funds from America and the friendship of Djemal Pasha. Another relief center was maintained at Suq-al-Gharb under the direction of Bayard Dodge and George Scherer,

[9] Cf. Antonius, pp. 203-4, 240-42.

former staffite and member of the American Mission. These stations saved the lives of many, but alas, all too few.

The year 1915-16 marked the fiftieth anniversary of the establishment of the Syrian Protestant College, and it had been hoped that a golden jubilee might be held, with several of the trustees participating. The war made all such plans impossible, but honor was paid at Commencement to the two remaining prime-movers by conferring upon D. S. Dodge, in absentia, and upon the President-emeritus, who was present, the honorary LL.D. degree. Little more than a month later, Daniel Bliss was granted a higher, a heavenly reward. He died peacefully in Beirut on July 27 at the age of ninety-three, following his beloved wife whose death had occurred in April 1915.

The fall of 1916 found the enrollment at its lowest level, 695 students. But in spite of difficulties, dangers and the depressing outlook in general the work of the College continued without interruption. There were some rays of light. Dr. Ward had returned from Constantinople in the late spring. Although it was learned early in 1917 that Professor Joy had felt it necessary to resign, strength was given to the faculty by the return on January 8, 1917, of Professor Nickoley, Miss Van Zandt, Margaret Bliss and Margaret West, the latter being the President's secretary. Byron Smith and Harold Close, former staff members appointed to the permanent faculty, and two new staffites, Leslie and Russell Leavitt, arrived at the same time. The odyssey of these travellers had taken them across central Europe in war time, but after many delays they had all arrived safely. They were a month late for the abbreviated Jubilee ceremonies held in December, but their arrival was occasion for another celebration.

The attitude of Turkish officials became somewhat more favorable because of the obvious sincerity, frankness and courage of President Bliss in his constant dealings with them. Throughout the war he maintained a consistent attitude of loyalty to the existing Ottoman Government, "believing that it had a right to demand from the College, as an institution affiliated with the educational system of the Empire, ready obedience, in so far as its demands did not violate the fundamental principles of the College."[10] But he was adamant when he felt that such violations threatened. He startled and impressed men who were used to servility, and their admiration for him and for the College led to genuine friendliness. In the last years of the war the College was given the opportunity to buy military supplies at cost and thus keep body and soul together.

Djemal Pasha and other commanders could not fail to be favorably impressed when they found that graduates of the American medical school were the only doctors who would willingly serve in typhus wards and in the front line dressing stations. It was Djemal who refused to permit the medical school to be closed when America finally entered the war. It is not an exaggeration to say that the graduates serving with the Turkish forces were, by their devotion to its principles, in large measure responsible for the continued functioning of their alma mater.[11]

1917-1918

On Sunday morning, April 22, 1917, the Vali, Azmi Bey, sent word to Dr. Bliss that diplomatic relations between the United States and Turkey had been severed, and that in consequence the College should be closed immediately. The buildings and equipment would be taken over by the Ottoman Government and administered by the Imperial Ottoman Medical School. A few days later the Vali modified this last statement to the effect that the College would not be taken over except in the event of war between the two governments. Policemen were stationed at the gates, ostensibly to protect the property and lives within from the "attacks of the furious mob that might attempt to destroy an American institution." The amusement resulting on the campus from this pronouncement lightened the tension considerably.

The College was closed, but student life went on as usual with the library and West Hall functioning normally. The Dental School alone was not shut down, for Dr. Dray was "doing some

[10] Al-Kulliyah, VI, 9:66.

[11] Thirty-two medical graduates gave up their lives in active service during the war. Their names are inscribed fittingly on a bronze plaque in West Hall.

artistic work on the jaws of the Vali at that time and, in consequence, had a forceps-grasp of the situation."[12]

On May 5, the Vali informed Dr. Bliss that the College might open on the 7th. This it did, and so after only a two weeks intermission all departments were able to resume their normal operation. It was the only time during the war that the institution was to close its doors.

The permission to reopen is explicable partly because of the intercession of Djemal Pasha. But Djemal Pasha would not have interceded if the United States had declared war on Turkey—and this it never did. Behind that fact lies a curious story which has never before been published.

During the war period Mr. Stepan Panaretoff was the Bulgarian Minister to Washington. Mr. Panaretoff was a graduate of Robert College in the class of 1871 and had been head of the Bulgarian Department of that college until 1914 when King Ferdinand had asked him to represent his country in America. Being devoted to the American educational work in the Near East, the importance of which he clearly realized, he was very gravely concerned at the prospect of a declaration of war by the United States upon Bulgaria and Turkey. In April 1917 he came to New York to call upon Mr. Cleveland H. Dodge, President of the Board of Trustees of Robert College, to see if there might be some way of preventing that declaration of war. Mr. Dodge succeeded in obtaining from Mr. Panaretoff an understanding that provided war were not declared, supplies would be sent at regular intervals from Bulgaria to Constantinople and that a certain proportion of these should be given to Robert College. It was apparent to both men that the work of the American colleges in Bulgaria and Turkey would be stopped by war.

Mr. Dodge called a hasty meeting of Robert College trustees and described his discussion with Mr. Panaretoff, urging that some action be taken. It was shortly agreed that the only possible action would be for Mr. Dodge himself to go to Washington and talk with President Wilson, whose intimate friend and supporter he was. Mr. Dodge was at first loath to go, for he took pride in the

[12] Al-Kulliyah VI, 10:78 (June 15, 1920). See below, p. 230.

fact that he had never asked a favor of the President in spite of their intimacy. He was quickly convinced, however, that in this case he would be asking no personal favor at all but rather would be urging a policy of vital importance to American influence in the Near East.

Mr. Dodge was a man of action. Before the meeting broke up an appointment with the President had been made by telephone, and Mr. Dodge left at once for Washington. Mr. Wilson promised to do his best to prevent a declaration of war on Bulgaria and Turkey. War was not declared, and the supplies for Robert College came regularly throughout the period of conflict. Furthermore, American citizens in Turkey did not have to be interned as enemy aliens, and Djemal Pasha was not prevented from permitting the Syrian Protestant College to remain open.

Happy as this turn of events was, the situation at Beirut was far from comfortable. The constant surveillance to which the College was subjected, the difficulties of securing the necessities of life, the sight of misery, starvation and death all around,[13] tended to produce in students and faculty alike despondency and depression. In this period West Hall was a constant blessing and though available movie films became more and more worn and dilapidated they helped to provide entertainment for the College community and for large groups from the city. Athletic equipment began to wear out. Tennis balls deteriorated and finally were to be found only in antiquated specimens four or five years of age. Footballs were patched, repaired, and patched again until what was left of them had to be reserved for the use of the regular teams. Hockey sticks were worn to slivers and could not be replaced. But the equipment was made to serve and the College remained the only fairly lively spot in Beirut. Too much credit cannot be given to Bayard Dodge and the other staff members who struggled constantly to preserve a semblance of normal life on the campus. Without their efforts the world would have seemed darker than it was and classroom work would have been much less efficient.

[13] It was said that "even the officers of the German Navy could not endure the sights of suffering in the streets of Beirut, and withdrew to their submarines in horror, to free their ears from the cries of starving children." Al-Kulliyah, VI, 11:81.

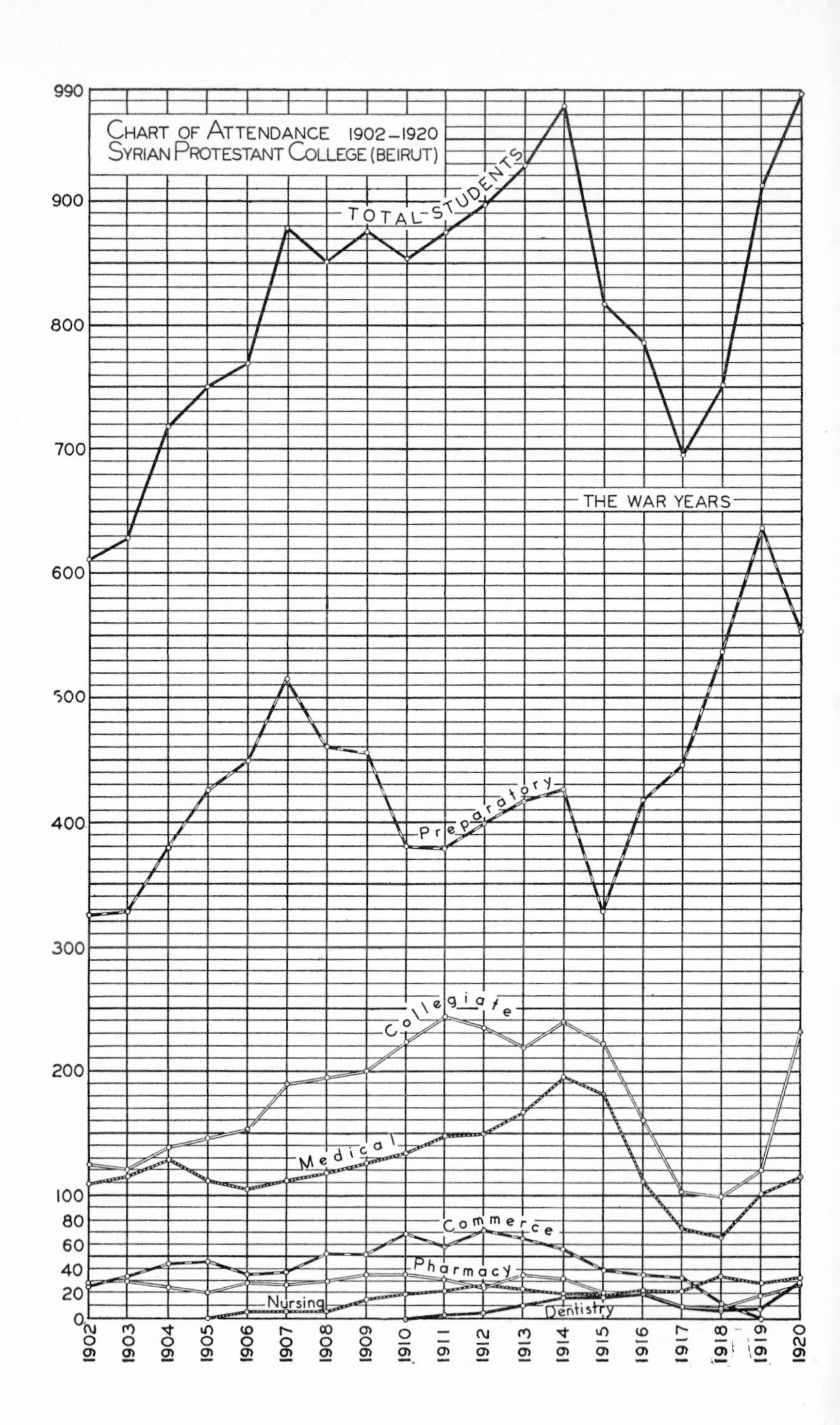

ALLEGHENY COLLEGE LIBRARY

Shortly after America entered the war summary notice was given from Germany of the severance of relations between the College and the Johanniter Order. Six months notice was required by the contract of 1871, and the College had until the second of January 1918 to find some substitute for the Johanniter Hospital. Under the circumstances, however, nothing could be done in the way of construction or even of money raising. Not until some time after peace was restored was it possible to make up for the loss of hospital space occasioned by this unnecessary and regrettable severance.

Hospital supplies had long been dwindling, and before the war was over they would have disappeared entirely had it not been for acquisitions from Turkish army stores made available by Djemal Pasha. An attempt had been made early in 1917 to send to Beirut a shipload of supplies, provided by the generosity of Cleveland H. Dodge and sent under the auspices of the American Red Cross,[14] but the cargo never reached the College. Pelion piled on Ossa created no greater mountain of discouragement.

In spite of the continuance of war, the fall of 1917 had shown an upward trend in the College enrollment to a total of 762 students. Before work began in the fall of 1918 the British and Arab forces had entered Damascus, and on the 8th of October a British division came up the coast and occupied Beirut. It was greeted with scenes of wild rejoicing on the part of those inhabitants strong enough to rejoice, and speedy efforts were made to distribute food and clothing to the destitute. French destroyers entered the harbor with more supplies, and the clouds of suffering began to disperse. Release from the bondage of war through the signing of the Mudros armistice on October 30 brought a rush of students to the College and the registration rose to 913. The end of the long night seemed at hand.

[14] The Trustees on January 30, 1917, voted to express their thanks to Mr. Dodge for the supplies sent on the *Caesar,* and to Albert W. Staub, Director of the Atlantic Division, American Red Cross, "for his untiring and effective efforts in purchasing the College supplies, carefully packing and shipping them." This was Mr. Staub's first effort on behalf of the Near East colleges.

X. PEACE

I. THE CONDITION OF THE S.P.C.

THE OCCUPATION OF SYRIA by the Allies marked indeed the dawn of a new day, but it brought no surcease in the administrative problems of the Syrian Protestant College. "For two days Dr. Bliss aided in meeting the new authorities with whom he had to comply in the direction of the huge College community. Then came many a day of frantic effort to arrange for food and care for some hundreds of Armenian orphans, left in a lamentable condition by the fast retreating Turks. Days of joy followed, as the land of bondage burst forth into freedom and the awful shadow of starvation faded into hope and light. But during these days of bright anticipation there was the strain of readjustment. Students and teachers became impatient. Financial values and sources of livelihood became confused, new demands were made upon the College by the British Army and many a favor was the President asked to perform. Such duties were joyful and full of cheer, but they meant constant going without meals and sitting up until very late at night."[1]

Just when it seemed that normal life at the College might be regained, Dr. Bliss was called in January 1919 as an advisor to the Peace Conference in Paris. He left Beirut on sixteen hours notice with a tremendous new burden of responsibility placed upon him by a nation which trusted him, whose call he could not refuse.

President Bliss spent years at Paris in a very few weeks. Constantly consulted on Near Eastern affairs, he made a great impression by his knowledge, his wisdom and his fairness. He struggled constantly for the principle that the people of the Near East should be given a chance to choose the mandatory power over them, rather than be subjected to a mandate not in accord with their wishes. (Appendix K.) In this he failed, perhaps fortunately, for the people

[1] Al-Kulliyah, VI, 11:83-4 (July 1, 1920).

would have chosen the United States of America as the mandatory power. Nevertheless the actual outcome of the Conference and the intrigues leading up to it were a disappointment to him.

Throughout his stay in Paris the chief care upon Dr. Bliss' mind was the effort to safeguard the rights of the College so that its work might go on regardless of the final settlement to be made. The question had not received satisfactory answer when Howard Bliss had to leave for America in precarious health, but it at length received definite formulation in the "Convention between the United States and France," signed at Paris, April 4, 1924 (Appendix H) and in the "Agreement" between Ambassador Herrick and President Poincaré. (Appendix I.)

President Bliss sailed for America in March and arrived a very sick man. In the words of his brother, "the lifting of the peculiar strain of four and a half years, the chill of a Paris winter, the change from a Spartan diet to one of greater variety—all these circumstances had an effect upon his constitution of iron."[2] He was forced to rest briefly in Jaffrey, New Hampshire, but then plunged at once into the attempted solution of the problems pressing upon the College. These he presented forcefully to a meeting of the Finance Committee of the Trustees on May 15.

The financial needs of the College were classified by Dr. Bliss under five heads:

1. Increase in salaries according to plans approved before the war, but never put into effect. The faculty had really suffered during the war, for they could not be paid in gold, and the paper currency they received had depreciated until it was at one time worth but 15 percent of its face value. At the same time prices of everything had gone up, in many cases several hundred percent. Occasional bonuses had been given but they relieved but slightly the real poverty of the teachers.

2. War emergency expenses. These included the uncontrollable universal price rises, exchange fluctuations, new taxes, and the very large item of emergency relief for stranded students, absolutely

[2] Bliss, Reminiscences, p. 227.

penniless for four years and dependent for food, clothing and shelter upon the College. This item alone amounted to over $80,000 and little of it was ever recoverable. The total indebtedness of the institution approximated $200,000.

3. Repairs of existing plant. Naturally no expenditures had been made on repairs and upkeep which were not absolutely essential. Four years without upkeep had played havoc with the physical plant as well as with the equipment of laboratories, classrooms, dormitories, etc.

4. Putting the existing departments of the College in a state of efficiency. Even before the war, increases of staff, apparatus and teaching facilities were badly needed in order to improve the quality of the work offered. In addition, the loss of the Johanniter Hospital required at least a new Surgical and Medical Pavilion, a new laboratory and considerable addition to the endowment. These were required simply for the continued existence of the medical school.

5. Expansion. In view of the period of reconstruction ahead, with its increased demands for trained native leaders capable of handling the responsibilities of government, the College would fail in its purpose if it did not grow to supply the broadened needs of the country. Dr. Bliss envisaged an expansion of the work in agricultural engineering, begun in 1914 under Professor Patch, into schools of agriculture (including forestry) and civil engineering. He also saw the need for work in law and theology. All these would require more teachers, purchase of land, new buildings, increased endowment. They seemed to the President to be essential if the position of leadership of the Syrian Protestant College were to be maintained, and its spiritual aims fulfilled.

At a meeting of the full Board of Trustees on May 26, it was voted to make an effort to raise $200,000 to cover debts, and $500,000 for increased endowment. Pending the attainment of that goal the Trustees would seek to raise $30,000 annually to pay the increased costs of operation. A new era of peaceful expansion was in process of organization.

2. THE NEAR EAST COLLEGE ASSOCIATION

Before the campaign for funds really got under way, a new development took place which was to be of far reaching importance in the work of the American colleges in the Near East.

Robert College was faced with problems similar to those which occupied the Syrian Protestant College. Both institutions had become so large that the business which had to be handled by the Trustees required more time than busy men could easily give. The additional problems of an extended financial campaign seemed to require the employment of some agency which could devote its sole efforts to the work, receiving guidance from the Trustees but relieving them of the immense amount of detail involved.

Mr. Cleveland H. Dodge, President of the Robert College Board, made the proposal that a joint office for the two colleges should be established, with an executive secretary in charge. The only alternative would be for each college to set up a separate office, with an unnecessary overhead expense resulting and a probability of duplication of activity if not actual mutual interference. Mr. Dodge magnanimously offered to carry the expense of the office himself and he even had in mind the man for the position of executive secretary. Albert W. Staub, former missionary to China, organizer of the Oberlin-Shansi Memorial Association, Director of the great Atlantic Division of the American Red Cross, had so impressed Mr. Dodge with his organizing ability, energy, honesty and idealism that he considered him the ideal man for the post. Mr. Dodge succeeded both in persuading Mr. Staub to accept the job and in getting the agreement of the two boards of trustees to the cooperative venture.

The Board of the Syrian Protestant College voted to unite in the Near East College Association, as it was later called, at their meeting on November 19, 1919. The following resolutions were embodied in the action:

1. That an Executive Secretary should be appointed as the representative of the Boards of Trustees in America to facilitate selection of teachers, purchasing and shipping of supplies, and collecting funds.

2. That Mr. Albert W. Staub should be appointed as the Executive Secretary.

3. That the present office and staff made available for the current year should be recognized by the Trustees.

4. That the Board of Trustees of each College appoint two members to act as a Joint Committee, of which the Executive Secretary shall be Chairman and the Presidents of the Boards of Trustees ex-officio members.

(Note: for the present year Drs. Bliss and Gates and Messrs. Fowle and Dodge shall also be members of the Committee.)

5. That this Committee shall organize itself for a year as it sees fit, and may add to its members such persons as it desires.

6. That the Joint Committee thus formed shall undertake to raise a sum of money for the coming year, the amount of which shall be determined by the Board of Trustees.

7. That during this campaign, all contributions specifically intended by the donor for either one or the other institution shall be paid to the Treasurer of that institution.

8. That all funds collected by the Joint Committee and not designated by the donors for one or the other College, shall be divided between the two institutions in accordance with a plan formulated by the Campaign Committee and submitted to each Board of Trustees.

9. That in general the money thus collected by the Joint Committee for the coming year, is to meet the actual running expenses of the two colleges, as money for paying off the war deficits must be raised independently, and money for new buildings and expenses will probably be raised independently through special appeals of teachers on furlough and other channels.

10. That the problem of paying off of deficits incurred during the war is to be left to independent action of each institution. The Joint Office is not to make a cooperative appeal to persons named by the Trustees of the two institutions as their most likely contributors to paying off deficits.

11. That each Board shall reserve the right to plan independently for additions to endowment, or for special funds, and that the Presidents, Trustees, Professors and returned teachers of the two institutions shall be free at all times to appeal to individuals on behalf of their institution, it being understood that the Joint Office shall be notified in writing so as to avoid duplication of appeal.

Mr. Staub was at once sent to the Near East to familiarize himself with the field, and the office which was established at 18 East 41st Street, New York, was placed temporarily in the charge of Luther Fowle of Constantinople, and Bayard Dodge, as acting executive secretary. This son of Cleveland Dodge had returned on a furlough from his unremitting labors in Syria during the war.

The start of the joint financial campaign gave him little opportunity to relax.

3. FROM S.P.C. TO A.U.B.

At the same meeting at which the cooperative venture with Robert College was accepted, the Trustees voted unanimously to change the name of the institution to "The American University of Beirut," applying to the Board of Regents of the University of the State of New York for an amendment to the charter which should comprehend the enlargement of function implied in the change of title. This amendment was granted on November 18, 1920. (Appendix F.)

The proposal to call the institution a university was not new. As far back as 1901 the Board of Managers had voted to change the corporate name to "Syrian Protestant University." To this proposal the Trustees had replied that "in the opinion of this Board it is desirable to postpone for a somewhat longer period the taking of the necessary steps to assume the title of 'University.'"[3] Daniel Bliss in his final report had spoken of the College as being on "the threshold of a university career." The faculty had brought the matter up in 1910, and consideration was then given by the Trustees to the actual title to be used. Howard Bliss, however, had not submitted specific recommendations until 1912, when he reported that the faculty, after long consideration, "would recommend that the term University be adopted to designate the character of the institution, the word to be used upon the occasion of the celebration of the semi-centennial anniversary of the founding of the College."[4] He noted that there was some reluctance felt about taking that step because of a feeling that the resources of the College were as yet inadequate for a university program. However, with four years to go before the fiftieth anniversary it was hoped that additional funds might be secured. In this recommendation the Trustees concurred.

The war, of course, interfered with the realization of this hope, but it was taken up again at the Trustees' meeting in May 1919. In view of the changed political situation in Syria it seemed pos-

[3] Trustees Minutes, January 30, 1902.

[4] Annual Report, 1911-12, p. 25.

sible to make the name "The American University of Beirut," rather than simply "Beirut University" or "Beirut Christian University," as had earlier been suggested. "Syrian Protestant University" was undesirable for two reasons. The institution was no longer Syrian, for its students came from all the countries in the Near East. It was inadvisable to continue the term Protestant because students and faculty now represented nearly every religious form in the Near East and there was no point in needlessly emphasizing sectarian distinctions. Likewise, although there was never any intention to weaken in any way the original principles of the founders, the inclusion of the term "Christian" in the title seemed to provide unnecessary emphasis on religious differences which might prove unfortunate. As a matter of fact, the University is accepted all over the Near East as being a Christian institution but one to which Moslems may safely send their children without risk of any direct proselytizing being attempted. The fact that nearly half the present enrollment of almost 2,000 students is Moslem is an indication of the trust placed in the school by the Moslem world.

The proposal to broaden the charter and change the name was submitted to the New York State Board of Regents, but though they approved of the charter change they objected to the name. Their position was that they had no right to grant the use of the term "American" to an institution in a prominent location where diplomatic relations might be delicate, and furthermore, to call it the "University of Beirut" might cause misunderstanding with the French or local educational organizations in the city. As it was deemed advisable to change both name and charter at the same time, the matter was referred back to the faculty for other suggestions as to title.

A flood of letters from Syrians insisting upon the name "American University of Beirut," was the result of this reference, and as it was apparent that this name was the overwhelming choice of those who might be expected to object, the Board of Regents reconsidered its action. The charter amendment was granted incorporating the name which the institution has since borne. The Syrian Protestant College was now the American University of Beirut.

4. JOURNEY'S END

Howard Bliss did not live to witness this metamorphosis. Worn out in body by the racking strain of the past six years he developed tuberculosis, and though every effort was made to save him he died at Saranac on May 2, 1920.

Dr. Bliss was without any question a casualty of the war. Far more than many a more spectacular rôle played on the field of battle did his work require a type of courage which merited highest honors. For four years, without any relief, he led what to many must have appeared a hopeless cause. He was the leader to whom all turned, but he was also the soldier who bore the brunt of the struggle. It is no exaggeration to say that the police and Turkish officials made trouble for Dr. Bliss at least twice a day every day of the four years. He expected to be called, at any hour of the day or night, to go surety for some student or teacher illegally seized for military service or arrested on some fictitious charge. Without consular representation, he was the official representative of the entire community of Allied nationals as well as of the Americans and students. He himself described the period to the Trustees as follows:

"The high government Turkish officials were, at the start, suspicious, hostile and eager for our downfall. The Germans were even more angry, bitter and malicious. We were watched at every turn. Our enemies were recruited by jealousy and mobilized by hatred. Our friends, of whom in times of peace we had many, were timid and powerless to help us. The possibility of deportation to the interior was always before us. A sudden order to evacuate the city was ever a menace. Mob rule was not an improbability. Provisions became more and more scarce. Starvation stalked through cities, towns and villages, cutting down thousands in Beirut and tens of thousands in Syria. The cries of the dying will ever ring in our ears. It became increasingly difficult to secure money, even at the most exorbitant charges for exchange. Government restrictions of all kinds became more and more harassing and arbitrary. Medicines and hospital supplies diminished at an alarming rate. Communications with our Board of Trustees were uncertain if not impossible. The generous supplies which were sent to us by the 'Caesar' did not reach us. Our consular officials were withdrawn. Our Capitulation privileges were abrogated. We were under martial law of the most arbitrary character. Almost everything we did aroused distrust. A single false step might have precipitated us into unspeakable suffering. The daily drain upon our sympathy knew no limit. The alternation between hope and fear was a continuous strain. Considerations of personal safety and ease strongly counseled closing the College till the storm was overpast. Considerations of simple duty, of unsurpassed opportunity counseled the uttermost struggle to keep the College open. We never had any doubt as to which counsels should prevail, as to what our government expected us to do, as to what the judgment of the Trustees would be. Such occasional and widely separated messages as reached us from the President of the Board of Trustees gave us boundless cheer. They assured us of their confidence, they guaranteed their support. We thanked God and took courage, and held on. And never for a moment did we regret our course."[5]

Another reason for worry which Dr. Bliss did not emphasize as a personal problem was the scarcity of food. "When households could not find enough to keep them fed, the task of supplying food for the assembly of teachers, students, and servants at the College was tremendous. Constant and difficult negotiations were carried on, which demanded skill and care. Although the Treasurer and Steward attended to the details, the actual responsibility came back upon the Executive, and many an anxious night he passed. . . . The cost of living became utterly unreasonable. It was a choice between allowing many of the families of the native teachers, as well as the teachers themselves, the poorer students and servants to starve, or else to run the College into tremendous debt." Without communication from the Trustees, "Dr. Bliss was obliged to assume the responsibility for a financial burden which weighed upon him more heavily than anyone realized."[6]

With the end of the war the pressure on Dr. Bliss did not slacken. After the Peace Conference he had the condition of the College on his heart, and his days in America were filled with speaking, writing and travelling. In the fall of 1919 he anxiously sought for permission to return to Beirut, but the Trustees, perhaps hoping that he might get some rest if he remained, asked him to stay in America. He could not let down however. He worked unceasingly, travelling about to make speeches, trying in every way to interest people in coming to the rescue of his work. Finally that

[5] Special Report, published in 1920 as part of the endowment campaign.
[6] Al-Kulliyah, VI, 11:82.

winter, during a speaking tour, he came down with an acute attack of tubercular pneumonia. He had over-run his strength.[7]

President Bliss was taken first to the Presbyterian Hospital in New York, where it became obvious that the end was not far off. With full knowledge of the fact, Dr. Bliss settled his personal affairs and as many items of College business as his strength would permit. No complaint ever escaped him, and he faced the end not only with philosophical calm but with the courage of a man dominated by the will of God. On March 8 he wrote thus to his colleagues in Syria:

"My doctor has just told me that the x-ray examination clearly indicates that I have tuberculosis. Of course this is very serious, and whatever the disclosures of the coming days may be, they will affect all my future, but whether that future be long or brief the news finds me undisturbed and solicitous only in the use of the time that remains in promoting the welfare of our beloved College. I am very grateful for having lived as long as I have. I am rich, as few men are rich, in friends, and I have a great and abiding faith in the College."

In April he was taken to Saranac Lake in the forlorn hope that he might find relief there, but the only relief was death. On May 2 he talked at length in Arabic, the language of the land of his birth. That evening he died, surrounded by the members of his family who were in America.

By his own request, Dr. Bliss was buried in the little church-yard by the Jaffrey church which he had loved to attend when his visits to America permitted. "As a company of devoted friends looked across his grave to the summit of Mt. Monadnock beyond, Dr. James Barton, Secretary of the American Board and Chairman of the Near East Relief, closed the service with a prayer that Dr. Bliss' students and friends might follow to the mountain heights to which he had led the way."[8]

The news of the death of Howard Bliss fell like a pall upon the Near East. Numberless expressions of regret and esteem poured in to the College from associates, friends, and alumni groups. Two

[7] The tuberculosis probably developed so quickly because the patient was worn down by diabetes. Dr. Bliss was a sufferer from diabetes, unfortunately, before the discovery of insulin.

[8] Al-Kulliyah, VI, 11:85.

particularly may be quoted here, the first being translated from the Arabic:

Damascus

In the death of President Bliss, who is well remembered for his numerous memorable deeds, the country has lost the corner-stone and the most energetic factor of its recent literary and scientific uplift. The sad news of this great affliction has fallen very heavily on the hearing of His Majesty, the King. He therefore ordered me to offer to you in his behalf, his sincere condolence. He believes that the affliction is so great that no words can express the real feelings. In closing he entreats God's mercy on the deceased, and patience and resignation for his honored family, and long life for you all.

Ihsan Allah Jabiri,
Chief Attendant on his Majesty, King Feisal

June 4, 1920
The Residency, Cairo

The death of President Bliss leaves a terrible blank and one that will be difficult to fill. I always look back with living pleasure to the day when I visited the Syrian Protestant College at Beirut, and I feel that I have lost a friend.

(signed) ALLENBY
High Commissioner for Egypt

In their tribute to the memory of Dr. Bliss the faculty presented a keen analysis of his administrative ideals which made clearly apparent the exceptional qualities of his leadership. A more touching testimony was given by the members of the Staff, the short term teachers who might have had small opportunity to know an ordinary president well. "He was," they wrote, "strong and hopeful when all others were weak and despairing; he rejoiced when the task grew difficult and trying; he was calm and patient when others were overcome with fret and worry; he counted nothing, no, not even life itself, too dear to be sacrificed in the interests of those holy ideals towards which he had set his face. And to us, Staffites, he was not only a wise and powerful leader, but also a true and loving father, reserved but sympathetic, dignified but not severe, enthusiastic but always humble, rejoicing to see us happy, grieving in our distresses, patient when we went wrong, forgiving when we repented."[9] Could any father of a real family hope for a finer appreciation from his children?

Howard Bliss himself left a most powerful witness of his masterful intelligence and devoted Christian idealism in an article published in *The Atlantic Monthly* for May 1920, only a few days before his death. To this article, "The Modern Missionary," and to its author, Professor A. D. F. Hamlin, son of the first president of Robert College, wrote a great tribute which was published in the *New York Evening Post* on May 20. Said Professor Hamlin: "No more powerful, convincing and eloquent apologia of the missionary enterprise as that is understood and conducted today has been uttered. Though in a grave among the New Hampshire hills his body lies, worn out by the privations and labours of the last six years, he yet speaks to the world in that masterly utterance and will long continue to speak words which in this distracted and selfish age sound like the inspired message of a divinely commissioned prophet. And such he indeed was."[10]

In the belief that this message should be made permanently available, Howard Bliss' article is herewith reprinted.

[9] Al-Kulliyah, VI, 10:73-4.

[10] Quoted in Bliss, Reminiscences, p. 230.

XI. THE MODERN MISSIONARY*

BY HOWARD S. BLISS

I

It was during the war. Ahmed Djemal Pasha, Viceroy of Syria and Minister of the Marine in the clever but infamous Ottoman Cabinet, had been visiting the American College at Beirut. For some time previous he had been taking note of the record of our graduates, and he made this request: "I want to send to your College, for a period of six weeks, Jamil Bey, whom I have recently appointed Director of the newly established Saladin University in Jerusalem. I wish him to live among your teachers and students, to study your methods, and to discover, if possible, the secret of the success which your graduates have attained."

Jamil Bey came. He did not stay six weeks, but he made good use of his brief sojourn. He was a man of intelligent, alert, and serious mind. His first survey of our campus, our buildings, our equipment (and they are not insignificant), brought him almost to despair. "How can we hope," he exclaimed, "to compete with all this?"

I assured him that the growth of the College had been slow; that it had taken fifty years to reach our present strength. "But we are here," I continued, "not as rivals: we are here to share with the people of the East the best things we have in the West, or rather to exchange the best things that East and West have received. For the whole world needs the whole world. We wish, moreover, to promote and not retard the native educational enterprises in the Near East. "In fact," I added, "it is our purpose to render ourselves, not indispensable, but, as soon as possible, *dispensable,* and we shall go elsewhere just as soon as the ideals of education and of life cherished by us are adopted here."

In my study, a little later, we reached deeper things. His eagerness to get at the hidden roots of our success became increasingly

* Reprinted from "The Atlantic Monthly" for May 1920 by permission of the editor.

apparent. He especially asked about the religious problem—for he knew of the astonishing variety of religious sects represented in our student body. I told him that our motto was: "Frankness and good-will"; that every student's theological and religious opinions were sympathetically respected. I illustrated our attitude in these matters by telling him how the College—missionary and Christian as it is—joins every year with its Moslem, Druze, and Bahai students in their religious celebration of Mohammed's birthday.

The scene is, indeed, impressive. I have in mind the last celebration: a great throng of reverent students—Sunnis and Shiites; white-turbaned sheiks scattered through the audience; the low chanting of the Koran; the serious and restrained orations—previously censored by the Moslem students themselves and thus rendering almost unnecessary any further censoring by the College authorities. In the closing address, given by a responsible officer of the College, the speaker makes it clear that, as a representative of the Christian religion, he is glad to have a sympathetic share in all efforts to strengthen the forces of righteousness in the world. Praising the splendid democracy that obtained in early times among Moslems themselves,—no rights withheld because of color, poverty, or social status—and commending Omar's massive declaration upon becoming Caliph: "By God, he that is weakest among you shall be in my sight the strongest, until I have vindicated for him his rights; but him that is strongest will I treat as the weakest, until he complies with the laws," he pleads that this spirit should not only be maintained among Moslems today, but extended by them so as to embrace all mankind. He bids them retain the sense of the nearness of God asserted in the Koran's memorable line, "God is closer to you than the great artery of your neck." He urges that they should remain true to their Book's injunction as to intoxicating liquors, at just this epoch when Western peoples are grappling with the evils of alcoholism. Characterizing as a stroke of genius the Moslem custom of calling men to prayer through the matchless human voice, rather than by means of bells, beautiful as these are, he begs all the students, Christian as well as Moslem, to turn their thoughts God-ward at the summons of the muezzin. And, finally. he pleads for an ever deeper, richer interpretation of the word

Islam, until everywhere it shall connote an active, personal, intelligent submission to the Will of God in body, mind, and spirit, and thus stand for a true and a sound conversion.

To all this, and to the recital of other illustrations which I gave of the attitude of the College toward his own and other non-Christian beliefs, Jamil Bey listened with wondering and deepening interest. He opened his heart. "We need your help," he cried, "all along the line, but especially in the training of our Moslem religious leaders. We are groping in the dark and we need a helping hand."

It was stretched out to him. In the earnest conversation that followed, I referred to the difficulties which the Christian Church had experienced and was still experiencing in adopting the scientific method of studying the Bible as represented by the principles of the Lower and the Higher Criticism, and I dwelt upon the final necessity confronting every religion of vindicating its truth by an appeal to the inner authority of a spiritual experience rather than to an external and mechanical norm. Sympathetically, but frankly, I pointed out to him that, as the orthodox Moslem belief concerning the inspiration of the Koran was more mechanical and rigid than any of the current theories regarding the inspiration of the Bible, his task would not be a light one.

The subject was renewed at other interviews. I hope he got some help. At least he took with him, for detailed study in his Theological School at Jerusalem, the latest catalogue I had of a leading American theological seminary, with its noble programme of up-to-date theological discipline, with its outlook wide as truth, with its sympathy for all religious aspiration.

Well, the Saladin University of Jerusalem has disappeared and disappeared forever; and Jamil Bey has disappeared (I hope not forever: he was a charming and earnest gentleman); but the episode just related serves to indicate the spirit in which many a modern missionary in all parts of the world today is working out his task. *Missionary,* I repeat, for this College of which I have spoken, the Syrian Protestant College at Beirut, is a distinctly missionary institution, typical of other missionary colleges and missionary enterprises. It has not, to be sure, the earmarks of the traditional missionary project. But while bending every endeavor to give its students a sound, modern education that shall make them efficient doctors, dentists, pharmacists, teachers, merchants, engineers, trained nurses, it does not consider its task as really begun—certainly not as ended—until it has made known to its students that which it holds to be of supreme worth in life: the adoption of the Christian Ideal as the best means of fitting a man to play a worthy part in the great drama of life.

Just what this expression—The Christian Ideal—connotes to the modern missionary will be indicated later; but just now I wish to make it as clear as possible that so deeply, nay, so passionately, does the College believe in the value of its conception of the Message of Jesus to the World, that it would fain persuade its students to absorb and assimilate, on the athletic field, in the class-room, in their social and religious life, in the communities in which they live, in their temples, synagogues, and mosques, in the forum, the counting-house, everywhere, this Ideal. That way lies the fullest life, the deepest joy, the sweetest peace, the truest success.

This, then, in the last analysis, is the *raison d'etre* of the College's foundation. Its classic expression took form in the words of Daniel Bliss, the first president, when, at the laying of the corner-stone of College Hall fifty years ago, he said, "The College is for all conditions and classes of men, without reference to color, nationality, race, or religion. A man, white, black, or yellow, Christian, Jew, Mohammedan, or Heathen, may enter and enjoy all the advantages of the institution for three, four, or eight years, and go out believing in one God or many gods or no God; but it will be impossible for anyone to continue with us long without knowing what we believe to be the truth and our reasons for that belief."

II

The Modern Missionary has been privileged to live in an age in which a flood of light has been thrown upon God's processes of creation. Trained in the scientific method, he has risen from his studies in the broad aspects of Evolution, in Comparative Religion, in the history and the philosophy of religion, in the history of civilization, in the Lower and Higher Criticisms, convinced as never before that a man's religious belief powerfully affects that man's happiness, usefulness, progress and salvation. He has scant sympathy with the superficial view which declares that so long as a man is honest it makes no difference what he believes. He is persuaded that Christ's message is a definite and distinct message, founded upon the knowledge of facts as facts. Christianity respects all that is good in Buddhism; but Christianity is not Buddhism. Christianity is not Brahmanism, it is not Mohammedanism, however near these religions may come in some of their teachings to the teachings of Christ. It is a Christian message, based upon a particular attitude to the universe, explicit, precise and unique. Men may reject it, but in rejecting it, they must reject something that is a definite interpretation of the great mysteries surrounding us.

Moreover, while painfully aware of the glaring defects of Christendom, and with every disposition to be fair and generous in his judgment, he is convinced as never before that the influence of the best of other religions upon the individual, the home, the state, has been incontestably far less benign than that exerted by Christianity. He is certain that the Christian view of the world is so superior to all other views as to make it infinitely worth while to proclaim this view to the uttermost parts of the earth.

In these beliefs he is in full accord with his predecessors. But his studies and his observation have forced him to a further conviction. He does not believe that Christianity is the sole channel through which divine and saving truth has been conveyed. And this persuasion he admits ungrudgingly and gratefully. For it at once enlarges his spiritual fellowship. All men who are themselves seeking God and who are striving to lead others to God become his companions and his fellow workers.

Our missionary has a new conception of the brooding of God's spirit over the soul of man, the soul which ever retains traces of the divine image, in which the light "which lighteth every man that cometh into the world" is never wholly quenched. Reverently he dares to apply to himself Jesus' pregnant discovery: "My Father worketh hitherto—*and I work.*"

Thus seeking and thus working, he discovers with a new humility that, with very much to give, he has not a little to receive from men of other faiths: the mystical element so prominent in Eastern religions; a becoming reticence in the presence of the great mysteries of life; a sense of the nearness of God; a recognition of the importance of religion.

This widened conception of the work of God in the world has a profound effect upon the missionary's method of presenting his own Christian message. He is not content to combat the error which looms so large in the creeds of other men. He is anxious to find the kernel of truth of which so often that error is but a distorted expression. He comes to supplement, not solely to create. He prays for all men with a new sympathy—for all mosques and temples and synagogues as well as for all churches. He will preach wherever he is invited. He speaks the truth, but he prunes his vocabulary of harsh phrases. He realizes that such words as "heathen," "infidel," "heretic," "pervert," are not brotherly words. The mere word "crusade" makes some of my Moslem students white with anger. I have known men who are separated indefinitely from the gospel's influence just because of these infelicitous, these poisonous words. On the other hand, how richly beautiful is Christ's vocabulary in this connection: the seed, the light, the leaven, the spring, the life!

I shall never forget how close we came to having a riot at the College because of a supposed insult leveled at the Koran. For thirty years a slurring reference to Confucius was remembered against a veteran worker in China. The modern missionary, profiting by these warnings, rejects epithets however telling if they are not quite just. He withholds arguments which, the tables turned, he would not think fair or generous if applied to his own belief. He seeks to practice, with a new sense of its importance, the Golden Rule.

Coming in contact with men who are as convinced of the truth of their own faiths as the missionary is of his, his appeal to them must be upon the common basis of absolute fidelity to truth. He must strive to be unflinchlingly, scrupulously honest in his own intellectual processes and habits. Our students at Beirut are repeatedly reminded of Coleridge's great aphorism, applicable to all religions as well as Christianity: "He who begins by loving Christianity better than truth will proceed by loving his own sect or church better than Christianity, and end by loving himself better than all." In our classes, and especially in our Bible classes, there is a tradition of absolutely untrammeled inquiry; and woe be to the teacher who gives the impression that he is suppressing or fumbling question and answer, however blunt, embarrassing, or indiscreet the inquiry may seem to be. Indeed, a chief advantage which a college offers the missionary as a rich field for his activity lies in the fact that here he has as his constituency a picked body of youth, the future leaders of their lands, singularly responsive to the presentation of new moral and religious ideas and ideals, provided the appeal is made in as straight and honest and rational a way as other ideas are taught in laboratory and class-room.

III

Like his predecessor, the modern missionary finds in the Bible the Great Book of Religion; but, spared the burdensome obligation of attempting to defend as errorless everything found in the Bible, whether in the realm of events, of science, of ethics or of religion, he is free to concentrate his attention upon its spiritual appeal. As it echoes God's voice speaking in the souls of men and of peoples, and awakening re-echoes in his own heart, it gains a new authority over him as a man of reason, of conscience, of intellectual and spiritual responsibility. Credible history he finds there, but still more matchless illumination and inspiration. Its cumulative wisdom, its profound devotion, its compelling eloquence, its mounting passion, its yearning appeal—all this has "found" him, to use Coleridge's quite adequate expression.

And he has gained something more. For while convinced of its incomparable superiority, he does not look upon the Bible as the sole body of literature that God has used as the vehicle of divine expression. Authentic echoes of God's voice he finds in other books.

Influenced by these views, and unhampered by a tradition based upon a more mechanical view of the inspiration of the Bible, which attached undue value to local habits of mind and to fleeting words and phrases, the modern missionary finds himself conceiving of the Gospel of Christ in simpler fashion than in earlier days. He has, indeed, scant respect for the popular cry against dogma, against theology, against metaphysics. He does not discourage the formulation of doctrine. He would destroy no historic creed. He would not tinker them. Back of every statement of belief, oecumenical or of narrower acceptance, he believes that there was some great truth seeking, with whatever success, to express itself, and that it was this element of truth which gave vogue to the creed in question. But to him the gospel of Christ is a thing so vital, so dynamic; words and phrases are in so great danger of becoming static ("polarized" was Oliver Wendell Holmes' word); the traditional distinction between the natural and the super-natural is so misleading and even mischievous—all this compels him to believe that the Everlasting Gospel can get itself expressed in an ever-changing world only in the ever-changing terms of personal experience and in today's phraseology; and hence he attempts to restate his interpretation of the Faith in modern language.

IV

What then is the missionary's message?

It is the proclamation of the Religion of Jesus as disclosed in his teaching and as exemplified in his career. Christ's religion is a world-religion because it deals with a craving elemental, instinctive, universal—man's craving for life. Christ claimed that He knew how men can live adequately, overflowingly. His message to mankind is a message that is astonishingly simple in its statement, naïve in its claims, ample in its outline, self-evidencing in its application. It is couched in terms that relate to universal human experiences, and hence that all men can understand. "If you wish to live," said Christ, "really to live,—not a life of mere animal existence, but a life human, divine, victorious, eternal, a life whose quality gives in itself the surest hope that it will survive the dissolution of your physical forces,—you must think of God as your Father, loving, righteous, wise, strong; and you must reverence and love Him and live with Him as such. You must think of yourself as God's child, docile, obedient, trustful; and you must love yourself and live with yourself as such, with a self-reverence that insists upon a standard of unstained conduct maintained at whatever cost; loss of goods, loss of hand, loss of eye, loss of life itself. You must regard your fellow man as your brother and love him and serve him and live with him as such. Thus living, you will live in such peace as the world cannot give and in such joy as nothing can destroy."

This is the message which Christ proclaimed in word and in life, and proclaimed with the unshakable conviction that all men needed it and that any man following in his steps would find his elemental craving for life richly satisfied. Christ's religion involves complete submission to the Will of God in filial, loving obedience. It links in indissoluble bonds creed and deed. As it regards the doing of God's will as that which brings Heaven upon Earth, so it looks with fear and with loathing upon sin as that which separates man from God, constitutes its own hell whether here or hereafter, and corrupts the very being of the soul.

Though possessed by a joy that nothing can destroy, life is not a comedy. Though passing through tragic experiences of suffering, sorrow, and sin, life is not a tragedy. Life is the unfolding of the Father's plan for the child's body, mind, and soul—with *perfection* as the ever-present, ever-receding goal. The pathway will not be an easy one, even as it was not easy for the Master—loving service always costs, whether it be God or man who extends the helping hand. Suffering and sacrifice will be inevitable. "Working out the beast" is no holiday jaunt: the "ape and the tiger" do not readily die. You cannot truly love God and self and man; you cannot really put righteousness, justice, mercy in the very forefront of life, without a willingness to give up ease and comfort and popularity and power. But the victory is sure: all the forces of righteousness in the Universe are on your side.

Much remains implicated in the Religion of Jesus that is not formally expressed: a Home beautiful and radiant: a spiritual and ministering Church: a just and benign social and industrial order: a truly democratic state. All these must inevitably follow when once the Christian Ideal has been adopted. Perfection, moreover, upon which Jesus insists as the goal of man's striving, will bring with it a due development of his intellectual and aesthetic nature.

Many details might, indeed, be added; but they are details—splendid details, but still details. Of course, it is absolutely inevitable, as it is absolutely proper, that Christ's message should be subjected to intellectual restatements as varied as is the mind of man; restatements more closely articulated in their various parts than this simple statement from the lips of Jesus. For his Message deals with the greatest and the deepest things in the world, the most mysterious, the most baffling; and it is natural that man should wish to explore more closely and explain more minutely and justify more completely the Message. But the plea must always be made, with full recognition of the perennial honor in which the theologian should be held, that Christ's essential Message must remain on the lips of his messengers simple in its assertions, ample in it outlines, universal in its terms. Faith in a loving, wise, righteous, and holy God; faith in self; faith in mankind; faith in truth, in love, in righteousness—this fulfills the conditions of the Catholic faith, *quod semper, quod ubique, quod ab omnibus.*

V

As a consequence of his belief in the vital character of Christ's Message, involving a personal relationship between the soul of man and the soul of God, the modern missionary rests the final proof of its authenticity upon the inner experience of the recipient: upon the personal satisfaction of the universal spiritual cravings and aspirations of humanity. "Taste and see!" is the first and the last appeal.

Do these values of the x's, the y's, and the z's, in the complicated problems of your life solve your equation? Substitute these values and establish the proof for yourself!

Does this key open the doors that lead to the "life that is life indeed?" Put the key in the lock and try it for yourself! And the missionary out of his own experience offers with confidence this key as the master-key that will unlock, in other hearts as well, the doors of Peace and Joy and Life and Power. Peace and Joy and Life and Power—these are the divine sanctions, these are the final tests; not a belief in this miracle or that, not a belief in any miracle at all, is the *sine qua non* of Christian discipleship,—is that which brings certitude in Christian belief,—but only the doing of the Will of God as interpreted by Christ!

VI

The missionary's views upon theological questions are of course to him of importance, and he imparts them freely to those to whom he preaches; but he does not do this dogmatically.

He strives never to forget that he is working among peoples whose mental habits and points of view differ from his own. Here there must be perfect liberty. Each temperament must be given its full freedom for speculation, for inference, for conjecture, for elaboration. The missionary does not shun discussion, controversy even, if the purpose is manifest that the real object is to clear the darkness, and not to gain the barren victory of party or of school.

His first concern, however, is always for something deeper, something more vital, than questions of theological and metaphysical speculation relating to the Person and the Work of Christ; to the Virgin birth (in which, together with other miracles, he may or may not believe); to the fine distinctions between the humanity, the divinity, the deity of Christ; to the nature of the Trinity, to the atonement. Upon just one thing he insists: that which touches, not the *bene esse* of the Christian faith, but its *esse*: the personal assimilation in the disciple's life of the teaching and the spirit of Jesus. It is this deliberate purpose, it is this passion that counts. Other questions may be important, but they can wait. What Christ put first, he would put first.

God is still a jealous God, but God is jealous about *things* and not about words and phrases and formulas. Christ was never concerned about the outward honor paid Him. He did not yearn to be admired; He yearned to be followed. He wished men to come to Him, not as a shrine, but as a door; not as a goal, but as a highway; not as a memorial tablet, but as a window through which they could see God and Self and Man and Life and Opportunity.

And so our missionary bids his hearers formulate their thoughts of Christ in their own way, provided they retain the authority of his leadership.

Does He save you from your sin? Call Him Saviour!

Does He free you from the slavery of your passions? Call Him Redeemer!

Does He teach you as no one else has taught you? Call Him Teacher!

Does He mould and master your life? Call Him Master!

Does He shine upon the pathway that is dark to you? Call Him Guide!

Does He reveal God to you? Call Him the Son of God!

Does He reveal man? Call Him the Son of Man!

Or, in following Him, are your lips silent in your incapacity to define Him and his influence upon you? Call Him by no name, but follow Him!

Oh, how our divisive names—Arminian, Socinian, Calvinistic, Trinitarian, Universalist, Roman Catholic, Greek, Protestant, Orthodox, Liberal,—shrivel up and disappear in the presence of actual discipleship and under the realities of personal experience!

VII

The modern missionary, while delivering the Christian Message in its great outlines, must, furthermore, expect and encourage the age in which he lives to work out in its own way the details of the meaning and the implications of these great simple statements, so few in number, but which go down into the deepest things in the universe. In every department of Christian thought and Christian organization,—theological, ecclesiastical, liturgical,—as well as in the larger circles in which the Christian spirit is dominant,—the home, the school, the state,—full scope must be granted for local development. Of course, the missionary will be ready with counsel, but he will be very careful how he attempts to legislate or coerce. In the history of his own church he has had ample warning of the danger of crystallizing non-essentials into permanent elements in the Church's creed, and he is on his guard lest he forge heavy chains upon the necks of those whom he would fain make free.

I have already emphasized the necessity laid upon the missionary of pruning his vocabulary in the interests of brotherly kindness; he must also be careful of his language from this standpoint of theological progress. He must not transmit words and phrases, or their equivalent, however much such transmission would free him from intellectual effort, if thereby he runs the risk of confusing the minds of the coming generations.

The missionary must approach his constituency intelligently. He must not underrate the task before him. He is not merely dealing with a sinful man; he is dealing with an ignorant man, or with a prejudiced man, or with a bigoted man, or a fanatical man; or he may be dealing with a man of great and profound intellect; and he must take these men seriously, he must acquaint himself with their religious creeds, and patiently and steadfastly must he strive to put himself into their minds and learn their logic.

If he feels the need of all available wisdom in order to understand the Eastern mind, he must try to realize that his own mentality is often just as perplexing to the Oriental.

If Jesus had been born in Labrador, it is as inconceivable that He would have conveyed his message in the language He used in Palestine as that He would have clothed his body in the garments of that land. Parables, similes, and formulas would all have been changed—the permanent abiding element would have been his message about God as Father, man as brother, self as child of God, all linked together in the kind of love with which He loved the world.

Had Paul been born a Confucianist instead of a Jew, or a Buddhist or a Brahman, and had still yielded his allegiance to Jesus in those far-off lands, epistles might still have been written by him, but in how surprisingly changed a form the everlasting gospel which he preached would have been presented! What strange omissions of arguments which we have been led to think of as indispensable, or as all but indispensable! What strange additions in historical allusions! What a new world of illustration and simile and metaphor!

The Master has given the only standard by which to measure all vocabularies, all phraseologies, indeed, all beliefs—*his own included:* "The words that I speak unto you, they are spirit and they are life!" Only thus measured are they binding upon us.

VIII

As he has found that the Message of Christ carries within itself its own proof of authenticity, so the modern missionary finds in the message itself his own sufficient credentials; Christ's Message is Christ's commission. The Message creates the Messenger. By its very terms it belongs to the whole world, and the man who has received it at all must in common honesty receive it as a message to be transmitted to the last man in the world. He too is "a debtor to the whole world." He too is in the grip of an Apostolic Succession! From him, too, escapes the cry, "Woe is unto me if I preach not the Gospel!"

Geographical boundaries do not count either this way or that: the missionary spirit is the decisive thing. The decisive thing: for he has had a vision which gloriously haunts him: the vision of a man made in the image of God and rising into his great inheritance from the kraals of Africa or from the huts of the Fiji Islanders. He has seen a Christian home displacing in a few short years a household of warring elements. He has faith in a coming state permeated with the purpose to make justice and righteousness and service its dominant insignia; he has beheld the City of God descending from the Heavens upon the Earth. And so he goes forth, not because he believes that the operation of God's merciful and saving grace is confined to the span of a man's earthly existence. But loving pity for the sufferings of his brother men; anxiety for those who have lost their way in the mazes of ignorance and error; solicitude for those who are enmeshed in sin and guilt; a chivalrous compulsion to share with all mankind a spiritual dynamic which belongs to all mankind—these are the motives that compel him to carry the comforting, enlightening, merciful, life-giving Message of Christ to all the world.

His task is not an easy one. He must realize that his message will have no meaning unless he himself is the product of the message, representing and living the life which he asserts is the true life. Never were Emerson's words more true than of the missionary: "What you are speaks so loud I cannot hear what you say." And here is found the reason why, nineteen hundred years after its proclamation, hundreds of millions of people do not yet know that God is their Father, that man is their brother. The reason, I say, is that our own lives have not kept up with our own words. "Speak *things,*" cried Emerson, "or hold your tongue."

So far as they will permit him, the missionary works in cooperation with all men of missionary spirit—living and letting live, respecting where he cannot share their religious and theological beliefs. He is often misunderstood by friend and by foe. The globe-trotter thinks him a fool; the zealot a weakling; the fanatic a traitor. But he is not thereby deterred from his work. He thinks indeed that he may learn much that is useful from each one of them.

Realizing that the result of his work must be in its very nature destructive of much that is venerable, he seeks to be as constructive as possible. He is hopeful. For, though he may see few results of his labor, he believes "that God cannot use a discouraged man," and "that things are never settled until they are settled right." If at times he is appalled when some dreadful and unspeakable perversion of human nature suddenly confronts him, he is, on the other hand, surprised and comforted at the discovery of how fair a thing this same human nature may become.

IX

How does the modern missionary measure his success? Certainly not by ecclesiastical statistics: he believes profoundly that "the Kingdom of God cometh not with observation." How then is progress estimated? Much as their work is measured by serious men at home.

Take the work of this American College at Beirut, as one example among many. The briefest sojourn on its lovely campus, among its two dozen noble buildings, with its superb views, eastward and northward, of opalescent Lebanon, and westward of the great blue sea; with a visit to its museums, its laboratories, its observatory, its library, its athletic fields, its hospitals, its Students' Building; interviews with its ninety teachers; contact with its thousand students of many races (Syrian, Turk, Tartar, Persian, Indian, Egyptian), and of many religions (Moslem, Druze, Jewish,

Bahai, and all the Christian sects), as they study, as they play, as they worship—a visit, I say, of this kind establishes the irrefutable conviction that here has been created a "psychological climate" from whose influence no student can escape. He is not, indeed, always aware of the changes in himself. With perfect sincerity he would probably deny that he is being affected so powerfully by his environment. The fruitage of this seed may not come till long after he has left the College campus. But a change is being wrought, and he is daily learning, not merely, not chiefly, from his books, lessons in fairness, in honesty, in purity, in respect for labor and learning and culture, in reverence, in modesty, in courage, in self-control, in regard for women, in the many forces which make for civilization. And wherever this man goes, he makes it easier to foster education, to overturn tyranny, to soften fanaticism, to promote freedom in state and church. The story of Bulgaria and Turkey and China and Japan and India amply attests this.

Few are the students from among the thousands who have studied at the Beirut College during the past fifty years who have not received a distinguishing stamp upon their lives which makes them to a greater or lesser degree marked men. And it was really this mark that Djemal Pasha was anxious to trace to its origin when he sent Jamil Bey to visit the American College at Beirut. It was because of this stamp upon our men that this same Turkish official declared that he considered the College as one of his "most precious instruments" in carrying out his plans for the educational development of Syria. And it was this mark upon the College as an institution—the habit of straightness, frankness and good will—that kept the College open during the difficult years of the war. And all this our missionary believes is very worth while.

But he is seeking something more definite than these more or less unconscious influences, valuable as they are. For among those thousand students—all worth educating—he has his eye upon a smaller group; the eager, earnest, future leaders of the Near East. These he is training to become teachers, doctors, merchants, pharmacists, dentists, engineers, nurses: men and women who are responding more consciously and more readily than their companions to the "psychological climate" of the College, and at the same time are being disciplined in a definite way to become centres of light and leading all over that region. Their professional standing will make it certain that many a "cup of cold water" will be proffered by them to a thirsty world. And it is these graduates—there have been twenty-eight hundred of them—whose services are in such demand. It is of these that Lord Cromer and Lord Kitchener and Sir Eldon Gorst and Sir Reginald Wingate and Field-Marshal Lord Allenby have spoken in such warm and generous praise for their splendid work in Egypt and the Soudan. It is for such men that Prince Feisal, son of the King of the Hedjaz, has recently made a personal demand; men of integrity, of trained skill, of the spirit of "the helping hand."

For all this our missionary is profoundly grateful. He thanks God and takes courage. But his chief hope is concerned with a still smaller group, whose size is unknown to him, but for whose enlargement he daily strives and daily prays—the company of those who have made a decision, intelligent, deliberate, whole-hearted, a decision to live their lives as sons of the Great Father in the spirit of Jesus Christ. "Conversion," "regeneration," "surrender," "consecration" were the old words, and they were, and they are, good words. But the *thing* back of them is better than the words and than the particular way in which this thing is brought about: the dedication of body, mind and soul to the Will of God as interpreted by Jesus Christ. For when a man so commits himself, with or without a resulting change in his ecclesiastical affiliation, the missionary is assured that a force has been started which will work miracles in that man's world—his world of personal, domestic, community, political relationships. This is leaven hid in three measures of meal: the whole will be leavened. This is the "cup of cold water" *at the well itself*. This is the religion at its source: human thirst quenched at the exhaustless Fountain of God.

X

Has the Modern Missionary any contribution to make to the church at home? He surely ought to have, with the advantage in perspective which his foreign residence gives him; with his daily opportunity of estimating the real strength of Christianity as compared with other religions; with his first-hand realization of the spiritual needs of other peoples; with a knowledge of the impression—so often painfully unfavorable—that nations, Christian in name, have made upon nations outside of Christendom.

He would, of course, reiterate the familiar protest, and cry out against the shameful waste of men, energy, time, and money involved in the hectic strife of sectarian rivalry at home. He would still more strongly deprecate the loss of good temper and of fairness, the jealousy, the meanness of spirit, and the narrowness of opinion involved in such conflicts.

He would bid the Church cease this ignoble strife, not by disregarding differences of conviction in matters of theological belief or ecclesiastical procedure, but by subordinating them to a more spacious, to a simpler conception of Christianity, as a world-religion. Deep, broad, strong, the foundations must be laid, for a *world* must stand upon them!

He would urge the Church to remember that "Christianity is nothing unless it is universal," and therefore he would plead with her to set forth the essential things in her faith in terms that all races, all temperaments, all mentalities can apprehend—reserving local terms for non-essentials. He would charge her to be bolder in making a direct appeal to man's spiritual nature; to have greater faith in truth, in reality; to be assured that a response will be forthcoming when the challenge is the outcome of the personal experience of the advocate. He would bid her rehabilitate in the vocabulary of religion the noble words *reason, rational, free-thinking, natural.*

Living among peoples where the blighting effect of dead formulas is so shockingly and almost incredibly manifest, he would warn his fellow Christians at home against the danger of repeating creeds which have ceased to mean for them the things that they meant for their framers, nay, have ceased in some of their articles, to have any real meaning at all. The supposed gain in the direction of the preservation of "continuity with the past," of "catholicity" (both admirable things), is offset in his opinion by the loss of frankness, of the sense of reality, and even of plain common honesty.

Finally he would beg the Church to send to the foreign field only men of intellectual, social, and apostolic power: godly men, world-men, modern men, resourceful men, moulders of civilization, who can get abreast of the width of the opportunity in these coming days of reconstruction in the world—men worthy of the weighty and glorious responsibility lying before them.

Of course, when all is said, the modern missionary is, in many things fundamental, not modern at all. He has not surpassed—in many cases he may not have reached—the zeal, the wisdom, the passion, the fearlessness of his predecessors. He has not overtaken St. Paul on Mars Hill and his Master is always far in the lead with his method, "inwardness"; with his secret, "self-renouncement"; with his atmosphere, "sweet reasonableness"—to use Matthew Arnold's inimitable characterization. But he follows after "without haste and without rest." He is sure of his message; he is sure of ultimate success,—

> *. . . gazing beyond all perishable fears*
> *To some diviner goal*
> *Beyond the waste of years.*

PART III

The Administration of Bayard Dodge

1922-

XII. INTERIM

I. FINANCIAL CRISIS

THE SENSE OF TERRIFIC URGENCY which had driven Howard Bliss beyond his strength was in no wise unjustified, for conditions in the College were really serious. Although it was announced in November 1919 that more than $100,000 had already been pledged to cover the indebtedness, it was only too soon apparent that the deficit was increasing instead of shrinking. Circumstances were such that this was unavoidable.

In the first place it was absolutely necessary to increase the field budget. For the past six years American faculty salaries had been on a basis which scaled down from a maximum of $2,000 annually for married full-professors who had served more than fifteen years. Lower academic ranks were paid proportionately less. Non-Anglo-Saxon full-professors, if married, could attain to an annual salary of $1,250 after a service of thirty years! To be sure, there were small allowances made for bringing up children. Nevertheless, with the immense rise in the cost of living, these salaries were plainly inadequate, even when paid in gold. A blanket rise in salaries had to be effected at once.

With the return of the enrollment to normal a considerable number of new teachers was essential. There had been no replacement of short-term men, or of permanent men either for that matter, throughout the war period. Thirty-four short-term American instructors were required to be sent out during the two years 1919 and 1920. Replacements for Dr. Moore, Professor Joy and Professor Reed, who had resigned in 1918, were needed on the permanent faculty. The death on February 27, 1922 of Professor Harris Graham left a void in the medical faculty which was like a mortal wound. The engagement of several new permanent men of lower rank was also a necessity. All of them had to be paid. Some provision was required for assisting all faculty members in the matter of housing, for rents in Beirut had soared to impossible heights.

Coincident with the rise in field expense came a drop in endowment income. Whereas in 1918 the endowment fund had produced a return of over $60,000, three years later the return was only $34,000. The actual net result was that by July 1, 1920, the American University of Beirut had an accumulated deficit of $510,258, much more than double the amount of the indebtedness at the close of the war. There could be no question but that an emergency of the first magnitude existed.

Under the careful administration of Professor Edward F. Nickoley, acting-president after Dr. Bliss' death, expenditures on the field were kept as low as possible under the circumstances. At the same time, Mr. Staub pressed vigorously the joint financial campaign. A memorial fund of $400,000 in honor of Howard Bliss was sought in 1920-22. Thanks to a conditional grant from the Commonwealth Fund of $37,500 which was matched by a contribution of $25,000 from Cleveland H. Dodge and one of $12,500 from Arthur Curtiss James, the College budget for the year 1921-22 was balanced, but the result of a general appeal was disappointing. Only some $5,283 was received from new contributors. It was apparent that more strenuous efforts were required in order to bring to the American public a proper appreciation of the situation in the Near East.

Accordingly it was decided early in 1922 to raise an emergency fund of $1,100,000, half to go to the American University of Beirut and one-quarter each to Robert College and the Constantinople Woman's College, which then entered into association with the other two institutions. The Laura Spelman Rockefeller Memorial appropriated one-third of the total on April 24, conditional upon the completion of the fund by July 1. The time limit was later extended to July 15, when the amount raised in cash and pledges was $1,100,511.05. It is hardly necessary to say that in the three months of the campaign a very intensive effort had been made through the joint office with the whole-hearted cooperation of the various trustees and powerful friends of the colleges like former Ambassador Henry Morgenthau and the Bulgarian Minister, Dr. Stepan Panaretoff.

The half-million dollars assigned to the American University as a result of this effort was sufficient to pay off all indebtedness, including restoration of endowment funds used for emergency expenditures. It likewise assured the balancing of the budget until the end of the year 1923-24. This was a marvellous recovery but it made no provision for future expansion. The University was actually as well off as it was before the war, but just as at that period there was a great deal of room for essential development.

2. REORGANIZATION

In spite of the hampering financial situation it must not be assumed that conditions in Beirut remained static. As has been indicated, there were large replacements in the Staff at the beginning of the years 1919-21. Even before that, aid had been brought to the college faculty by the transfer in 1919 of Professor Brown to the professorship of Astronomy and the observatory directorship in place of Professor Joy, and by the appointment to the professorship of Physics of Arthur A. Bacon, formerly of Hobart College. The medical school faculty was strengthened by the permanent appointment of Dr. William T. Van Dyck to the professorship of Comparative Anatomy. Dr. Van Dyck shortly transferred to the chair of Zoology but continued to have charge of courses in Physiology and Hygiene. He "retired" in 1922, but as professor-emeritus continued for several years to give regular lectures in Zoology. He played a valuable and stimulating rôle in the college community almost until the day of his death in 1939 at the age of eighty-two.

In the fall of 1919 Dr. William Douglas Cruikshank of the University of Toronto was appointed as Lecturer in the medical department and became associate professor of Pathology in 1922. Five years later he became professor of Surgery and occupied that chair with great distinction until 1938. Dr. Harry G. Thomas was appointed as adjunct professor in the medical school to occupy the Allenby Chair, established in 1920 by an unknown English donor.[1] Dr. Arthur E. Hurt at the same time became associate professor of Dental Anatomy and Histology and Operative Technique.

[1] Unfortunately the necessary funds were forthcoming for one year only, and the Allenby Chair had to be given up.

Among the numerous appointees of 1919 and 1920 were three who became members of the permanent faculty. These were Laurens H. Seelye of Amherst, William A. West of Princeton and Rudolph J. Pauly of Whitman. Seelye was made professor of Philosophy and Psychology in 1922, later becoming also director of West Hall. After his return to America in 1935, he became president of St. Lawrence University. West, the son of Professor Robert H. West, taught Mechanical Drawing and Mathematics for two years, and then, after two years of graduate work in America, returned as adjunct professor of Chemistry. Pauly was for three years instructor in Chemistry and returned in 1927 as adjunct professor of Pharmaceutical Chemistry. Both West and Pauly are still serving on the faculty.

Two former staffites who had returned to Beirut after an absence for study were raised to faculty rank when Harold W. Close was appointed professor of Inorganic Chemistry, and Byron P. Smith was taken from the associate principalship of the preparatory department and made professor of English. At the same time Dr. Habib Rihan, a graduate of the Syrian Protestant College in 1908 who had completed a dental course at Harvard in 1915, was appointed Lecturer in Prosthetic Dentistry and Orthodontia. He was made associate professor in 1922. In 1920 Dr. Philip K. Hitti, formerly instructor in History after his graduation in 1908, returned from America where for five years he had been teaching at Columbia University. He was appointed professor of Oriental History. Professor Hitti, who is now the distinguished professor of Semitic Literature at Princeton University, is one of the outstanding alumni of Beirut who have made a distinct contribution to world culture.

A number of the Syrian staff were raised to permanent rank and several of them have since become heads of departments. Among these were Said Himadeh, '14, now professor of Applied Economics; Anis Khuri al-Makdisi, '06, now Margaret Weyerhauser Jewett Professor of Arabic; and Asad Rustum, '16, now professor of History. Several of the Syrian medical staff were also given permanent status on the medical faculty and have served their alma mater and humanity with distinction.

The building up of an adequate faculty was accompanied by a revision upward of the salary scale and, in view of the change to university status, a reorganization of faculty rankings to eliminate confusion and inequality between American and non-American teachers. Five classes of teachers were provided: Instructors, on definite term appointment, ordinarily for three years; Lecturers, either definite or indefinite term, as occasion warranted; adjunct professors, indefinite appointment; Associate professors, indefinite appointment; and Professors, indefinite appointment. The phrase "indefinite appointment" meant "without definite term of contract." No appointments were to be considered permanent, but men on indefinite appointment would retain their positions indefinitely unless given a year's notice of termination by the proper authorities. It was fully understood that retention of position depended upon continued efficiency.

It was distinctly stated in the Trustees Minutes for June 29, 1920, that "hereafter no distinction shall be made between Anglo-Saxon and non-Anglo-Saxon teachers and administrators in regard to ranks or categories of promotion, but all, having once been given an indefinite appointment, shall be expected to pass through all subsequent categories in normal course of advancement, with a longer or shorter occupancy of each grade as qualifications and preparation may indicate." The day of the non-voting professor was at an end. Thereafter non-Anglo-Saxon and American had an equal voice in the conduct of faculty affairs. Five formerly non-voting professors immediately took their seats in the General Faculty and these five, Dumit, Khauli, Ladakis, Jurdak and Tabit, were shortly followed by others. Acting-president Nickoley reported that "the General Faculty is not only numerically strengthened but its efficiency is materially increased by permitting the non-Anglo-Saxon professors and associate professors to share in the responsibility resting upon that body."[2]

The reorganization likewise provided that the General Faculty should be divided into departmental faculties under their respective deans. (Professor Hall was head of the Preparatory, Professor Day, Dean of the College, Professor Nickoley was principal of the School

[2] Annual Report (1920-21), pp. 9-10.

of Commerce and Dr. Dorman was then acting-dean of the medical department.) These men, together with the Secretary of the Faculty (Professor Nelson), the President and the Treasurer (George B. Stewart) were to compose an administrative council which would serve as an executive committee of the General Faculty. The relations between the various parts of the organization are shown on the attached chart.

3. SELECTION OF A PRESIDENT

Among the pressing problems which faced the Trustees, not the least was the finding of a successor for President Bliss. This was officially undertaken at the annual meeting following the death of Dr. Bliss, when a committee of trustees was appointed for the purpose. From that January 1921 until August 1922 various candidates were suggested by the faculty and friends of the College and their merits were carefully investigated. Finally a decision was reached, and on August 22, 1922, Mr. Bayard Dodge was unanimously elected first President of the American University of Beirut.

Mr. Dodge was magnificently equipped for the presidency both by nature and experience. Son of Cleveland H. Dodge and great-nephew of D. Stuart Dodge, he carried on the family tradition of service to the Near East. After graduating from Princeton in 1909 he had planned to enter the ministry, and took his divinity work at Union Theological Seminary. He first became engaged in work at Beirut in 1913 when he was appointed Director of West Hall and executive secretary of the College Y.M.C.A. All during the war he gave splendid service to the College community and assisted materially in the relief of the starving inhabitants of the Lebanon. On furlough in America in 1918-19 he had helped to establish the joint office and conduct the financial campaign begun in those years. He returned to Syria in 1920 and gave his services as Director of the Near East Relief for Syria and Palestine, winning the love and gratitude of Arabs, Jews, Armenians and many other national and religious groups. He learned to know the country, the people, and all phases of the College administration far better than men lacking his experience could possibly have done.

The attitude of the faculty toward the new appointment was expressed in the last annual report of Mr. Nickoley, in which he spoke of Mr. Dodge in the following terms: "He is optimistic and buoyant with hope for the future, he is endowed with an unusual capacity for continuous application and arduous labor, and, best of all, he has the good-will and the confidence of the entire University community in Beirut, as well as of all the friends of the University throughout the Levant. With the newly inaugurated President thus equipped, it is more than a mere formality or the expression of a pious hope to prophesy an era of success and prosperity for the University during the years to come."[3]

Mr. Dodge was married to the eldest daughter of Howard Bliss in 1914, thus uniting the two families most closely associated with the College from its foundation. Mrs. Dodge, with her gracious and sympathetic spirit, has been a wonderful asset in her husband's great effort to advance the cause of Christian education in the Near East.

Mr. Dodge was in Syria when his election was announced. He at once set about a study of the most important needs of the University in consultation with the faculty. He was then able to return to America and present specific recommendations to the Board of Trustees at its annual meeting in January 1923. After a period of intensive work in Paris, preparing himself in fluent use of the French language, President Dodge returned to Beirut for his formal inauguration, which took place at Commencement on June 28. The third administration of the institution was officially launched, three years after the death of President Bliss.

Great credit is due to the exceedingly capable acting-president, Edward F. Nickoley, for the preservation of high quality in the educational work during the three year intermission. It was a period of financial stress, of diminished capacity for the most efficient operation, when readjustments of all kinds were required from students and faculty alike. The assumption of control over the country by the French brought numerous problems in its train as well as the possibility of jealousy, friction and active antagonism to an American institution. New requirements such as French in-

[3] Annual Report (1922-23), pp. 3-4.

struction for all students living in the proposed mandate, and a new fifth year in the medical school for all who wished to qualify for the government examination, worked considerable hardship on the University in view of its very straitened circumstances. But it pulled through the crisis with no loss of prestige and with uniformly improved relations with the French authorities. The quiet, careful, firm control of Professor Nickoley was to no small extent responsible for the basic soundness of the institution which the new president found ready for his further guidance.

4. TRUSTEE CHANGES

The period of reorganization immediately following the war extended to the Board of Trustees, though in its case the reorganizing factor was Time itself. During 1918 death carried off Dr. Edwin Bradford Cragin, who had been a distinguished member of the Board since 1913. His experienced guidance had been of very great value, particularly in the administration of the medical school and hospitals. Early in 1919 Samuel S. Dennis, secretary of the Board, was forced by ill health to resign from that post and in May he found it necessary to retire entirely from the Board, having devoted a trusteeship of twenty seven years to the service of the Syrian Protestant College. Albert W. Staub, Executive Secretary of the joint office, became the permanent secretary of the Board, succeeding Mr. Dennis.

The retirement of Mr. Dennis reduced the membership of the Board to eight, for Dr. Francis Brown had died in 1916 and his place had not been filled. In May 1919, therefore, the Board elected three new members with a fourth in prospect. The three were the Rev. Dr. William Adams Brown, Franklin A. Dorman, M.D., and Mr. James H. Post. Mr. Clarence Phelps Dodge was elected a trustee in 1921, thus completing the roster of twelve members.

The president of the Board, D. Stuart Dodge, was not at all well following the last years of the war, and to provide him some relief from responsibility, the office of vice-president was created in January 1918. This position was filled by the election of Arthur Curtiss James. But Dr. Dodge's health did not improve, and early in 1922 he died. His place as president of the Board was taken by

BAYARD DODGE
President (1922-)

ALLEGHENY COLLEGE LIBRARY

DAVID STUART DODGE
President, Board of Trustees, 1908-1922

ALLEGHENY COLLEGE LIBRARY

William M. Kingsley who also retained his former position as treasurer.

The loss of Dr. Dodge was keenly felt, for he truly represented in his person the entire history of the institution. He had been present at the counsels which led to its establishment. He had been its first professor and had spent several years on the campus. He had an intimate knowledge of the political, social and religious conditions in the Near East, refreshed by constant study, unflagging interest and repeated visits.

Long before he became a trustee, D. Stuart Dodge acted as secretary of the Board on behalf of his father, William E. Dodge. Until he succeeded Morris Jesup as president of the Board he kept the minutes in his own handwriting. From 1870 to 1908 not more than four meetings were recorded in any other script, and the minute books were carefully annotated by him in red ink for ready reference. No man could have had a more profound knowledge or more sympathetic understanding of the problems which had faced the College throughout its existence. Since 1882, when he was elected to the Board of Trustees, he had been successively secretary, treasurer and president, holding the former office for twenty-five years, the latter for fourteen.

Dr. Dodge had personally been responsible for the hiring of almost the entire American teaching force at Beirut from the earliest years. Until he was handicapped by painful physical disability, "he was entrusted," said the memorial minute drawn up by the Board of Trustees, "with the whole burden of the practical execution of the purposes of the Board. Notwithstanding the limitations imposed on him by his ailment, his usefulness to the College was not seriously affected."[4] Mr. Staub considered it one of his pleasant duties to report to Mr. Dodge in his hotel sick room at least every two weeks, and he invariably found his interest keen, his comprehension penetrating. He was so highly respected by his fellow trustees that they would rarely, if ever, consider acting in opposition to his judgment.

Some indication has been given in these pages of the really great financial contribution which D. Stuart Dodge made to the Syrian

[4] Trustees Minutes, May 12, 1922.

Protestant College. No one will ever know its full amount. But far more important than his material aid was the idealism, the enthusiasm, the faith with which he inspired his colleagues at home and in Beirut. "To him," wrote the Trustees at his death, "the American University of Beirut was more than a conglomerate of buildings in a far-off land. It was a human enterprise, a body of men and women, most of whom he knew by name, and of students whom, without seeing, he yet loved.

"He wished the College to respect every man's faith and personal beliefs, and thus to promote the principle of loyalty to each individual conscience. In full consistency with this attitude, it was also the heartfelt desire of Dr. Dodge that every student should carry to his people the message of Christ's power to transform the character of individuals and of nations.

"During the long critical period of the war, when little was heard about the College, his faith in its destiny sustained him. His sane optimism was cheering and refreshing to all those who were solicitous about the outcome of events. Nor did the financial difficulties in which the University became involved as a result of the war, weaken his belief in its future career.

"During his long service to the College, Dr. Dodge transmuted faith pure and profound into activities beneficent and far-reaching. For many years to come, the influence of his life in the Near East will be an abiding and vital force in the reconstruction of its lands and the regeneration of its peoples. Our tribute to his memory is that of warm affection and reverential regard. He will be missed, but his leadership was such as to inspire all who continue the work he loved."[5]

In one sense the death of D. Stuart Dodge imposed upon the Board of Trustees the necessity for a complete reorientation. Dr. Dodge had always been the point of contact between the Board and the faculty to such an extent that his fellow trustees had really lacked personal contacts of their own. At the time of his death, of all the active Trustees, only Mr. James had ever visited Beirut. None could say that they knew the various members of the faculty in any way approaching the intimacy of Dr. Dodge. But they all

[5] Trustees Minutes, May 12, 1922.

knew Bayard Dodge and were anxious to cooperate with him in reestablishing the close relations between faculty and Trustees which had been severed by the deaths of Dr. Bliss and Dr. Dodge. Several of them visited Beirut as soon as they possibly could. The new administration saw reestablished a liaison which had always been the true source of the institution's strength.

XIII. OPPORTUNITY

1. THE MACEDONIAN CALL

"THE YEAR 1923-24 marks a new chapter in the history of the American University of Beirut." Thus wrote President Dodge in his first annual report to the Trustees. Without any question the statement was true. Quite aside from the fact that a new president was in office and that the staggering load of debt was being lifted, the University faced such an opportunity for augmented service to its constituency as has rarely occurred in the annals of higher education. The Macedonian call was heard from no less than ten countries, created *de novo* since the war or wakened to new life by its jarring influence. "Send us men," they begged, "leaders to man our public offices, guide our development, educate us in a way of life that may make us strong. Send us men of vision, men we can trust, men with principles, men who know what is right with courage to do the right."

From Lebanon and Syria, Palestine and Transjordan, 'Iraq, Arabia, Bahrein and Kuwait, Persia, Ethiopia, Zanzibar and the Sudan came the call. It came to the American University of Beirut with special force because for fifty-eight years the College had been supplying just the kind of men who were needed. Too, no other institution was in a position to answer. The new Egyptian National University could serve Egypt, and the Université de St. Joseph in Beirut could help train Catholic groups in Lebanon and other sections under French control. Systems of education were in process of development elsewhere, but it would be years before they could turn out college graduates, to say nothing of trained teachers, doctors, pharmacists, dentists, engineers, economists, political scientists. In no other institution in the Near East was there a school of commerce like that at Beirut, training men for business life. Many Beirut graduates, like Sir Said Pasha Shoucair, '86, Director of Finance for the Sudan, were already in major positions of honor and trust. No wonder the call came urgently to the American University, "send us men."

It is still well-nigh impossible for Americans to realize the amazing situation which arose in the Near East following the war. The ratification of the Treaty of Lausanne in the summer of 1923 definitely established the mandates system which looked toward eventual autonomy of new nations formerly under Turkish control. Turkey herself by that treaty escaped from the domination of the western powers and set out on her meteoric career of progress under Kemal Atatürk. Lebanon and Syria, under French control, and Palestine, Transjordan and 'Iraq under the British, felt that they were headed for statehood as soon as they could show themselves capable of autonomy. That meant the setting up of a parliamentary form of government which could at length take over control from the mandatory power. That in turn required capable officials, few of whom had been developed under the Ottoman régime.

Before the war Arabia was divided among a number of tribal rulers, with Ottoman troops maintaining precarious control in the interior and British ships patrolling the coasts. One of the Arab rulers was a young giant by the name of 'Abd-al-'Aziz ibn Sa'ud, whose family home was at Riyad. He proved to be a most astonishing person. After the war, in which he had sided with the British, he came into conflict with Husain, Sharif of Mecca and King of the Hedjaz. Husain was defeated and exiled to Cyprus, while Ibn Sa'ud became King of Hedjaz as well as Sultan of Nejd. As absolute ruler of northern Arabia he set about modernizing the country—no small task considering its history and the roving nature of its scattered population. What higher education Arabia could use must very largely come from the American University of Beirut, the only center outside of Egypt where Arabic culture and the most modern education could both be found together.

Soon after the opening of the academic year 1923-24, the University was visited by the Shah of Persia, who was greatly impressed by the useful service which the institution might render to the young men of his country. At that time there were twenty-two Persian students enrolled. Not long after the Shah's visit he was overthrown by Riza Khan, who, at the close of the war, had been an officer in the Persian army. Riza Shah Pahlevi can fairly be compared with Atatürk and Ibn Sa'ud in his powerful effort to modernize his country, control banditry, develop communications and commerce, eradicate ignorance and superstition. He had a very long way to go but he has made remarkable progress. Relatively few Persian students could afford to make the five-day trip to Beirut and study there, but the government was willing to make the way easy for some by providing bursaries for them. Courses in the Persian language were instituted at the University and the attendance of Persians was encouraged. The possibilities of service to that vast country were almost endless.

One other great personality was intent on building up his country, and he too looked to the American University of Beirut for help. This was Ras Tafari of Ethiopia, who in 1930 became the Emperor Haile Selassie. Ethiopia had been admitted to the League of Nations in the fall of 1923 and under the guidance of Ras Tafari set out on a career of internal development. Even before the World War a number of Ethiopian students had come to Beirut, and on their return had greatly pleased His Majesty. When he set out to develop a secondary school system he sent seven students to Beirut to be trained as teachers for the government schools. The succession of these Ethiopian students was only broken by the Italian conquest of the country in 1934-36. It is to be hoped that it may now be resumed.

When Kitchener occupied the Sudan before the World War, he organized the government in the following manner: the important positions were given to Englishmen, and educated Arabs were appointed as assistants in all of the intermediate positions, with native Sudanese doing the unskilled work of the government. The British authorities were few in number compared to the Arabic speaking officials, many of whom were Egyptians or Syrians. The large majority of these trained Arab officials were graduates of the Syrian Protestant College. They occupied important posts in the Health Service, the Army, and almost every other department of government. Except for Syria, no other land had been so much influenced by the institution which was now the American University of Beirut. Even at the present day, when officials for the Sudan government are appointed from among the people of Lebanon, Palestine or Syria, the president of the University is usually asked to make the appointment. The University is also asked to give medical examinations to such officials as are appointed.

Following the war, enviable progress was made in the Sudan, not only from the standpoint of commercial development but from that of cultural advancement as well. Gordon College at Khartoum was enlarged to train more and more of the native Sudanese. A medical research laboratory was set up in Khartoum and a model Department of Health was organized. In all of these movements graduates of the American University of Beirut had an important part. Medical graduates from Beirut were largely responsible for keeping sleeping sickness from crossing the border from French Sudan. Said Shoucair was made a pasha and was knighted for his services in controlling the sugar traffic so as to maintain price stability and at the same time pay off a heavy government debt. He later became financial advisor to the government. In 1928 fourteen Beirut alumni were teaching at Gordon College, and in that year six black Sudanese from Gordon were finishing work at Beirut, preparatory to teaching in Khartoum. Since then more of these fine natives have sought a higher education at Beirut, and the Sudan continues to maintain its close contact with the University.

In 1934 the Director of Education of the Sudan wrote to President Dodge of the government attitude toward the University. "The Sudan," he said, "is developing rapidly, but the native students who are able to benefit from a University education are too few to justify the expenditure which a University must entail if it is properly staffed and properly equipped; for many years to come it would be unjustifiable to divert to the education of a few, sums of money which are so badly needed for the economic and educational development of the many.

"In this respect, I think our situation is not unlike that of some other countries in the Near East, and to all such countries a residential institution like the American University of Beirut offers the best solution to a difficult problem."[1]

[1] "American University of Beirut—Description of Its Organization and Work," 1934, p. 43.

Similar sentiments have been expressed from time to time by the Director of Education in Palestine and officials in 'Iraq and Transjordan. The first said in part:

"The American University of Beirut holds a position which is unique in the Near East. No other institution in this part of the world offers the same opportunities of higher education, and the students include, in addition to Greeks, Armenians and Persians, natives of Syria, 'Iraq, Palestine, Arabia, Egypt and the Sudan, among whom Arabic is the common language. The fact that English is the medium of instruction, while great attention is paid to the study of Arabic, the native tongue of the majority of students, and that courses of study are offered in various higher branches of learning, renders the University peculiarly adaptable to the needs of those countries of the Near East under British influence, and to none more than Palestine."[2]

Of the relation of the University to the youth of 'Iraq, a former member of the Department of Education there wrote as follows:

"There is as yet no 'Iraq University, and for some years to come, there cannot be any college of high standing. In the interval, Beirut acts as a magnet, attracting students from all over 'Iraq. The young 'Iraqi sees there a center of learning which invites him to be discontented with a secondary education and to go on and prepare for a professional career. Beirut sets up a standard of scholarship, which is independent of any political influences and the present high standing of a few former medical graduates in their local communities is sure evidence of the real worth of the College training."[3]

There was no limit to the new horizon of opportunity which spread before the American University. To the task of surveying it and supplying the needs of an awakening world, the new administration was to dedicate its efforts.

2. THE ANSWER

No man was more ideally fitted than President Dodge, both by nature and experience, to realize in full and to make the most of

[2] Quoted in "American University of Beirut—Description of Its Organization and Work," 1934, p. 45.

[3] Ibid., p. 46.

the new opportunities which faced the University. A natural diplomat, he at once set about establishing friendly relations with the authorities in countries which the University was qualified to serve. At the same time he directed the development of curriculum which should best fit the needs of those countries. It had never been the policy of the College to demand that students fit themselves to a program adapted chiefly to American life. In the administration of President Dodge, apparently radical steps were sometimes taken to make the program fit the needs of the students. The development of a French school within the institution, the division of courses at the end of sophomore year, with qualified men going on for three years more to attain the M.A. degree, the removal of emphasis from the B.A. degree, the establishment of an agricultural course for land-owners' sons—these and many other innovations were put into effect over an extended period of time. The story of the latest administration has been one of constant expansion of the great influence which the University already possessed. The expansion was geographical as well as ideal.

The distances from which students sometimes had to come to reach Beirut were so great that occasionally parents asked the University to become a foster parent of their children for the period of their education. Principal Hall of the Preparatory department reported on some of these cases in 1924. They are striking evidence of the widespread confidence which was placed in the American University.

"A boy of twelve years from the Sudan was sent here in the fall of 1922. His father is a Moslem merchant in Port Sudan. The boy spends his summers in the Summer School where the students have lessons in the forenoons and recreation in the afternoons. Money is sent as we demand and we must look after his clothes, shoes, and spending money; care for him in illness, direct him in his lessons, and report regularly to his father. He is entrusted to us for all his training, mental, moral and spiritual. He is likely to remain for at least five or six years without even seeing his parents.

"Two Persian students, one from Teheran, the other from Hamadan, were sent here by their grandmothers, one of whom is a princess and the other a countess. They are large landowners. The boys are twelve and fourteen years of age. They arrived at the School a year ago, about one month before the close of the year. In those far-off countries not much account is paid to the times and seasons for the opening and closing of schools. The grandparents wish to have the boys trained. They have come to believe that this School is able to do that and to return their sons as grown men with a suitable education and with characters that can be relied upon.

"Another example is a group of three from the city of Aden, on the Arabian coast of the Red Sea. Their parents are prominent merchants in that city. These boys, like the three mentioned above, are Moslems. Their parents are earnest and devout but are confident that the School is going to respect their faith while at the same time it will build into their sons' lives those qualities that make for honest manhood. The fathers are apostles for the College, seeking to make it known along the coast of Arabia, wherever their business takes them.

"Still another case might be given of one who has now completed the Preparatory School, but who was the ward of the School for some four years. He was a Jew from Jaffa whose father was dead.

"The administrator of the estate placed him entirely under the care of the School for his period of education. The relations became so intimate that when, after two years of college work, he wished to go to America to complete his studies in engineering, the American Consulate required from the School certificates, not only as to education and character but also as to his financial ability to be supported while pursuing his studies.

"Other cases might be cited of boys from Busrah, from upper Egypt, from Baghdad and Mosul. But the above are sufficient to illustrate what is becoming a chief function and opportunity in the Preparatory School."[4]

These cases are quite different from that of the boy who was sent by his Bulgarian father to the University a very few years ago. As the father was apparently unable to provide the necessary fees he wrote to President Dodge as follows: "Honored Sir: In the name

[4] Annual Report (1923-24), pp. 10-12.

of the Lord Jesus Christ, I present my son Benjamin as a gift to your University." It was with some difficulty that the father was made to understand that the University could not accept such unbounded generosity.[5]

The stabilizing of the mandates system in 1923 permitted the development of permanent relations with the newly established governments, and exceedingly fine cooperation was achieved. General Weygand, then High Commissioner for France, was very friendly, and through his interest Dr. Dray was asked to assist in examining candidates for the dentist's license. Dr. Dorman and Dr. Cruikshank were asked by the Governor of Grand Liban (Lebanon) to aid in examining candidates for the Lebanon sanitary service.

Professor Khuri, head of the Department of Arabic, was sent on a visit to 'Iraq, where he was shown the greatest cordiality in centers like Baghdad, Kerbela and Mosul. An important 'Iraqi cabinet minister visited Beirut and urged the University to start a preparatory school in Baghdad and train men for all kinds of professional service in 'Iraq. The Ministry of Defense in 'Iraq asked that the University appoint a number of army doctors, and the Department of Education was provided with a group of teachers through the good offices of the University.

Four students were sent to Beirut by the government of Palestine to prepare for teaching in government schools. The Director of Education and his assistants visited the University several times during the year to consult on educational matters, and the British High Commissioner was very friendly and appreciative.

The Director of Education for the Sudan also visited Beirut and arranged to send men to the University for teacher training. The government of the Sudan asked Dr. Dodge to appoint a number of medical officers and dispensers for official service. The University was also asked to appoint boards to examine employees of the Sudan government who were taken ill while on vacation in Syria.

[5] The father lived at Monastir, which before the Balkan Wars was in Turkey and after the World War was in Jugoslavia. As the father was a Bulgarian, his son was liable for military service in the armies of Bulgaria, Turkey and Jugoslavia. Consequently he sent the boy to Beirut. He was kept in the University one year, worked in West Hall for two more, and then found a job with Socony-Vacuum in Sofia, Bulgaria.

This was only the beginning of diplomatic relations which expanded and grew firmer with the years, as more and more graduates proved their worth in the countries of their service. By 1928 the 'Iraq government had paid for forty-one students to be trained as teachers alone. Palestine had supported twelve, Transjordan five, the Sudan six and the Sheikh of Bahrein eight. This last ruler sent a fifteen-year-old member of his family, 'Abdallah ibn Ibrahim al-Khalifah, to study in the preparatory school. When Professor Tabit, then head of the preparatory, visited Bahrein in 1928, he was not only royally received by the Sheikh but was sent back to Beirut at the Sheikh's expense. His return was followed by a request for the University to send a graduate to be Supervisor of the Bahrein schools.

In Transjordan a number of graduates were taken into the school system which was developing. Another graduate was made head of the Transjordan Department of Health and he naturally drew liberally upon his fellow medical alumni for assistance.

The enumeration of such cases could be continued ad nauseam. It will suffice to show the 1928 figures of alumni in strictly *government* service in medicine, education, and civil service throughout the Near East.

	Medicine	*Education*	*Civil Service*
Egypt	27	—	15
Sudan	41	14	11
'Iraq	5	20	2
Palestine	31	15	21
Transjordan	5	3	—
Cyprus	1	—	1
Syria	10	1	6
	120	53	56

The number of alumni in *private* medical work at the same time was 635; the number in private education was 119; and the area served by them included Turkey, Persia and Ethiopia in addition to those countries listed above. Eighty-four of the medical alumni were scattered in Europe, the United States of America, England, Australia and South America.

In 1934 a rather detailed description of the organization and work of the University was prepared, which listed some of the important positions held by graduates and former students since the war. When to it are added some recent appointments, one has a list which is by no means exhaustive but which is significant of the influence which alumni of the University possess. It is a partial indication of the part which the University has played in the building up of thirteen nations.

Lebanon

Prime Minister
Minister of Public Works
Minister of Health
Minister of Agriculture
Members of Parliament (several)
Secretary, Department of Education
Vice-President Municipal Council, Beirut
State Director of Mines
Municipal Engineer, Beirut
Judge, Palace of Justice, Beirut

Syria

Minister of Justice and Education
Director of Agriculture, Jebel Druze
Cabinet Ministers (4)
Professor of Dentistry, Arab University, Damascus (2)
Professor of Law, Arab University Damascus
Government Translator, Aleppo

Transjordan

Director of Public Health
Director, Departments of Health (several)
Supervisor of Education
Customs Officer, Amman

Palestine

The Administrative Officer, Southern District
The Administrative Officer, Northern District (2)
The Administrative Officer, Haifa
The Public Prosecutor, Jerusalem
The Senior Magistrate, Haifa
Magistrate, Tel Aviv
Senior Assistant Treasurer
Inspector of Pharmacies, Jerusalem
Headquarters Inspector, Education Department (2)
District Inspector of Education (2)
Lecturers, Government Arab College (3)
Senior Horticultural Officer
Assistant Settlement Officer (3)
Land Officer
Assistant District Traffic Superintendent
Senior Inspector, Arab Schools
Director, Arab College (Normal School)
Manager, Jewish Labor Bureau, Haifa
Senior Bacteriologist, Jerusalem
Senior Probation Officer
Junior Assistant Treasurer
Auditor
Director, Government Laboratory, Jerusalem
Director, Arabic broadcasting
Head of Bahai Council (Shoghi Effendi)

'Iraq

Secretary to the King (several)
Advisor for Education
Director of Education
Director, Teacher's Training School
Professor Royal College of Medicine (2)
Officers, Department of Health (several)
Officers, Civil Service (several)
Director of Higher Education
Director, Engineering School
Director, Army Medical Service
Chargé d'Affaires, London
General Inspector of Education
Sheikh of Sheikhs, Shammar Bedouin

Arabia

Director, Department of State (Foreign Minister)

Yemen

Physician to Royal Family

Bahrein

Directors of Education (2)

Kuwait

The Crown Prince

Egypt

Associate Director, Government Publication
Director, Army Medical Corps

Sudan

Medical officers (several)
Military and Civil officials
Director of Finance
Head, Government Press

Ethiopia

Director, Government Hospital, Addis Ababa
Ethiopian Consul, Paris

Persia

Professor of Physics, National University, Teheran
Director Secondary School, Teheran
Director, Sabzevar Hospital

Such a list omits any reference at all to the much larger numbers of municipal officers, civil servants and teachers whose positions are not outstanding. It does not mention the entrepreneurs, business men, farmers, and professional men who have, in innumerable cases, contributed largely to the development of national life in their respective countries. The introduction in the Near East of fruit preserving, dairy enterprise, soda fountains, 5, 10 and 15c stores, talkies, as well as the development of orange growing, banana and vegetable plantations in Arab districts in Palestine, soap and oil industry, salt works, poultry raising and many other valuable interests have been due to graduates and former students of the American University. Many have been and are newspaper owners and correspondents, ministers, civil engineers, agents and employees of American and English business concerns, oil companies and the like. Fifteen medical graduates were employed by the 'Iraq Petroleum Company as medical staff for the construction of the great oil pipe-line, running across the desert from 'Iraq to Palestine, which was built in the early thirties. The list of interesting and valuable occupations is well-nigh endless.

The period of opportunity, however, is as extensive as the desire to meet it. In the Near East there is no such saturation of trained men as is to be found in the West. College graduates of quality are no drug on the market. The American University of Beirut, even with the facilities it now possesses, cannot begin to supply men for all the calls upon it that are made. It cannot expand materially, for it will not lower its standards. Its service to the Near East can be as great through acting as a measuring rod for the work of other institutions as by its direct contribution of high-minded, ambitious men. In both regards it still is faced with undiminished opportunity for meeting the needs of that vast area.

The Macedonian call still rings clear.

XIV. PROGRESS

I. FINANCIAL AID

THE EMERGENCY FUND campaign of the spring of 1922 had assured the balancing of the budget throughout the year 1923-24, but it was only too apparent that the relief afforded was temporary. The increase in operating costs was, on the other hand, permanent. Immediate measures were necessary if the recent financial gains were not to be dissipated.

In the winter of 1923 Mr. Staub again visited the Near East to make a careful survey of the situation in all the cooperating colleges. On his return, plans were developed for a Fund for Near East Colleges which should provide operating expenses for a period of five years, 1924-29. The new campaign, for $2,500,000, was set up to include the needs of the reorganized American College of Sofia and International College of Smyrna, which then joined the original triumvirate of participants in the joint operations.

The Fund for Near East Colleges, launched in the spring of 1925, was successfully completed on January 1, 1926. It provided approximately $950,000 for the American University of Beirut. But even before a start on this fund was made, plans were being laid for an immense endowment campaign which should obviate the need for periodic efforts to meet annual deficits. As early as January of 1924, Mr. Staub had outlined for the Beirut alumni a plan for doubling the present endowment of the institution, and he began at that time to revivify and reorganize the alumni association. A number of new branches of the association were organized at the time of Mr. Staub's visit. Under the leadership of Mr. Shehadeh A. Shehadeh, '92, newly elected executive secretary of the association, a campaign was begun to raise $150,000 among the alumni. The illustrious Sir Said Pasha Shoucair agreed to serve as General Treasurer for the alumni. The Cairo branch subscribed its quota of $10,000 at its initial meeting, and by 1929 the entire amount was successfully raised. The total, while small in proportion to some other contributions to the work of the University, represented

NEW MEDICAL SCIENCES BUILDING

THE OUTPATIENT CLINIC

ALLEGHENY COLLEGE LIBRARY

NURSING GRADUATES (Class of 1937) AND NURSING STAFF
(Miss Van Zandt fifth from right, seated)

STUDENT NURSES IN THE HOSPITAL GROUNDS

ALLEGHENY COLLEGE LIBRARY

nevertheless a very considerable sacrifice on the part of graduates and former students scattered all over the world. Many Syrians who had no direct connection with the University also gave liberally to the Alumni Fund.

The great Endowment Fund campaign got under way in the fall of 1926. Athens College in Greece, which had been organized the year before, joined the group of Near East colleges and brought to a total of six the institutions participating in the campaign. Following the death of Mr. Cleveland H. Dodge in June 1926, the joint office of the colleges had been incorporated as the Near East College Association, with Mr. Staub as Director. Under the new organization the attempt was made to bring the endowment of the American University of Beirut and Robert College to $4,500,000 each; that of the Woman's College to $2,500,000; that of International College to $1,000,000. It was also planned to provide $500,000 for endowment and $500,000 for buildings for both the American College of Sofia and Athens College. The total amount needed for the six colleges was $15,000,000, of which approximately three million represented the existing endowments. At the time, the endowment of the American University of Beirut was $1,226,347.

The story of the Endowment Fund Campaign should properly be told elsewhere. Here it need only be said that on January 1, 1930 the entire amount required had been raised, with all conditional gifts satisfied. Events in the early 1930's materially reduced the amount of the new endowment thus gained but they did not diminish the very real achievement of securing it. At the beginning of 1930 the financial stability of the University seemed assured.

2. THE MEDICAL SCHOOL

The establishment of French control over Syria after the war brought a new problem to the medical department which had had such a difficult experience in securing official Turkish recognition. The situation was not as difficult this time, but the determination of educational standards by the French Department of Public Instruction forced upon the school a revision of curriculum. The principal change was in a direction which had been adopted in principle and ratified by the Trustees before the war, namely, the establishment of a fifth year of medical work to provide clinical and practical hospital experience. The chief difficulty in the way was the inadequacy of the hospital plant, which, because of the severance from the Johanniter Hospital, was less satisfactory even than it had been in 1914.

Until the definite establishment of the mandate in the summer of 1923 the fifth year of study remained only a likely prospect, and graduates of the four year course were permitted to take the French government examinations for license on the understanding that they would complete another year of internship. After 1924, degrees were given only to those who had completed the full five years of medical work.

Lack of hospital facilities, up-to-date laboratory equipment and adequate staff were a terrible handicap to such a forced expansion but in the hour of greatest need substantial help came. The election to the Board of Trustees of Dr. William S. Ladd brought the number of medical men on the Board to two in 1923 and assisted greatly in concentrating the Board's attention on the improvement of the medical school. Through the assistance of General Weygand, the French Foreign Office approved the granting of permission for students of the University to spend their fifth year in France, and arrangements were made to admit fifth year students to the Universities of Montpellier and Lyons on certificate. The M.D. degree of the American University of Beirut was to be given on receipt of evidence that the year's work in France had been satisfactorily completed.

At the same time the Rockefeller Foundation began to take an active interest in the work at Beirut and promised its assistance. Dr. Victor Heiser of the Foundation visited the University first in the spring of 1921 and again in 1922, inspecting the medical school and making valuable suggestions. In 1923-24, Dr. George E. Vincent, then President of the Foundation, and Dr. Richard M. Pearce, director of the Foundation's department of medical education, both came to Beirut. As a result of their recommendations, the Rockefeller Foundation made a grant of $125,000 to be spread over the five years 1924-29. The money was to be used only for the development of new work in the medical school. The Foundation also provided scholarships whereby some of the younger members of the medical staff could go to America for postgraduate study.

The Rockefeller appropriation made possible a complete reorganization of the departments of study in the medical school and assisted in providing additional well-trained and competent instructors. Professor William M. Shanklin in Histology, Dr. Pierre Lépine of the Université de Lyons in Pathology, Dr. Stanley Harris in Internal Medicine, and Dr. Stanley L. Kerr in Biochemistry, came to Beirut in 1925. A year later, Dr. Bennett F. Avery in Anatomy and Dr. Telemachos Rossides in Pharmacology were engaged, and Dr. Raymond Goodale succeeded Dr. Lépine. These men, in addition to Drs. Leland W. Parr and Edward L. Turner who had joined the faculty in 1923, very greatly increased the efficiency of the medical school and relieved the fine but overworked triumvirate of Dorman, Ward, and Webster. Dr. Adams had unfortunately been incapacitated by a stroke in 1924 and until his death in 1928 was unable to carry on any regular work.

A start was also made in building up an adequate medical library, for which, in 1924-25 alone, an appropriation of $2,200 was made by the Foundation for books, journals and back files of periodicals. The following year the Foundation grant supplied a competent medical librarian in the person of Miss Ida Burtnett. Dr. Ladd, of the Board of Trustees, personally made very valuable contributions to the medical library over an extended period of years. The research facilities which the library provided were a very great asset to the medical school and have proved their value in the stimulation they have given to individual investigations by faculty, students and graduates.

The yearly appropriation from the Rockefeller Foundation was to be used for the development of new work and was not available for plant expansion, but it mightily stimulated the University's efforts in that direction. During the year 1924-25 a total of $68,350 was spent on new buildings and the remodelling of inadequate older structures. The chief new buildings included a kitchen-laundry, donated by Mr. and Mrs. Arthur Curtiss James; a laboratory building for pathology, bacteriology and parasitology; and a nurses' home, named the Mary Bliss Dale Home in honor of the beloved first superintendent of the hospital, who had turned over her work in 1922 to the wife of Dr. Graham. The money for this construction work was largely provided by special gifts, like that of Mr. and Mrs. James and was secured in addition to the Fund for Near East Colleges, then being raised.

The new construction helped materially in increasing the capacity as well as the efficiency of the hospital, for it relieved the crowding in buildings which could then be used for strictly medical purposes. By the end of 1926 the capacity of the University hospital was 200 beds in all categories. Though this was scarcely adequate for the demand, efficient operation secured the utmost use of all the facilities.

Dr. Ward succeeded Dr. Dorman as dean of the medical school in 1924 just as the five year course was being put into effect. Dr. Dorman had requested relief from administrative duties in order to give his full time to the department of Gynecology and Obstetrics. Dr. Ward thus had the satisfaction of seeing the University medical department develop into a Class A school under his administration, with full recognition as such being accorded by the Regents of the University of the State of New York, under whom the institution was chartered. The Regents' recognition meant that the work was accepted as meeting the academic requirements of New York State. The chief reason why the Beirut medical school is not now listed by the American Medical Association is that it was found to be impossible for the University to support the expense of bringing an inspection commission of the Association from the United States.

Another step toward the improvement of medical work was taken in 1926 when an international board was invited to examine students of the various medical classes. Since the termination of the visits from the Imperial Ottoman examining committee ten years before, examinations had been conducted by professors only. The new plan had the aim of making the examinations more impressive and more exhaustive, as well as more thoroughly satisfactory to the various government authorities.

The examining board for 1926 was composed of the Director of the French Military Hospital in Beirut and another French officer representing Syria; the Director of Health for Palestine and the Director of Hospitals of the Baghdad Lewa—both British; the Acting-director and another professor from the Kasr-el-Aini Medical School in Cairo, Egypt. It was an impressive group for second, fourth and fifth year students to face, but they had to do it and they have faced similar boards ever since. The effect upon the students was electric, for failures in that first year incited a marked increase in devotion to study.

Early in November of 1927 the Rockefeller Foundation, impressed with the value of the work which was being done at Beirut, voted to capitalize their appropriation which had been granted in 1924. The wording of the resolution was as follows:

"Resolved, that the Foundation hereby pledges itself to pay to the American University of Beirut a sum not to exceed one million dollars ($1,000,000) with the understanding that $250,000 of this amount shall be used for building and equipment of the medical school and may be appropriated by the Executive Committee at any time, and with the further understanding that $750,000 shall be used toward endowment of teaching in the medical sciences and shall not be available until after the expiration of the Foundation's present five year agreement with the University as of June 30, 1929."[1]

The $250,000 for buildings and equipment was made available at once and as soon as plans could be prepared, construction of three new units was begun. These consisted of a new chemistry building, a medical sciences building and an out-patient clinic. The first, completed in 1929-30, contained up-to-date laboratories for general, analytical, physical and industrial chemistry, as well as private laboratories for research and a large lecture room, reading room and class-rooms. The medical building housed the departments of anatomy, histology, biochemistry, pharmacology and physiology, providing large and well-ventilated laboratories, a large lecture room, and class-rooms, and an animal room on the top

[1] Trustees Minutes, January 26, 1928.

floor. The Out-patient Clinic building had, in addition to the clinic itself, space for the Public Health Center[2] and the medical library, as well as for a number of private offices. The attic story was used as a dormitory for fifty medical students.

It is interesting to note that the funds available for construction went approximately four times as far in Beirut as they would have done in America. The average cost per cubic foot of the three buildings was 13.7 cents, whereas in America equivalent structures at the time cost from 45 to 75 cents per cubic foot. Local materials and workmen were very largely employed and much of the woodwork and furniture was made on the campus. As a result, the University had three large, well-equipped buildings instead of the one which the same funds would have built in the United States.

Late in 1934 a further raising of the standards of the medical school was put into effect with the requirement of three years of collegiate training as a prerequisite for entrance into medical studies. This change was in accord with the long-cherished desires of the faculty, as well as with the policy of the New York Board of Regents and of the Lebanese Government. Since October 1935 students entering the medical school must have completed a minimum of three years of college work.

The improvement of the medical school, of which this change in entrance requirements is symptomatic, was made possible by a further grant from the Rockefeller Foundation which was made at the end of 1931. The new appropriation was originally a total of $450,000 to be spread over a period of seven years, on condition that by 1935 the University should have secured from other sources $350,000 to be used for construction of a hospital building. During the Depression this money could not be raised, but the Foundation gave $50,000 a year for the seven years, half the money going to the medical school proper and half to nursing and pre-medical sciences. In 1939 it agreed to capitalize the grant at $1,000,000 provided the University would raise $500,000, a part of which should be used for hospital construction. With $50,000 contributed from

[2] The Health Center was established in 1927 through an additional grant of $10,000 for two years from the Rockefeller Foundation. It was intended to conduct Public Health work in cooperation with the Clinic.

the Alumni Fund and $110,000 donated by Arthur Curtiss James, it was found possible to secure the entire amount required before the end of 1939. The faculty themselves gave over $1000 toward completion of the fund.

Plans for building the new hospital were drawn up and approved, but events in 1940 prevented the start of construction. The coming of war brought to a halt the intended development of the medical school's capacity for humanitarian service.

3. THE DENTAL SCHOOL

The improvement in the medical work which was made possible by the Rockefeller grants was paralleled by advances in the schools of dentistry, nursing and pharmacy. Dr. Arthur Dray, founder of the dental school, reorganized the work in 1925 to provide a much more comprehensive course than had previously been given. The dentistry building itself was remodelled to provide a lecture room and prosthetic laboratory in addition to work rooms on the ground floor. Upstairs, the public clinic was rearranged and equipped with twenty-eight modern chairs, which were in addition to the chairs in the examining and extracting rooms. Private clinics with laboratories attached, and a demonstration room for minor surgery were arranged, as well as satisfactory x-ray and sterilizing rooms. The crown and bridge laboratory was improved, and a good deal of new equipment was added. Another full-time professor in the person of Dr. Edward E. Fox, was added to the staff.

Entrance requirements were raised to include at least two years of college work as a prerequisite to the four-year dental course. The curriculum was revised to provide a greater amount of work in the medical sciences as well as a larger laboratory and clinical experience. The dental school was ready to receive the Regents' recognition which had already been accorded to the medical school.

Just at this point a terrible tragedy occurred. On March 4, 1926 Dr. Dray was shot and killed by a deranged servant, who thus savagely brought to an abrupt end the career of one of the great servants of the Near East and a benefactor of the College.

Dr. Dray was a remarkable man as well as a fine dentist. He was born in London in 1875 but his father, who was a dentist, early brought him to Beirut where he grew up. He studied at the Syrian Protestant College and then set out on what was to prove for him a long road toward becoming a dentist. After many unique experiences as a "practical" dentist in Palestine and Cilicia, he finally succeeded in getting to America. In due time he graduated from the dental and medical schools at the University of Pennsylvania, and before returning to Beirut to open the dental school he practiced for a number of years in Philadelphia.

Dr. Dray was without question the finest dentist in Syria and was much sought by Ottoman officials, who learned to respect and trust him. It was this fact which helped to gain him exemption from imprisonment during the war. It also enabled him in a singular way to be of the greatest service to the College. The story was told by President Dodge shortly after Dr. Dray's death:

"A very high German official was fired at by an assassin and his jaw was badly injured. Dr. Dray was summoned to Jerusalem so that he could perform the operation. He left Damascus in a private car. Dr. Dray performed a remarkable operation and saved the official's life. Jemal Pasha was so much pleased that he asked Dr. Dray what he wanted and gladly offered to make it possible for the University to continue its work.

"It was an evening early in October when Dr. Dray returned from this experience. He happened to come right back to a meeting of the faculty. The professors were wondering how they could open college that year, and had almost voted to postpone registration. New teachers from America were on a ship in the harbor and could not gain permission to land. Native teachers were wanted for military service. Students were also needed for the army, and supplies were hard to procure.

"Dr. Dray explained the favors that he had procured from the head of the army. The next day the American teachers landed, Syrian teachers were excused from army service, foodstuffs were provided to the University at military prices, and only certain categories of students were forced to go to war. From that time on Jemal Pasha kept the University going throughout the war."[3]

[3] Near East Colleges News Letter, Vol. VII, 2:7 (June 1926).

It seemed peculiarly tragic that Dr. Dray should be killed just as his dreams came true: when he had built up a dental department which was spoken of in America as having higher standards than any other dental school outside the United States. But Dr. Dray had built well and the work could now go on without him. He was succeeded by his former student, Dr. Habib Rihan, whose experience as an instructor at the Harvard Dental School and as an officer in the Dental Reserve Corps of the United States Army had helped to prepare him for his work at Beirut. Under his guidance the dental school was to continue to maintain its high standards until circumstances forced its closing in 1940. The Regents' recognition for which Dr. Dray had so earnestly worked was granted on October 28, 1926, only seven months after his death.

The closing of the School of Dentistry was a direct result of the Depression, which forced a curtailment of University expenditures, and of the unwillingness of the University either to lower its dental standards or to oversupply the country with dentists. Few have been the cases in history where a school has voluntarily closed its doors because it has ceased to supply the needs of its constituents, but at Beirut this was actually done. The action is typical of the way in which the University has ever tried to adapt itself to the conditions which surround it.

As early as 1934 President Dodge reported to the Trustees that "as the (dental) schools of the Université Saint Joseph and the Syrian University (at Damascus) are not attempting to adopt high American standards, and as few young men can afford to pay for the installation of an expensive dental office during the depression, the University dental school is meeting with difficulties."[4] Two years later he reported: "Government regulations do not discourage low standards of dental education and professional work. During a period of economic depression comparatively few people care to pay for first-class work. Accordingly, students prefer to enter a number of short and inexpensive dental courses, rather than the difficult course of the University."[5] What was of course implied was that students prepared to do fine work could not com-

[4] Annual Report (1933-34), p. 18.

[5] Annual Report (1935-36), p. 14.

pete economically with dentists who could afford to charge lower fees. The condition had arisen whereby an oversupply of dentists for the capacity of the country made impossible the preservation of high standards of training.

It was impossible for the dental school to lower its standards and preserve its raison d'être, and equally impossible to consider turning out dentists who were not desired and who could not support themselves under the conditions which existed. The Trustees therefore reluctantly voted, in March 1936, to accept no new predental students in the fall of 1936 and to take in no first year students in 1937 and 1938. In the latter year the situation still showed no prospect of improving and it was therefore decided to close the school entirely as soon as the classes then enrolled should graduate. The last of these received their degrees in 1940, and the dental school ceased to function. Its thirty years of unique and useful service were brought to a period. Whether it may again reopen when happier days return will depend upon whether they ever do.

4. PHARMACY

At the time when the New York Regents officially recognized the medical school, they extended recognition to the School of Pharmacy and the School of Arts and Sciences as well. During that year (1925-26) the work in pharmacy was improved to require three full years of study in that department. Previously, students entering the University from other institutions had been permitted to go into the second year of pharmacy, the first year being under the control of the School of Arts and Sciences. Thereafter all students were required to pass through the reorganized and developed first year which was transferred to the School of Pharmacy. Preliminary training in the sciences, particularly chemistry, was required for entrance to the first year of pharmacy, instead of being included in it.

This development took place under the leadership of Dr. Ladakis, '01, Director of the school, and was aided materially by the Rockefeller appropriation. It became possible to secure an additional permanent member of the faculty of pharmacy in the person of Dr. Rudolph Pauly, a former staffite who returned to Beirut in 1927 as adjunct professor of Pharmaceutical Chemistry. At the same time an improvement of equipment was secured.

The construction of the new chemistry building in 1930 released the old structure for the exclusive use of pharmacy and permitted a further expansion in its facilities. Shortly thereafter the course was lengthened to four years in addition to a year of practical work in an approved pharmacy. At the same time the entrance requirements were adjusted to fit into the government training programs of the various countries from which students came. Admission to the first year of the school was granted to holders of the Lebanese, Syrian, French or Egyptian Baccalaureate diplomas, provided they could pass a special English examination, and to possessors of the Palestine or London Matriculation Certificate or the Oxford and Cambridge School Certificate. This adjustment was consistent with the aim of the University to meet the needs of the countries it could serve and to fit in with their educational systems, varied though they were. One result of the change was to increase the enrollment in the school by more than 100 per cent even though the course had been lengthened.

5. THE SCHOOL OF NURSING

Since its foundation the School of Nursing had been involved in a constant struggle to get suitable student material. In the Near East the work of a nurse was generally regarded as menial, and it was extremely difficult to set up any respectable entrance requirements to the school because of the danger of cutting off all of the few applicants for admission. The situation was bad enough when the association with the Johanniter Hospital provided a number of well-trained foreign nurses to handle the nursing work and large numbers of student nurses were not required. But when that association was broken and the College had to provide its own nursing force, a considerable number of students was essential in order to carry on the work in the wards. Entrance requirements had to be low in order to admit even the few girls who showed any inclination toward the profession.

Furthermore the hospital had no facilities for making a nurse's life in the least attractive. Probationers had to sleep in hospital lofts or wherever room could be found for them. On the relatively few occasions when they were off duty and not sleeping they had no recreational facilities, no place where they could rest and relax in any privacy. Like the policemen in the "Pirates of Penzance," the nurse's lot was not a happy one.

Not until 1924 was it possible to do much more for student nurses than to instill in them the high idealism and spirit of service which were so manifest in their leaders, Mrs. Dale, Miss Van Zandt and later Mrs. Harris Graham, who succeeded Mrs. Dale as Superintendent of the Hospital. At last, however, through the practical interest of the ladies on the Board of Trustees, funds were raised to build the Mary Bliss Dale Home for Nurses, a beautiful and practical building, the cornerstone of which was unveiled on June 26, 1924. To the original two stories of the Home a third with a roof garden was added in 1927. At last the students could feel that they had a home of their own, and could hold up their heads as a recognized part of the medical school.

Further recognition was accorded the girls in 1925 when the nursing graduates were awarded their diplomas on the main commencement platform before a great audience which then could not fail to appreciate what the University thought of the profession.

These were but first steps. The Rockefeller grant for the medical school made it possible in 1926 to engage a larger number of attendants and graduate nurses to handle the hospital work, thus lifting some of the burden from student nurses and permitting a limitation of enrollment in the school. This in turn permitted not only a raising of entrance requirements to completion of one year of high school work (in 1927) but made it possible to enrich the course with more class-room instruction and laboratory work. The first five months of the three year course could be given over almost wholly to study. Miss Van Zandt was given a year in America in which to study recent developments in methods of instruction and to engage additional staff.

Progress was necessarily slow and it was not until 1932 that graduation from high school could be required as a prerequisite for entrance to the School of Nursing. However, in the meantime additional opportunities for practical work were provided. The establishment of the Public Health Center in 1927 offered experience for students in the novel field of Public Health and gave them a chance to work in homes and schools. In the same year a course in mid-wifery was opened for graduate nurses, and the government license was granted to those who passed it successfully. The following year the University took over a small maternity hospital, originally established by the Near East Relief, next to the great Armenian refugee camp on the outskirts of Beirut. This provided additional training in obstetrics both for medical students and for nurses.

The Rockefeller grant of 1932-39 provided $18,000 a year for the School of Nursing and the work developed markedly under this stimulus. One Syrian graduate of the school, Miss Hilda Hakim, was given a year of Public Health instruction in America and on her return in 1937 established a health center in the tiny mud village of Marj in the Boq'aa plain, over the mountains from Beirut. This isolated outpost is visited weekly by a pediatrician from the medical school, and student nurses take turns serving for a period with Miss Hakim, helping to improve conditions of health in the Arab villages in the vicinity. It is a remarkable, lonely, exacting work, which has produced almost incredible results.

When, in 1939, a large group of Armenian refugees moved to the Boq'aa from the Sanjak of Alexandretta, recently ceded to Turkey by the French, the nursing services of the University were expanded. The support of an Armenian graduate of the School of Nursing was assured by the Howard Karagheusian Commemorative Corporation in New York. This nurse, Miss Elizabeth Shorvoghlian, was to devote herself chiefly to the refugee camp at Anjar, but conditions during that winter were so bad that both girls had to work unceasingly with the refugees. They were helped by relays of student nurses, government doctors and both doctors and medical students from the University.

Such experience has given the pupil nurses and graduates alike a new vision of the opportunities for helpful service, as well as priceless practical training and development in self-reliance and initiative. Working under the most difficult conditions in far from pleasant circumstances they have accomplished results worthy of the greatest admiration.

In his annual report for 1939-40, President Dodge cited an instance illustrative of the courage and energy of these graduates of the Nursing School, as well as of their matter of fact treatment of difficult problems. "One evening," he reported, "the nurses were late in returning home as they had been seeing patients all day. A drunken refugee held them up on the road. They blew the horn of the Ford and flashed the lights but he refused to let them pass. Miss Hakim got out of the car and asked him to let them pass by, but he refused and pushed a revolver into her face.

"She hit him an uppercut which laid him flat. Then she arranged him neatly on the side of the road, folded his arms and put the revolver on his chest. Finally she returned to the car and drove her companions home to supper."

XV. CONTINUED PROGRESS

I. REORGANIZATION OF CURRICULUM

A GLANCE AT THE ENROLLMENT CHART for the years following the war shows that a very rapid increase in attendance at first occurred, which brought the total number of students up with a rush from its low of 695 in 1917 to a high of 1001 in 1920-21. There followed a falling off in the two succeeding years, as local and government schools were organized, emigration set in and economic conditions improved somewhat, enabling some students to take up jobs. But in 1923-24 the tide began again to rise when the opening of the automobile routes to 'Iraq and Persia permitted students from those countries to supplant the abating local attendance. With that development the increase in numbers was rapid throughout the twenties until the Depression provided a temporary setback. By 1937 that loss had been made up and in 1941, in spite of the war, a total enrollment of 2000 was nearly reached.

It was and is still a romantic sight at the opening of each college year to see the big cars with "Desert Route" painted on their hoods roll on to the campus fairly bursting with boys who have crossed the great caravan routes of days gone by as nonchalantly as Americans drive from New York to Amherst or Yale. It is a twenty-four hour drive across the desert from Baghdad to Beirut, but to attend the American University some hundreds of students make the round trip annually.

The inauguration of President Dodge, coincident with the political crystallization of the Near East, made possible a much needed revision of the entire curriculum in accord with a long range plan of development. Much attention was given to the effort to adapt the work of the University to the stabilizing conditions in the Near East, and a uniform plan of organization from elementary to professional levels was worked out. The principal changes envisaged may be summed up as follows:

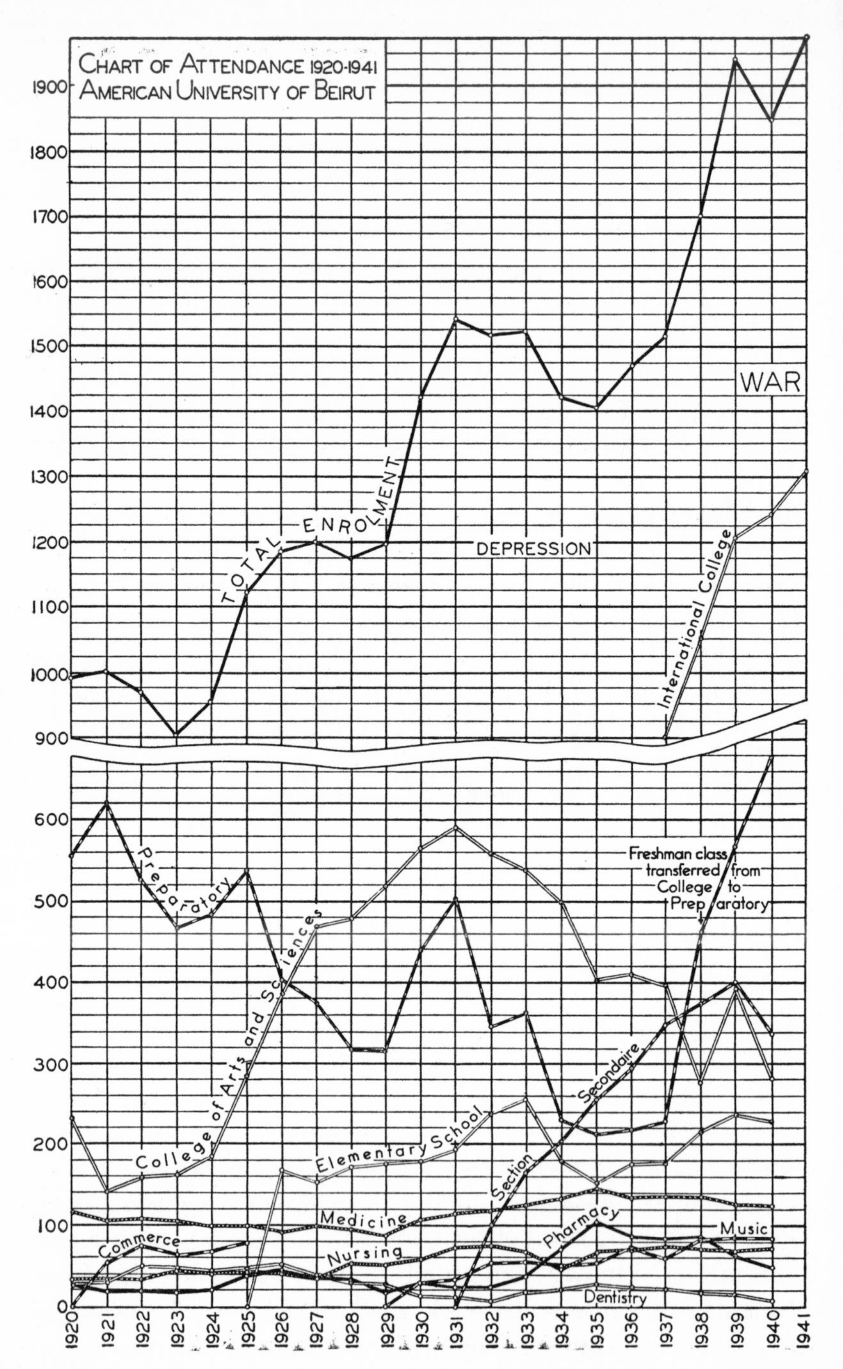

Departmental figures for 1941 were not available for the chart. See Appendix O.

ALLEGHENY COLLEGE LIBRARY

1. Establishment of an improved elementary school under the supervision of the Preparatory Department, to provide an ideal primary education in the Arabic language. This school could serve as a greatly needed model for the country and as a laboratory for advanced students of education who needed practice teaching.

2. The inclusion of additional French instruction for boys from French mandates, and more Arabic for others, applying both to courses other than purely language studies. The French courses eventually became a special French section.

3. The organization of a summer school for boys from the Preparatory, providing opportunity for students to remedy special deficiencies.

4. Division of the Preparatory into Senior, Junior and Primary schools, with headmasters for each under the guidance of the Principal. The Senior school was later called the Freshman school and was placed under the supervision of the Dean of the College.

5. Inclusion in the Senior school of Freshman college year with the secondary certificate being given at the end of Freshman year. This served the purposes of providing a broader cultural base before major specialization or, for those who did not go on to college, a more thorough education. It also made the secondary certificate more nearly the equivalent of the French and English certificates.

6. Inclusion of the School of Commerce in the School of Arts and Sciences thus simplifying the administration. A two year business course was put in the freshman school while the advanced commercial work was raised to B.A. level.

7. Development of departments in the college to provide adequate major studies which must be selected in Sophomore year. Even in 1925-26 majors were available in relatively few subjects outside of the pre-professional fields, with the greatest weaknesses being shown in the so-called Social Sciences.

8. Admission of women to all classes above Freshman.

The unification of educational plan and the raising of standards which it entailed provided the basis on which, in 1926, the Regents' recognition was awarded to the secondary and college work. At the same time the faculty voted to limit the size of the various parts of the institution, to require strict entrance examinations and to raise fees so that the University might not outgrow its capacity for doing a high grade of work. The policy was definitely stated, and has since been adhered to, that "the function of the institution is not to turn out a great quantity of half-trained men and women, but rather to rear up picked leaders who can make their influence felt throughout the Levant."[1]

2. THE PREPARATORY DEPARTMENT

The new plan was put into effect under a revised administration. Dr. Ward succeeded Dr. Dorman as Dean of the Medical School and Professor Nickoley succeeded Professor Day as Dean of Arts and Sciences, the latter having in 1924 resigned the post in order to devote his full time to teaching. On January 8, 1927 William H. Hall, Principal of the Preparatory Department, died after a severe illness. Mr. Hall had come to Beirut as a staffite in 1896, and after his three year term had studied for the ministry. However, instead of taking a pastorate he returned to Beirut as associate principal with Professor West, and on the latter's removal to the college Mr. Hall became Principal. Except for the enforced vacation of three years demanded by the Turks during the war, all of his time had been devoted, with great success, to building up the Preparatory Department.

Professor Hall's death was a serious blow to the school, but an excellent replacement was available. This was Professor Khalid Tabit, '01, who had been teaching in the Preparatory since his graduation and had for a number of years been head of the Junior school and the Elementary school (Ras Beirut school). Professor Tabit was the first non-American administrator to be appointed head of a school, and he fully justified the confidence placed in him. Until his retirement in 1935 he carried on with marked success the tradition of fine leadership which the Preparatory Department had had from the time of its first principal, Frederick J. Bliss.

The need for providing more thorough instruction in French for the benefit of students coming from French mandates, led in 1926-27 to the establishment of a separate French section in the Preparatory school. Beginning with 25 pupils, the section grew

[1] Annual Report (1924-25), p. 7.

so rapidly that it soon developed into an important branch of the school, offering a complete course similar to that of a French lycée and preparing students for the Syrian, Lebanese and French government examinations. By 1931 it had become so important a part of the preparatory work that it was organized separately as a French School under the administration of M. Robert Widmer of Paris. With his guidance it speedily developed into a first-class lycée offering preparation for the baccalaureate examinations, première et deuxième parties. Students in the French School were required to study a certain amount of English so that at graduation they were ready to enter the upper classes of the School of Arts and Sciences.

The reasons for the development of the French School were chiefly two, as stated by President Dodge. "In the first place," he wrote, "it is essential for an institution as large as the University to encourage the new government program, just as the Spanish schools in the Philippine Islands were expected to adopt English when the American occupation took place.

"In the second place, it is equally important for the University to be a part and parcel of the state in which it is located, rather than an exotic agency for the training of students from the British territories where English is used."[2] The University could satisfy neither requirement if it could not enable students from French mandated territories to complete their secondary studies and at the same time be in a position to profit from the advanced courses which the institution offered, even though they were given in English. The French School proved to be an exceedingly successful solution of a very difficult problem.

Paralleling the development of French instruction was that of the English section of the Preparatory school. Its problems were somewhat similar to those which caused the organization of the French School. For years it had been the outstanding college preparatory school in the region and had set the standards of secondary school education. But the establishment of the British mandates made it necessary for the school to adapt itself to the English educational system rather than the American. This was an addi-

[2] Annual Report (1932-33), p. 18.

tional reason for including the college freshman year in the preparatory, for it provided a course leading up to the English matriculation examination, as well as preparing for entrance into the University proper.

Both the English and French schools were fed by the Elementary school, which was in itself a unique institution. In the French mandates there were no government elementary schools because it had been desired to avoid competition with the parochial and mosque schools already established. Since it was much superior to these, as a rule, the Elementary school at once became very popular as soon as it was established in 1925-26. The language of instruction was chiefly Arabic, with considerable attention being devoted to English and French. The course was planned so that the graduate of the first six grades was fitted for the examinations leading to the government primary certificate. Thereafter the pupil could choose whether to enter the junior high school course (English) or the Classe de Sixième de l'Ecole Française.

The development of three schools in place of one might have overtaxed the facilities of the old preparatory department had not the total number of students involved remained fairly constant. The elementary school was accommodated in a remodelled private house which relieved pressure on the class-room buildings. The growth of numerous government and private secondary schools which were less expensive than the University's school reduced markedly the enrollment therein, particularly in the English school. It was therefore possible to maintain both the English and French schools in the buildings which had formerly housed the undifferentiated preparatory department.

The transfer in 1936-37 of International College from Izmir (Smyrna) to Beirut brought about additional changes and developments in the Preparatory school which was absorbed into it. That story will be told in the chapter dealing with International College.

3. ARTS AND SCIENCES

The major problem facing the School of Arts and Sciences at the start of the new administration was that of securing an adequate faculty. In 1922-23 there were but twelve full professors under contract, of whom five were in the sciences, and two in history. Six other men had reached lower professorial rank, and of them two were in French and three in Arabic. All the rest of the teaching was in the hands of short term instructors whose interest in and hope of obtaining permanent rank was slight under existing financial conditions. Lack of funds made it impossible to hire more expensive men, even though the salaries of professors were hardly large enough to be enviable.

The first step in improving the lot of the faculty was taken at the Trustees' meeting in January 1925, when it was decided to provide annuity payments for retirement of permanent faculty members at the age of sixty-five. This constituted in practice a ten per cent raise in salary which was the more welcome in its insurance form because of the lack of opportunity for investment in Syria. It constituted likewise a considerable inducement for young teachers to accept permanent status at Beirut.

The following year a grant was made by the Laura Spelman Rockefeller Memorial Foundation to aid in building up the work in the social sciences, which was very weak. This grant of $7,400 a year for five years made it possible to secure and train a number of fine men to teach commerce, economics, political science and sociology as well as to build up the library in those fields and provide additional equipment and material for demonstration and study. In 1931 this assistance was continued by the Social Science Division of the Rockefeller Foundation which promised $10,000 a year for three years. In 1935 the Foundation made a final grant of $45,000 to this work, the money to be distributed on a descending scale over the years 1935-40.

Under this stimulus the social sciences assumed a position of real importance at Beirut and made a very distinguished contribution to the life of the Near East. The results of research carried on intensively by teachers and students in those fields have had far reaching effects on the political and social development in that area. The labors of Stuart C. Dodd, Sa'id Himadeh and Walter H.

Ritsher,[3] to mention only three of the men directing the work, are worthy of the high respect they have won in Europe and the Near East.

The Fund for Near East Colleges and the Endowment Fund campaign made possible a further general improvement in the condition of the faculty of Arts and Sciences during the late twenties. Seventeen men above the rank of instructor were added by 1930 to the number on the faculty in 1922-23. This increase not only made possible an enrichment of course offerings but permitted a decided improvement in the quality of the teaching. Definite steps could be taken to raise the standards of all departments.

A symptom of this raising of standards was the installation in 1929 of a system of comprehensive examinations, written and oral, for promotion from junior year and for graduation at the end of senior year. At the same time a serious effort was made to bring about a greater measure of uniformity in the courses offered by different departments as requirements for graduation, with the definite purpose of advancing the requirements for the bachelor's degree in each department. The plan involved a grouping of allied or cognate departments in order to promote cooperation between them and integration of their offerings with the field of major study.

The seven groups were as follows: 1. Biology—Chemistry; 2. Physics, Mathematics, Engineering, Astronomy; 3. Oriental Studies; 4. Modern European Languages; 5. History, Politics, Economics; 6. Commerce and Business Administration; 7. Religion, Philosophy, Psychology, Education, Sociology. Some overlapping in the personnel of the different groups was planned so that cooperation between groups as well as within them might be enhanced. It was expected that the groups would make a more or less continuous study of means by which their course offerings should be strengthened and brought into line with the developing needs of the students.

As a result of these studies it became apparent that a segregation of students should really be made at the end of sophomore year,

[3] Professor Ritsher died in a tragic accident in Beirut in the fall of 1939. The others are still serving on the faculty.

which coincided quite closely with the French Baccalauréat, deuxième classe. Many students were not really qualified to go farther, and there was no particular reason for encouraging them to get the B.A. degree, inasmuch as that degree was essentially meaningless in either the British or French systems. What seemed advisable was to select the most promising students at the end of sophomore year and direct them on a specialized three year course leading to the M.A. degree. Those not selected would be given a certificate showing completion of the highest grade of secondary work. The B.A. degree would gradually be eliminated or de-emphasized.[4]

Such a program could not immediately be put into effect, though the selective process was emphasized as early as 1931. The development of faculty necessary for the offering of more individual, specialized, tutorial work in the upper classes was seriously hampered by the Depression but by 1937 it was possible to offer "honors work" in four courses of study. President Dodge described the system briefly in his annual report for 1937-38:

"Certain students are permitted to take a two year course, leading to the B.A. degree and resembling the "pass" course of a British university. The program of this course is a general one with few expensive electives.

"A brilliant student is encouraged to specialize in some definite field of study and to spend three years of "honors" work, so as to obtain the M.A. as well as the B.A. degree. This "honors" work—is largely conducted in the form of seminar and tutorial conferences, reading in the library and assisting the professors with their investigations. There are difficult comprehensive examinations and the number of students eligible to go on to the final M.A. year is, at any one time, limited to thirty."[5]

The year 1937-38 was further marked by the announcement of a "Ten Year Plan" to guide the development of the School of Arts and Sciences in the direction of the European conception of true university work. The first important step in this direction was

[4] The plan outlined is similar to the suggestions of Pres. Hutchins of the University of Chicago, though it was developed independently at Beirut, where it has been in partial operation since 1932 and definitely in prospect since 1928.

[5] Annual Report (1937-38), p. 11.

taken in 1939 with the transference of sophomore year to International College (which had taken over the expanded secondary work). This permitted the Division of Arts and Sciences to concentrate on a limited enrollment in its three year curriculum. The move explains the considerable drop in registration apparent on the enrollment chart of the School of Arts and Sciences.

The plan contemplated no addition of new chairs but rather a development of instruction in existing departments, the establishment of teaching fellowships, the improvement of library and research facilities. Tutorial work is inevitably more expensive than lecture room methods and it was estimated that the annual budget would need to be increased by some $22,000 by the end of the ten year period. The attainment of this goal has been made very dubious by the war, but the goal continues to exist. In the meantime the development of the plan goes on within the limitations of circumstance.

4. NEW CHAIRS AND FIELDS

The expansion of offerings in the School of Arts and Sciences has been almost continuous throughout the administration of President Dodge, but four contributions to it deserve special mention. Three of these were the establishment of new chairs; the fourth was the development of work in industrial chemistry.

As early as 1922 the Union Congregational Church of Upper Montclair, New Jersey, undertook to support the professorship of English in the University with an annual contribution in memory of Howard Bliss, former pastor of the church. The chair is known as the Upper Montclair professorship and it has been occupied since its foundation by Byron P. Smith.

In 1929 Dr. James R. Jewett, then Professor of Arabic at Harvard, endowed the chair of Arabic at the University in honor of his wife, Margaret Weyerhaeuser Jewett. In making his magnificent gift Professor Jewett wrote to President Dodge: "The thought of a professorship of Arabic attracted me both because of my own interest in the subject and because I feel that a strong department of Arabic will in itself be a distinct asset for the University. I hope that the founding of this chair by an American may be regarded by the Syrians and other Arabic-speaking peoples as an evidence of a sympathetic understanding of their cultural ambition, and may increase the already strong hold which the University has on their affection and their esteem."[6] In addition to serving the purposes mentioned, the Margaret Weyerhaeuser Jewett professorship very greatly broadened the usefulness of the department of Arabic. Under the leadership of Prof. Anis Khuri al-Makdisi, '06, much important work has been done to revive the flower of Arabic culture, long in a withered and quiescent state.

The third chair to be established was that of Archaeology, the money to support which was given in 1931 by a Syrian woman in New York who modestly requested that her name be kept secret. Up to that time the study of archaeology and the building up of the University museum had been carried on more or less as a hobby by some members of the faculty, and though the collections were extensive and valuable the organized study of them had not been possible for students. Thanks to the provision of this chair the magnificent archaeological opportunities of the Near East were at last made available to qualified members of the student body.

In the early days of the S.P.C. much had been done by the Rev. H. H. Jessup, Dr. Cornelius Van Dyck, Dr. Post, and especially Professor Porter to make the museum important. Now, however, a trained archaeologist in the person of Dr. Harald Ingholt of Copenhagen, could be engaged for a period of five years to improve the collections and give regular courses. Dr. Ingholt, who had already conducted extensive investigations at Palmyra and Hama, proved to be a most fortunate appointment, for he was a magnificent instructor as well as a first rate archaeologist. During his tenure at Beirut he edited and published *Berytus,* the archaeological journal of the University, and though his contract ended in 1937, when he returned to Copenhagen, he continued to issue the magazine. It is much to be regretted that the Depression prevented the continuance of the professorship.

In order to give practical emphasis to the work in chemistry, the department had long been anxious to devote attention to the in-

[6] Al-Kulliyah, XV, 6:143-4.

dustrial applications of the subject. With the completion of the new building in 1930 a start was possible. Advanced students were assigned some local product as a subject for study and experimentation, with a view either to improving the product or to using similar raw materials to manufacture some other article not locally manufactured.

The plan was further outlined by Prof. Close as follows: "Whenever through the joint efforts of teacher and student, a commercial product is thus obtained which is of really high grade and for which we believe a market could be found, that article will be manufactured on a small scale and put on sale in the local community. The privilege of making and selling the article will be granted as a sort of prize either to the student who has helped work out the process, or to some other student who has shown particular ability in his work in chemistry."[7] Students would thus gain experience both in manufacturing and selling, and might gain insight into the possible development of new local industries. They would also have the opportunity to share in any profits derived from their efforts.

Products thus manufactured were labelled "Iclaub Products" (Industrial Chemistry Laboratories of the American University of Beirut). The first of these was an olive oil shaving cream, and the list rapidly grew until in 1934-35 no less than twenty-one products had been developed. These included table salt, jams and jellies, canned fruits and vegetables, fruit syrups, pectin, flavoring extracts, numerous toilet preparations, soap, soap powder, inks, library paste, etc. The list has since expanded, and some of the articles have become the basis of productive industries in the Near East. The only limitation put upon the possible range of products was that they should be composed of materials available locally. It is readily apparent how much potential value such investigations might have for the non-industrial Near East.

5. RESEARCH

The work in industrial chemistry was typical of the orientation toward research which developed under the stimulus of the Rocke-

[7] Al-Kulliyah XVIII, 1:6.

feller grants and the acquisition of an expanded personnel. Before the war some work had been done in the field of medical research but relatively little publication was attempted. In other fields there was either no staff at all or the existing faculty was so pressed with teaching duties that it had no time to devote to extra-curricular studies.

In an article printed in the *Al-Kulliyah Review* in 1939, Professor Stuart Dodd described the development of this phase of the University's activities: "During the twenties research was not developed in all the departments of the University equally, but rather in four definite fields or specialties for which special resources or a unique need existed for the A.U.B. in her situation in the Near East. These four were the medical sciences, the social sciences, oriental studies and industrial chemistry."[8] The support of the first two was in large part provided by the Rockefeller grants. The Oriental studies were aided somewhat by the Alumni Fund and by a library appropriation from the Carnegie Endowment for International Peace (1931). The industrial chemistry work was largely self-supporting. One recent phase of it, the development of a local squill plant for use in rat poisoning, has been assisted by a small appropriation from the K-R-O Company in the United States. Research is expensive and the University is constantly seeking sources to provide the money for it.

In addition to problems of finance and personnel, Dr. Dodd continued, "there have been the peculiar difficulties here that data are inaccessible, the stimulation of professional colleagues is absent, and the appreciation of the value of research in the region is very meagre. To one accustomed to rich libraries, well indexed and equipped with abundant bibliographies in the West, the absence of such aids to scholarship is very striking in the Near East. Towards filling this need, the first project of the Social Science Research Section was to compile a bibliography in eight small volumes gathering together the publications in the Post-War decade about the Near East published in the seven chief languages. Much fundamental information is never published at all. As one illustration, when we needed the detailed figures for the census

[8] Al-Kulliyah Review, vol. 6, 7:2 (February 3, 1939).

of the Lebanon, it required a series of twelve calls at different government offices ranging up to the President of the Republic before the permission was granted to copy by hand the one copy of the census figures which the Government possessed. In most countries this information would have been published, or a photostat copy would be readily securable by writing to the appropriate department.

"The absence of other research specialists working in one's own field with whom problems can be discussed is a real handicap to research out here. Most of the departments of the University are one-professorship departments and even where the department has more than one professor, their research specialties do not coincide. The result is that the research man is scientifically lonely and has to depend upon journals and correspondence and occasional visits abroad and a large dose of persisting internal enthusiasm for his field of investigation. Gradually, professional conferences of scientists and scholars will develop in the Near East. A small group of a dozen or so professors from Cairo, Damascus and Beirut in the Oriental Studies have been meeting once a year or so in a group that may become a stimulating and effective academy of Arabic studies. Difficulties of different languages and diverse points of view and habits of working in isolation make it difficult to develop such conferences for inter-stimulation in other fields. In 1932 we organized a conference of the Near East Colleges between Sofia, Teheran and Asiut, but this had to be postponed on account of the depression.

"Another difficulty is that the public in general does not appreciate the value of research. Energies here are so largely absorbed in catching up with advances made elsewhere in the world that there has been little surplus for advancing into the region of the unknown and bringing additions to the world's knowledge. When scholarly works are published, there is very little demand for them. Such volumes, for instance, as Mr. Himadeh's economic series, which are fundamental knowledge for all economists and business interests, sell only a few dozen copies a year in the Arabic edition through the chain of bookstores who are our booksellers in the chief cities in the Near East."[9]

In spite of the difficulties, the amount of publication which has been done is surprising, including not only articles published in professional journals but approximately one hundred major books and pamphlets printed by the University. The list which had been compiled by 1934 occupied eighteen pages in President Dodge's "Description of the Organization and Work of the A.U.B." In spite of the Depression, a respectable collection has been published since then, including six complete volumes of *Berytus,* the archaeological journal. Professor Himadeh's authoritative volumes on the economic organization of Syria, Palestine and 'Iraq, published both in English and Arabic, have been issued since 1934, as have a number of other less imposing but equally valuable studies in other fields.[10]

One of the extremely interesting investigations now going on is that of Dr. Asad Rustum, '16, professor of History. In 1919 Dr. Rustum began a study of the relations between Egypt and Syria during the period 1805-49. In 1935 His Majesty, King Fuad, placed the Egyptian national archives entirely at Dr. Rustum's disposal and provided him with the numerous secretaries necessary for an extensive investigation. This assistance was continued by His Majesty, King Farouk, when he ascended the throne.

Of this work Dr. Rustum recently wrote: "The Royal Archives of Egypt for the period 1805-49 contain over a million documents. As 55,000 of this million relate to my subject, I owe it to my successors in my field of study to devote my time for ten years at least to preliminary work. With this in mind, I am preparing, to begin with, a guide for the Royal Archives of Egypt in matters pertaining to relations of Egypt with Syria and the Sublime Porte."[11] One gains some impression of the practically limitless opportunity for research in this almost untouched mass of material. Similar opportunities await students in Arabic literature and law,

[9] Ibid.

[10] The University prints a catalogue of its publications. It is too extensive to be reproduced here.

[11] Near East Colleges News Letter, vol. 19, 1:13 (November 1939).

in commerce, politics, religion, anthropology, archaeology and numerous other fields which are slowly being penetrated.

Impetus has been given to research at Beirut by the fairly frequent visits of scholars from America and Europe who have devoted extended periods to teaching and study on the campus. Among them have been Sir Arthur Smith Woodward, formerly head of the Department of Geology of the British Museum; Dr. C. U. Ariens-Kappers, Head of the Neurological Institute, Amsterdam, who taught for a full year (1929-30); Prof. Herbert A. Miller, then Professor of Sociology at Ohio State; Prof. E. G. Mears of Leland Stanford; Louis C. Karpinski, Professor of Mathematics at Michigan; Harold W. Temperley, Professor of History, Cambridge University; Dr. George Sarton, editor of "Isis," Professor of the History of Science at Harvard; Dr. Harold E. Vokes, Assistant Curator of Invertebrate Palaeontology of the American Museum of Natural History. Since the persecution of the Jews began in Europe, several distinguished European scholars have visited Beirut and helped to stimulate the spirit of scientific investigation. It is very much alive at the American University.

6. COEDUCATION

During the first year of the new administration, the faculty voted to admit women students to all classes of the School of Arts and Sciences above Freshman year. Although there had been women in the School of Nursing since 1905, and though for three years they had been allowed to study pharmacy and dentistry, the new decision represented an extremely radical step. Moslem women still wear the veil in Syria in spite of its abolition in Turkey, and in 1923 there was ground for serious doubt that Moslem girls would be permitted to enter classes with men. Furthermore, the idea of providing an education for women was almost totally new to the southern Near East. Woman's place was considered to be in the home and only in the home. She could talk only with other women or her husband, and her sole duties were to keep him comfortable and provide him with a family. Why should she be educated? It might give her ideas!

Another objection to admitting women to the college was the fear that it would be too much for the boys. Reared, as many of them were, in the strict Moslem tradition, they had never talked to or seen the faces of any women but their mothers or sisters. To allow bare-faced women in the classroom with these boys might put a terrible strain on their self-control and give *them* ideas which would be bad for them. It is not surprising that considerable hesitation was felt about taking such a momentous step.

But the administration felt that the time had come to provide an opportunity in Syria for that emancipation of women which was being legislated into existence in Turkey. It was a considerable satisfaction to have seven women enroll in the School of Arts and Sciences in 1924, in which year also the first woman to receive a degree from the University graduated from the School of Pharmacy.[12] It was a particular pleasure to find that one of the seven was a Moslem woman, Madame Ihsan Ahmad, a special student from Egypt. The experiment was beginning well.

The following year thirteen women were enrolled in Arts and Sciences and two of them were Moslems. President Dodge reported that they had attended classes without embarrassment. For the first time the B.A. degree and the degree of D.D.S. were granted to women graduates. Two other girls were enrolled in dentistry and one in pharmacy, while several of the Arts and Sciences group had expressed the hope of going on into medicine.

In 1926-27 a plan of cooperation was worked out with the Presbyterian Board of Foreign Missions, whereby the Board established a Junior College for Women at Beirut which would offer the work of Freshman and Sophomore year. Thereafter women students were not admitted to the University until the beginning of Junior year,[13] though they were given access to the laboratories and library of the University while enrolled in the Junior College. The plan had the double advantage of providing better preparation for college entrance and at the same time a place for women students to live while at school.

[12] This was Miss Sara Levy, a Jewish girl from Palestine.

[13] Specially qualified girls are permitted to enter the "Classe des Mathématiques Elémentaires" of the Section Secondaire, equivalent to sophomore science work. Few other schools in the country offer this course and girls are therefore allowed to enroll.

The Junior College developed so rapidly that in 1932-33 it became necessary to construct a new building and provide a campus for it. Even the new quarters, however, could not continue to accommodate both the students of the Junior College and women attending the University. Of the latter there were, in 1939-40, fifty-seven exclusive of those in the Institute of Music and the School of Nursing. The University was forced to rent a private house to serve as a girls' hostel, and the probability is considerable that at no distant date it will be necessary to provide a more suitable women's dormitory.

The number of Moslem women students has steadily increased, and they have come from surprising distances and from all ranks. The daughter of the former Sharif of Mecca graduated from the Institute of Music in 1931 and in 1935 the Prime Minister of 'Iraq and a distinguished Moslem sheikh of Palestine both enrolled their daughters as co-eds. Higher education for women is becoming an accomplished fact in the Arab countries. Literally and figuratively the veil is being drawn from their eyes. "The Near Eastern woman has entered the field of enlightened action to help her brother in trying to solve the social problems of these lands. There are many fields of action for uplifting society in the East, where women are better fitted to serve than men."[14]

7. THE INSTITUTE OF MUSIC

One of the fields in which women of the western world typically add to the enjoyment and grace of life is that of music. In the East this has not been so true, and in general it may be said that in the Arab world music has not been a scientifically cultivated art. Thus it was that the establishment of an institute of music at the American University of Beirut was in the nature of another radical step away from or beyond tradition, and it was the result only of a preliminary process of education.

"After the War," wrote President Dodge, describing the development of the school, "a number of Russian refugees found their way to Beirut. One of them was Professor Arkadie Kouguell, at one time acting director of a conservatory in the Crimea. When he

[14] Al-Kulliyah, XIX, 4:100 (March 15, 1933).

VILLAGE WELFARE CAMP NEAR SHTAURAH

DINNER TIME AT THE SHTAURAH CAMP

DEMONSTRATING A MODERN BEEHIVE

PATIENTS WAITING OUTSIDE THE MARJ CLINIC

ALLEGHENY COLLEGE LIBRARY

CAMPUS PANORAMA NORTHEAST FROM INTERNATIONAL COLLEGE

THE UNIVERSITY STADIUM FROM THE CAMPUS

ALLEGHENY COLLEGE LIBRARY

reached Beirut, he started to give private lessons and to organize concerts at the University. At first the people of the country did not enjoy classic European music. It was only by subsidizing the concerts that an audience could be gathered together.

"Gradually the music became so popular that Professor Kouguell was able to arrange for fortnightly concerts given by a symphony orchestra of thirty-five pieces, to audiences of five or six hundred people. Many high French officials and their wives encouraged the music and the students became enthusiastic. . . . In the symphony orchestra there are Russians, Armenians, French, Americans and members of other nationalities. Professor Kouguell has also organized a student orchestra."[15]

In the fall of 1928 M. Kouguell obtained government permission to start a private conservatory of music, but he was delighted at the opportunity to make it a department of the University. The Institute of Music of the American University of Beirut opened in the fall of 1929 with the famous Directeur de l'Ecole Normale de Musique de Paris, M. Alfred Cortot, as Honorary Director. M. Cortot himself visited Beirut in 1930 and examined the advanced pupils. During his stay he gave a delightful concert in West Hall.

In the Institute the language of instruction is French, and the elementary, secondary and higher courses are recognized by l'Ecole Normale de Musique de Paris. Graduates of the "Higher Stage" who satisfy the general requirements are awarded the Diploma of the Institute by the University Faculty.

In the year 1939-40 there were eighty-three students in the Institute exclusive of those University students who were taking lessons or classes but whose major interest lay in other fields. Many of the eighty-three had come from distant places to enjoy the privilege of competent musical instruction. Men as well as women are now profiting by the opportunity to enrich their lives in familiarity with the finest art. President Dodge, in a letter dated December 9, 1940, reported from war-isolated Beirut: "This is the first year that the students have been interested enough in music to buy tickets and to come to the concerts. . . . The effort of the Institute

[15] Annual Report (1928-29), pp. 21-2. Professor Kouguell also played the organ for the University Chapel services which his music greatly enhanced.

to produce a love of music amongst the Arab students and the Arab community at Beirut is proving to be a success."

8. TWENTY YEAR SUMMARY

In 1939 President Dodge presented in his Annual Report a recapitulation of the developments which had taken place in the institution during the previous twenty years. When the significant figures are placed in parallel columns, an astounding picture emerges of the progress which the University has made in the past two decades.

		1918-19	*1938-39*
Land Owned by the University (acres)			
This includes the great athletic stadium given by V. Everit Macy in 1926. Since the War the land has been irrigated, a number of roads have been paved and numerous gates and iron fences have replaced old boundary walls.		40	80
Buildings	*Large*	21	29
Electricity, telephones (given by an alumnus, D. A. Himadi, of New Jersey), better furniture, improved plumbing and modern equipment have improved all the buildings.	*Small*	8	20
	Total	29	49
Endowments (Including International College)		$1,079,000	$6,340,000
Library books, pamphlets and bound journals		18,000	67,704
Registration (combined)		913	1,938
Teaching and Administrative Force			
Professorial Rank		30	77
Instructors, graduate nurses, assistants, technicians, secretaries, clerks, etc.		68	209
	Total	98	286
Student Fees (Two Semesters)			
Tuition (upper classes)		$48.60	$130.00
Lodging (Minimum)		9.72	25.00
Board (Minimum)		243.00[16]	78.00
Appropriations and Grants from America required to meet expenses after deducting local income from student fees		$58,652.93	$237,073.87

[16] Food was abnormally expensive because of recent war conditions and the presence of a large foreign army.

Time had taken its toll from the faculty over this period. Eight professors, all of them outstanding men whose names have appeared before in this story of the University, were taken by death. The list includes Dr. Walter B. Adams (1928), Alfred E. Day (1930), Jebr Dumit (1930), Daud Kurban (1935), Edward F. Nickoley (1937), James S. Crawford (1939), Dr. William T. Van Dyck (1939) and Walter H. Ritsher (1939). To these should be added the name of Dr. Harald Krischner, a brilliant young pathologist who, in the three years of his service to the Medical School, had shown definite promise of real greatness and was at the time of his death in 1931 the head of the department of Pathology. Dr. Krischner died as the result of an infection acquired during a post-mortem demonstration.

Professor Nickoley, who had succeeded Professor Day as Dean of the School of Arts and Sciences, was succeeded by Professor Julius A. Brown who now is Dean. Dr. Ward, the very successful Dean of the Medical School, was forced by illness to resign in 1931, and his place was taken by Dr. George H. Miller, formerly of the University of Iowa and a staffite at Beirut from 1910-13. Dean Miller has occupied the post since coming to Beirut.

Dr. Webster reached the retirement age in 1928 but until the late war continued to live in Beirut where he assisted his colleagues as professor-emeritus of Ophthalmology. In 1940 he was joined in retirement by Professor A. A. Bacon, head of the Physics department, and by Miss Jane E. Van Zandt, who had been the valued head of the School of Nursing ever since its inception in 1905. During the academic year 1941, retirement is due for Dr. Harry G. Dorman, Professor Bulus Khauli and Professor Triantaphyllo Ladakis, head of the School of Pharmacy. To readers familiar with the University in its earlier years it must appear that the pillars of the institution are crumbling. They may be assured that new supports are safely in place.

Numerous changes have also appeared in the Board of Trustees during the past twenty years. The full roster of twelve members attained by the election of Clarence Phelps Dodge in 1921 was successively broken by the retirement from the Board of William Adams Brown, the death of D. Stuart Dodge in 1922 and the resig-

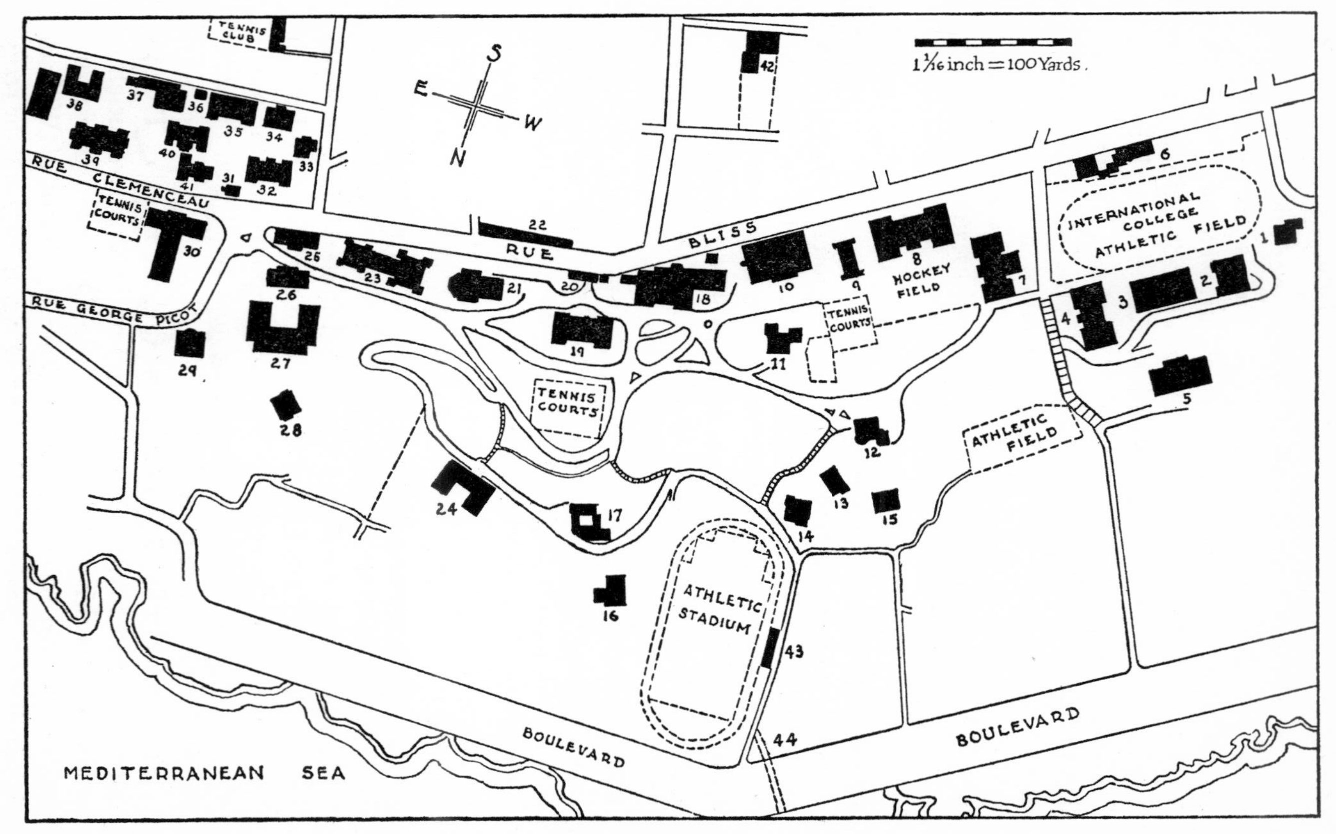

ALLEGHENY COLLEGE LIBRARY

LEGEND

1 Martin House, residence of Principal, International College
2 Thomson Hall
3 Rockefeller Hall
4 Sage Hall
5 Refectory, International College
6 Elementary School
7 Bliss } Housing the
8 Pliny Fisk Hall } "Intermediate Section"
9 Morris Jesup Hall, dormitory for medical students
10 Robert H. West Hall, religious and recreational activities
11 Marquand House, Faculty room attached
12 Observatory
13, 14, 15, 16, 28 Professors' residences
17 Workshops
18 Ada Dodge Hall, administrative offices, dining hall, physics department
19 College Hall, University library, classrooms, upper-class dormitory
20 Old gate house, administrative offices
21 Chapel
22 Medical annex, dormitory
23 Post Hall, University Museums, Department of Biology
24 Chemistry Building
25 School of Pharmacy, Dispensary
26 Old Medical Hall, Department of Biochemistry
27 Medical Sciences Building
29 School of Dentistry
30 Out-patient clinics
31 Hospital gate house
32 "Eye Pavilion"; Medicine, Eye, Ear, Nose and Throat
33 X-Ray Building (second floor internes' quarters)
34 "Personnel House" for overseas nurses
35 "Pathology Building"; Bacteriology, Parasitology, Pathology labs.
36 Ambulance garage
37 Hospital kitchen and laundry, storerooms
38 Mary Bliss Dale Home for student nurses
39 "Women's Pavilion"; Obstetrics, Gynecology, Pediatrics
40 "Children's Pavilion"; Surgery
41 Adham House, Administrative offices (destroyed by fire December 1939)
42 American Community School
43 Stadium grandstand
44 Tunnel under Boulevard to Swimming Facilities

nation on account of illness of V. Everit Macy at the same time. The three vacancies were filled in 1923 by the election of Dr. William S. Ladd, Mrs. Van Santvoord Merle-Smith and Mr. Vanderbilt Webb.

Dr. Franklin A. Dorman, who had entered the Board in 1919, died late in 1927 and his place was filled by the election of Mr. Acosta Nichols. Miss Eleanor de Graf Cuyler died in 1933 and her death was followed by that of Alfred E. Marling in 1935. Clarence Phelps Dodge found it necessary to resign in 1936, and James H. Post, elected in 1919, died in 1938. Mr. Arthur Curtiss James found it necessary in the same year to resign after thirty-two years of service to the University.[17] These vacancies were filled by the election in 1936 of three members of the International College Board and in 1938 of Mr. Harold B. Hoskins, son of the former Principal of the Preparatory School and missionary, Franklin E. Hoskins. In 1939 Mr. H. Irving Pratt, Jr. was elected to fill the remaining vacancy. In 1940 Mr. William Fellowes Morgan, Sr., who had served continuously since 1908, resigned from the Board, and his place still remains to be filled. Mr. Pratt resigned in the spring of 1941 in order to enter the Navy. He was replaced by Mr. Lawrence C. Marshall.

Mr. William M. Kingsley resigned his position as president and treasurer in 1938, but agreed to remain on the Board. He was succeeded as president by Vanderbilt Webb and as treasurer by H. Irving Pratt, Jr., who in turn was succeeded by Mr. Marshall. The place of Mr. James as vice-president was filled by the election of Mr. Hoskins.

At the annual meeting of the Board on January 22, 1941, it was voted to increase the membership of the Board to fifteen, if a revision of the charter to that effect should be granted by the Regents of the University of the State of New York. This revision of the charter, granted on May 16, 1941, marks the beginning of a new chapter in the history of the American University of Beirut. The last has been given a period by the present war.

[17] Mr. James died in June 1941, leaving a considerable legacy to the University.

XVI. INTERNATIONAL COLLEGE

1. HISTORICAL SKETCH

IN 1903 the Commonwealth of Massachusetts granted a charter to the Trustees of International College of Smyrna, Turkey, for the purpose "of providing a thorough practical education for boys and young men in and around Smyrna, Turkey, on a distinctly Christian basis." The institution which was thus raised to college rank had started in 1891 as a boys' high school operated by the American Board of Commissioners for Foreign Missions. Under its energetic founder and principal, the Reverend Alexander MacLachlan, the school developed so consistently that it became first a collegiate institute and finally a college.

Through the interest of Mr. and Mrs. John S. Kennedy, International College in 1910 was able to secure a beautiful campus on the outskirts of the city of Smyrna. The new plant was ready for operation in 1914 and the future looked very bright. But the war came, and the Near East was plunged into misery, famine, cruelty and bloodshed. Through it all the College carried on, and was able to render great service in giving comfort and relief to the people of the area.

The World War ended, but in 1919 a Greek army landed at Smyrna and for three and a half years occupied that portion of Asia Minor. To all intents and purposes International College was then in Greece and the charter was altered in 1921 to make the name "International College of Asia Minor." The student body was largely Greek, and the curriculum had to be designed to fit its needs.

By September of 1922 Smyrna was in flames, the Greeks were driven out, and Dr. MacLachlan himself was shot by renegades and nearly killed. But the College persevered, reorganized its curriculum to suit the requirements of the new Turkish population and began once more to grow.

In 1926 International College became a member of the Near East College Association and through the great Endowment Fund campaign acquired for the first time an endowment large enough to make unnecessary an annual search for funds. Until that time the College had never had an endowment of more than eleven hundred dollars. It came through the campaign with a total fund of one million dollars.

The development of the Turkish Republic, with its institution of new Turkish schools and new requirements for foreign schools, began to diminish the usefulness of International College, and in 1934 the Trustees regretfully voted to close the work in Smyrna. After an extended survey of possible alternative plans, the Trustees decided in 1936 to move the College to Beirut and begin afresh in cooperation with the American University, taking over the work which had been carried on by the preparatory department of that institution. The move was originally made for a trial period of five years, but so great was the success of the new "Kulliyah al-Thanawiyah al-'Amah," that in 1940 the Board of Trustees adopted the following vote:

"That the relation between the two Boards at the end of the five year period, terminating July 1, 1941, be continued on an indeterminate basis, with the understanding that a year's notice would be given on the part of either Board in case of discontinuance and with the understanding that the amount to be appropriated for the budget would be determined year by year by the International College Board."[1]

With its move to Beirut the college which had been International in name became international in fact, for in its new student body were to be found representatives of thirty-seven nationalities and sixteen religious groups. Its enrollment, which at Smyrna had never exceeded 310 jumped at once to 901, and in the years since 1936 the number has increased steadily until at the opening of the year 1940-41 a total of 1,272 students was registered.

Among the students are to be found representatives of the most powerful families in the Near East as well as boys whose backgrounds are obscure. A direct descendant of Saladin, son of a former Prime Minister of Syria, finds himself in association with a coal-black former slave boy, who incidentally was freed by his master, the Vizier of King Ibn Sa'ud, in order that the boy might

[1] Trustees Minutes, International College, February 7, 1940.

accompany the Vizier's two sons to college. Two boys are the sons of wealthy Arab traders at Singapore. Two others come from Bombay and three from Zanzibar. The former Director of Education for 'Iraq, the Director of Health at Mecca, the Postmaster of Jiddah, have all sent their sons to International College and Sheikh Muhammad al Khalifah, brother of the ruler of Bahrein, brought his two sons to Beirut in person from that fabulous island in the Persian Gulf.

These Moslem boys may find themselves in classes with a group of long-haired, black-gowned Greek Orthodox monks, sent to International College by the leading ecclesiastics of the Patriarchate of Antioch and the East. In the five years since International College moved to Beirut almost every religious group in the Near East has had its representatives among the students—and they all live together in peace and amity. It is probably the most cosmopolitan campus in the world, and is a constant source of inspiration to those who believe in the practicability of world brotherhood.

2. REORGANIZATION

Only three of the Smyrna faculty stayed with the College in its move to Beirut. These three, Professors Maynard, Fowler and Seylaz, were all that were left of the original staff. President Cass Reed, who had succeeded Dr. MacLachlan[2] as president in 1926, spent the year 1934-35 at the American University as visiting professor of Religion, and then accepted a call to the pastorate of the Congregational Church of Pomona, California. Others of the Smyrna faculty found positions elsewhere during the interim of the inactivity of the College. President Dodge became the new head of the institution, with Archie Stuart Crawford as Principal. Mr. Crawford, a graduate of Beloit, had been associated with the University since 1921, and, having been brought up in the Lebanon, had the great advantage of speaking French and Arabic with fluency.

Under Mr. Crawford were placed the three heads of the separate branches of the College. Leslie W. Leavitt continued as head of the

[2] Dr. MacLachlan became a member of the Board of Trustees. A Canadian, he died at Kingston, Ontario, on September 8, 1940.

Preparatory Section, the work of which was given in English. M. Robert Widmer remained Director of the Section Secondaire, or French division; and Professor George D. Shahla, '23, was placed in charge of the Elementary School. Professor Shahla also continued his position as adjunct professor of Education in the University.

The new faculty was almost as cosmopolitan as the student body, with ten countries represented. Fifty-two of the teachers came from Lebanon and Syria, eleven from America, ten from France, and two or three each from England, Switzerland, Spain, Iran, Palestine and Egypt. They represented also ten different religious groups. A number of the University teachers devoted part time to the Freshman class in order to assure high academic standards and continuity between the work of International College and the University.

In order to achieve closer contact between the boards of trustees of the two allied institutions, three members of the International College Board were elected to membership on the Board of the American University. The Reverend William W. Patton, Mr. Loren H. Rockwell and Mr. Whitney C. Colby thus became trustees of both colleges, assuring a thorough understanding of mutual problems in the United States as well as in Beirut. Mr. Colby found it necessary in 1940 to give up his membership on the two boards of trustees and his place on the American University of Beirut Board was filled by the election of Mr. John Wallace Young, who since 1933 had been a trustee of International College.[3]

At the annual meeting of the American University of Beirut Trustees in 1939 it was voted to transfer to International College the entire Sophomore class of the University, thus making International a complete junior college in both the English and French systems. The Section Secondaire was already giving work equivalent to sophomore year in its advanced lycée courses, and the change brought the English offerings to a par with the French.

[3] The present Board of Trustees of International College is composed of the following: William W. Patton, *Chairman*, Loren H. Rockwell, *Treasurer*, Herbert E. B. Case, *Clerk*, Paul M. Atkins, Enoch F. Bell, J. Seelye Bixler, Daniel Bliss, George E. Cary, Miss Mabel Emerson, William F. English, Frederick A. Gaskins, Fred F. Goodsell, S. Ralph Harlow, Mrs. Ivan Hekimian, Ashley D. Leavitt, Paul Monroe, Donald B. Perry, John W. Young.

Incidentally the new arrangement dovetailed perfectly with the "ten year plan" of the University, permitting it to devote all its energies to intensive upper class work leading eventually to the M.A. degree.

There were practical as well as purely logical reasons for this reorganization. The delineation of these reasons made by President Dodge gives an inkling of the serious problems which face institutions in the Near East which try to be more than mere educational factories:

"Most of the private schools and missionary institutions prepare students to enter the Freshman class. The graduates of government schools in the British territories come to Beirut either as Freshmen or Sophomores. Usually two-thirds of the Freshmen and one-third of the Sophomores are new boys who have come to Beirut for the first time.

"Many of them are Muslims from the state schools of the backward areas. They have never had girl friends outside of their own families or had any contact with Christianity. When they come to a Mediterranean seaport like Beirut, with its free social life, its cabarets and licensed prostitution, its horse races and bar-rooms, they are completely bewildered. Their first feeling of disgust for what they think of as Christian civilization is soon followed by a desire to taste the fruits of European life for themselves.

"They naturally find it difficult to use English as the language of instruction, so that they need extra coaching for at least a number of months. They do not know how to do independent study or laboratory work, as most of their training has been memory work. When they do begin to understand the problems of science, it is apt to produce a cynical and agnostic spirit.

"The transfer of Sophomore year to International College has made it possible to organize a junior college unit, so that special discipline and supervision can be given to this difficult group of students. They are to have their campus life . . . in residence buildings of their own. Dr. Habib Kurani, the Registrar, will be in immediate charge of this section and will try to unsnarl the difficult problems which arise when students come from Arab, French,

Italian, Armenian, Hebrew, Greek, Iranian, English, German and American preparatory schools."[4]

The war has interfered with the completion of these arrangements, for Dr. Kurani was prevented by it from returning to Beirut after a year of special preparation at the University of Michigan. In his absence, however, a picked group of teachers has been assigned to the "Intermediate Section," as the Freshman-Sophomore class is termed. The Section is housed as a unit in Fisk and Bliss Halls, surrounding the hockey field, and it thus has a kind of campus-within-a-campus for itself. (See plan, p. 258.) The experiment has proved to be very successful.

3. FARM MANAGEMENT

There are almost innumerable interesting facets to the life of International College which merit description, but perhaps the most interesting and significant of them is the unusual course in farm management which is offered to the sons of landowners. It is typical of the efforts of the institutions at Beirut to supply the needs of the countries they serve.

The Near East still presents as accurate a picture of feudal life as is to be found almost anywhere in the world. Agriculture is the chief occupation, and much of the arable land is still owned by a relatively few families of great influence who count their wealth in villages rather than in money. Their lands are tilled by tenant farmers, and if an owner sells some property the tenants go with the property, transferring their allegiance to their new landlord.

In far too many cases the sons of these feudal lords have flocked to the cities, there to spend their substance in riotous living, squandering their income and going into debt. When they have inherited their fathers' estates they have farmed them out to agents who have exploited both the land and the peasants. In many instances the heirs have mortgaged their lands at ruinous rates of interest in order to support themselves in the cities.

Labor has been looked upon by these men as degrading, and even exercise smacks to them of work. The story is told of a wealthy father who called at a mission school to visit his son and

[4] International College Annual Report (1938-39), pp. 3-4.

found the boy playing tennis. Turning to the principal he said, "Does my son have to do this work?" "No," replied the principal, "he likes to do it." "Very well then," said the father, "but he doesn't need to do it. I could perfectly well hire a servant to take care of it for him."

The aim of the farm management course in International College was, from the start, to interest these boys from wealthy families in developing their estates. The work was open only to them because it had been found from past experience that when boys from peasant families took special agricultural courses they usually classed themselves as "effendis" and became too proud to do practical work. The rich boys also were certain to have family estates on which to exercise their new knowledge and the example they would set could not easily be avoided by their tenants. If the lord works with his hands, it behooves the serf to labor with extra diligence.

Experiment had also shown that it was unwise to urge landowners' sons to study abroad until after they had gained some practical experience in their own country. Too often they returned from foreign parts enthusiastic about methods of work which were ill adapted to the Near East. On the other hand, if the student could do preliminary work at the American University and gain some years of practical knowledge on his father's estate, he could then profit greatly from further study abroad.

The farm management course is set up to cover two years of work, roughly equivalent to the last year of high school and freshman year of college. About a third of the student's classroom time is devoted to subjects of a general and cultural nature. Another third is given to commercial subjects, which may be studied either in French or English. The final third is devoted to agricultural courses in Arabic, presenting a general introduction to the more important aspects of agricultural work as well as special studies in science and farm administration.

In addition to their classroom instruction the students have a great deal of practical work. "Nowhere else in the country," writes President Dodge, "could one find sons of rich landowners willing to dig in the soil, trim fruit trees, plant vegetables, push wheelbarrows of manure, and perspire in the hot sun, clad in blue jeans or shirtless shorts."[5] The boys do their work mainly on the University grounds where there is a splendid herd of Jerseys and half-Jerseys, 1,500 chickens, 300 rabbits, bees, Angora goats, sheep, citrus and olive groves, a tree nursery, alfalfa, vegetable gardens and fruit trees. During week-ends, vacations, and particularly during the summer months, trips are taken for the purpose of studying farming conditions in the interior. For part of the summer the boys work on a large farm in the Boq'aa where they gain experience with crops not found on the coast.

The work was begun in the fall of 1937 with eight students. The following year the number jumped to fifteen and in 1939 it rose to twenty-four. The most recent report (December 1940) states that "ten of the students who entered last year have returned to complete the studies of the second or final year of the course. Over forty candidates applied for entrance to the first year class. Twenty-six were accepted, seven were refused because of insufficient preparation and seven others were refused to avoid overcrowding."[6] Thus in spite of the war, or perhaps because of it, this important work continues to gain in influence. It is entirely self-supporting, for the students are all able to pay respectable tuition fees.

Who are these boys who are willing to pay for the privilege of working as they have never worked before? One is the son of Diab Agha, a chieftain in the region of Kala'at el Husn. Another is the son of a feudal landlord of the Aleppo district who owns five villages and grows cotton as well as fruit and olives. One student is a member of the famous 'Azm family of Hama, owning fifteen villages. A Damascus boy of Kurdish descent is the grandson of the famous 'Abd-al-Rahman Pasha Yusuf, who was a great landowner and master of the Mecca pilgrim caravan. This year one boy has been sent by the Patriarch of the Greek Orthodox Church, in the hope that he can be fitted to help manage the extensive lands of the Church. Two of the new students come from Palestine, ten from Syria and fourteen from Lebanon.

In March of 1940 several teachers and eleven students made a ten day tour of Palestine. They visited government farms, Jewish

[5] Special Report, Farm Management course, 1940-41. [6] Ibid.

colonies, schools, factories and experimental stations. "Although," said President Dodge, "most of the students were Arabs, they formed excellent relationships with Jewish agencies and were glad to observe the modern methods of their Jewish neighbors. Everywhere they went, the students found that the people were greatly pleased because International College was making a serious effort to improve the conditions among the farmers in countries which are three quarters agricultural."[7]

[7] International College Annual Report (1939-40), pp. 12-13.

XVII. SOCIAL SERVICE

I. PUTTING NATIONALISM TO WORK

THE COURSE IN FARM MANAGEMENT at International College is symptomatic of the constant effort being made at Beirut to interest the students in the welfare of their own countries. Dealing as it does with the class of wealthy landowners, that course is but one small phase of a social movement, originating at the University, which in the last decade has attained a very considerable importance in the life of the Near East.

Since the World War, the flame of nationalism, so searing in Europe, has spread to the Levant where it has been given fuel by the continued domination of mandatory powers whose reluctance at giving up their control has aroused no little antagonism among the people. The fair prospects of independence, which thrilled the long-oppressed peoples of the Near East when first the system of mandates was established, gradually faded into the distance as both France and England maintained their firm control. The release of 'Iraq and Egypt only strengthened the desire of Syria, Palestine and Transjordan for autonomy. In 1936 Syria was promised independence, but in 1939 a new French government withdrew the promise. Resentment and bitterness were the inevitable result.

In recent years the Pan-Arab movement has gathered strength, seeking to revive among all Arabic speaking people the ancient glories of Arab civilization. The movement transcends state boundaries and religious differences. It is a force which, if unrestrained or unguided, might cause untold damage as the nationalistic spirit has already done in Europe. Controlled it might bring about a renaissance in the Near East.

Nationalism may, and frequently does, mean demonstrations, riots, revolutions, wars. On the other hand it may be sublimated into sacrifice for the welfare of country, recognition on the part of educated people that they have the privilege and the obligation

AN INTERNATIONAL STUDENT GROUP
With forty nationalities represented

ALLEGHENY COLLEGE LIBRARY

DEDICATION OF BUST OF YAQUB SARRUF, '70, IN FRONT OF FISK HALL
(June 20, 1937)

L. to R.: Abd al Kadir Bey al'Azm, Rector, Syrian University, Damascus; Faris Nimr Pasha, '74; Yusuf Bey Aftimus, '85, President, Alumni Association; President Bayard Dodge

ALLEGHENY COLLEGE LIBRARY

to do what they can to improve the lot of their countrymen. In the Near East the opportunity for such improvement is still enormous.

An English author visiting Beirut in 1937 was astounded to find how successful the American University had been in developing among Arab students an interest in social service. He asked President Dodge how it came about, and was told that it developed "through nationalism."

"Nationalism?"

"Yes. The young fellows realize the dreadful and antiquated conditions in which their families and their former friends are living in the mountains, even in the towns. Nowadays nationalism is the fashion. All our students want to see their country strong and prosperous. But they begin to realize that this cannot be achieved unless they, with their greater knowledge and better opportunities, set out to improve the conditions of their less fortunate fellows. I guess this is the most productive way of using Syrian nationalism."[1]

The principle of this "new" nationalism was stated in one of the early reports of the campus organization known as the Village Welfare Service. The student, says this report, "must be made to feel that in accepting the privilege of an education he thereby incurs increased responsibilities. He has contracted a debt which he can discharge only by bringing the knowledge and experience he has gained to bear upon the problems of the community which sent him to be educated, whether from city or country. If the privileged few were to consider themselves as delegates sent to the fountain of knowledge for the purpose of bringing back to the thirsty community a refreshing drink, then rural life would be resuscitated and with renewed energy and a strengthened morale we could grapple with the fundamental problems with vision and confidence."[2]

Students of the University had for many years been somewhat interested in social problems, and the West Hall Brotherhood had long conducted a night school for poor boys in the vicinity of the

[1] Landau, Rom—"Search for Tomorrow" (Nicholson and Watson, London 1938), p. 127.

[2] Third Annual Report, Village Welfare Service (1935), p. 2.

campus. But in 1930 very great impetus was given to their social interests when the Near East Foundation, successor to the Near East Relief, decided to make an effort to improve the condition of agriculture in the countries at the eastern end of the Mediterranean. In order to take advantage of all available experience and facilities, the Foundation sought the cooperation of the American University of Beirut. Both students and faculty welcomed the occasion to extend their opportunity for service.

2. THE INSTITUTE OF RURAL LIFE

With the financial backing of the Near East Foundation, the Institute of Rural Life of the American University of Beirut was organized with the stated purpose of "inspiring landowners and tillers of the soil to cooperate in the use of scientific knowledge for the improvement of rural life." The administration was placed in the hands of a committee of seven faculty members, with the president of the University as chairman. Later a salaried director of field work was provided. The present director, Mr. Halim Najjar, is a Druze from the Lebanon, a former student and teacher at the American University of Beirut, who received his Master of Science degree in agriculture at the University of California. Being a native of the country, he has the confidence of the people and has worked wonders with them. Recent word from Beirut states that he has been appointed Minister of Agriculture for the Republic of Lebanon. As such he will probably have to give up his work with the Institute of Rural Life.

After experimenting with the formal training of agricultural teachers in Palestine and Lebanon, it became apparent that the problem of the improvement of rural life was too complex for such an approach. It was then decided to try a method which had been suggested by the efforts of a group of students and teachers from the American Junior College for Women at Beirut, who had begun volunteer work for women and children in a rural center. Accordingly the Institute of Rural Life, in the spring of 1933, organized students and faculty of the University in what was called the Village Welfare Service. A five-day training conference was held in June, after which small student groups went to southern

Lebanon and Palestine to explore the possibilities for student activity along lines of health, agriculture, home life and recreation. The Near East Foundation expert assisted and the Palestine Department of Education gave its cooperation. The students paid their own expenses.

The following summer the experiment was continued on a larger scale with about sixty volunteers participating. Three centers for work were established: one in the Acre district of north Palestine; one in the Sidon district of south Lebanon, and another in the Akkar district of north Lebanon. This last was in the form of a stationary camp—a home and training center for volunteers—which concentrated its work on three neighboring villages. The Sidon center limited its contact to one village and concentrated on health improvement. The Palestine center was a movable camp, with the volunteers moving from village to village, staying in each place as long as the situation demanded.

The summer's experience proved the first type—the stationary camp—to be the most effective method, and the others were subsequently abandoned. During the years, other camps have been established at the request of villagers and local governments until in 1939 there were four centers: the original camp at Jibrail, near Tripoli; the Boq'aa camp, near Shtaurah, in the great plain between the Lebanon and Anti-Lebanon ranges; a camp seven miles east of Damascus, and another on the outskirts of Aleppo, 250 miles north of Beirut. A new center was to have been established in the summer of 1940 at Liwa Ajlun by request of the Transjordan Government, but because of the war the project had to be suspended. There are now more than three hundred teachers and students who have shown their willingness to devote a considerable part of their summer vacations to this volunteer service. Except in rare instances the volunteers have paid all their own board and traveling expenses.

The work which has been accomplished at these camps is astounding. Here is the outline of a typical day at the Jibrail camp which serves the villages of Jibrail, Tikreet, and Dahr:

7:00 A.M. Breakfast

8:00–12:00 Village projects such as—

a) Health Survey in Jibrail (under a doctor and medical students from the medical school).

b) Clinic at the camp for peasants from neighboring villages.

c) Digging pit for latrine in Jibrail (remember these students have come from a class to which manual labor is considered degrading).

d) Classes for girls in Jibrail (conducted by University co-eds and Junior College students).

e) Meeting with Village Committee (elected by villagers to facilitate cooperation and make suggestions).

f) Preparing for athletic games in the afternoon. (Each volunteer takes part in the particular project to which he has been assigned, except those to whom special duties at the camp have been allotted.)

12:30 P.M. Lunch

1:30–2:30 Meeting to discuss distribution of duties for the coming day and to review the experiences of the morning.

4:00–6:00 Organized athletic games for boys from the villages. (Most peasants have never known what it is to play games.)

6:30 Supper

7:30 Night school volunteers go to Tikreet (to teach the villagers to read and write). Other students attend informal lecture by some member of the faculty. Sometimes games and stunts replace the lecture.

8:30 Free time until one feels like sleeping.

Each volunteer takes his turn at camp duties, such as waiting on table, keeping the camp tidy, carrying water from the spring, etc. Meals are prepared by a professional cook who has a woman to help in the kitchen and do the laundry for the group.

Involved in the activities of this camp were health projects (clinics), sanitary projects (lectures on public hygiene, removing rubbish, manure piles, and building sanitary latrines), athletics and recreation, agricultural projects (training in diversification of crops, planting fruit trees to replace mulberry trees), preserving fruits and vegetables (never before practised in the villages), survey of economic conditions with a view to improving markets and production, classes in home economics for women, a literacy campaign in Tikreet and numerous other activities.

One of the major engineering projects taken up was the cleaning, draining, protecting and beautifying of the great spring which supplies Jibrail with water. Villagers had been accustomed to water their stock there as well as secure their own drinking water. The land surrounding the spring was levelled off, drained, sanded, and fenced to keep out the animals. A concrete swimming pool was constructed nearby, the stone, sand, and labor being furnished by the village, the cement by the Village Welfare Service. The village of Jibrail thus has the foundation for a public park which will offer most unusual opportunities for recreation. An athletic field is being developed, on the principle that if village life is to be improved the young men must be interested. Their cooperation can best be gained through athletics.

At the camp in the Boq'aa, a permanent health center has been established, with nurses in residence throughout the year and a doctor from the University paying regular weekly visits. The expense of this work is borne jointly by the University and the Near East Foundation. Miss Hilda Hakim, the head nurse, lives at the camp throughout the year. Pupil nurses take turns staying with her and learning rural health work.

The nurses have an ancient Ford in which, early each day, they go down to the small village of Marj in the center of the plain. Every morning, summer and winter, they operate a health clinic in a rented room. Frequently they visit families and help young mothers learn how to care for their babies. During the summer they hold clinics in two other villages, Istubl and Maksah. (Istubl is the Arabic name from which the word "stable" is derived. Maksah is the place in which Mark Twain's *Innocents Abroad* spent their first night in the Lebanon.)

Work in the Boq'aa district was greatly complicated in 1939 by the influx of some 15,000 Armenians who moved out of the Sanjak of Alexandretta when it was turned over to Turkey by the French. Six thousand of them settled in the Boq'aa at Anjar, where a town was eventually erected with government help. Health conditions among the refugees were very bad and the increase in work was too great for the Marj Clinic to handle. With financial and medical help from the government, the Institute of Rural Life set up five new clinics at other villages on the plain, with two graduate nurses and a student nurse to work in them. A twenty-two bed hospital and clinic under the charge of one nurse and an assistant were established near the refugee camp at Anjar. On successive Sundays in October 1939, a dozen doctors, nurses, and medical students went out from the University medical school and vaccinated 5,800 refugees for typhoid, the vaccine being manufactured at the University pharmacy.

The success of the Village Welfare Service work during its first few years aroused great interest on the part of both government and people. Officials in the districts served were invariably enthusiastic, from the Administrator of the Boq'aa and the Agricultural Agent, down to the Mukhtars of the villages. As an example of government helpfulness, when it was shown by the volunteers that Marj and neighboring communities were suffering from a lack of good drinking water, their supply coming from an open canal used by cattle and washerwomen, the Administrator of the Boq'aa sent to Marj a boring machine which the volunteers had discovered at Shtaurah. Excellent artesian water was found at a depth of 60 meters and the village acquired a safe water source. The government then sent the machine to other villages and bored artesian wells for them.

In 1936 a group of the leading young people of Damascus formed a group to organize a camp near the village of Jidaydah. They asked the American University of Beirut to show them how the camp should be conducted. The Prime Minister of Syria gave a handsome donation toward the work. The government contributed two agricultural experts as well as a motor truck, a doctor with medical supplies and several teachers for adult education. Well-bred Damascus women made a practice of leaving their homes in the morning and driving out to the camp, where they would throw back their veils and spend the day teaching the children and helping the peasants.

It was particularly pleasing to have this happen in Damascus, for since the end of the war, Arab nationalism there had meant political intrigue or violent street demonstrations. Furthermore, religious antipathies had been bitter. In Jidaydah village, however, both the priest in the church and the Imam in the mosque exhorted the people at the Sunday and Friday services to trust the volunteers and to cooperate with them.

The example of Damascus was followed by a group of young people in Aleppo, far to the north. They established a camp at a village on the outskirts of Aleppo and invited the Village Welfare Service of the University to help them. The Syrian Government, highly impressed with the value of the work, allotted 3,000 Syrian pounds to be divided between the Aleppo and Damascus branches. An additional agronomist from Beirut was assigned to the Damascus area.

In 1939 a group of students was delegated by the Department of Education of Transjordan to get the training of the University camp in the Boq'aa with the idea of starting a similar camp in Transjordan. Mr. Najjar went to 'Amman to make the preliminary arrangements. On his way back to Beirut he discovered in Jerusalem a group of young Arabs laying plans to start a camp in Palestine. They were entirely independent of the University but they had heard of the work of the Village Welfare Service and wanted to extend it to their own area. As Mr. Najjar said later: "At this period of history, when destruction is being wrought upon human society, it is most heartening that some of us out here are thinking of such constructive work."[3]

The war forced the postponement of the Transjordan experiment and made it impossible to open any of the other camps in 1940 and 1941. But the spirit of service has not been suppressed. It will continue to thrive, and the eventual return of peace will give it richer opportunity for ever-wider expression.

3. AGRICULTURAL EXTENSION WORK

The camp activities of the student volunteers must necessarily be confined to the summer when they are free from their college duties. This seasonal aspect of the movement was felt to be a weakness and the Institute of Rural Life has striven to overcome it. The Near East Foundation agricultural expert, Mr. Najjar, has been made director of the Village Welfare Service, and throughout the

[3] International College Annual Report (1939-40), p. 11.

year he gives continuity to its efforts by his agricultural extension work throughout the country. Not only does he visit the farmers in the villages and issue simple instruction pamphlets in Arabic for their use, but he periodically gives short courses at the University which the farmers are invited to attend free of charge. The January (1940) course, devoted to fruit growing, was attended by more than eighty farmers from Lebanon and Syria who devoted six days to the study. Included in the group were one woman, an ex-minister of finance, four sheikhs and five priests. Forty-five villages were represented. Mr. Najjar gave twenty-five lectures, most of them illustrated by motion pictures, slides, photographs and diagrams.

In March of 1940 the annual course on bee-keeping was offered to an enrollment of fifty-one bee-keepers. The first conference in 1937 was attended by only twenty. As a result of the third year's course, five members were chosen to apply to the government for the right to form a bee-keeping syndicate which would promote interest in bee-keeping, protect the sale of honey by checking adulteration, and gain release from the import duty on sugar used for feeding. It is estimated that there are between 40,000 and 60,000 old style hives in Syria and Lebanon and about 1,000 modern hives which yield 750-1000 per cent more honey. Gradual substitution of new for old will come as a result of the classes given by the Institute of Rural Life, and a considerable augmentation of farm income will be obtained.

Attendance at the farmers' courses has grown steadily as their value has become known and considerable public interest has been aroused. An Arabic daily, *Al-Nahar,* speaks of the Village Welfare Service as "the Mecca of farmers." And in reference to the fact that a rich sheikh from Damascus sat next to a priest from a monastery, and both were surrounded by peasants throughout the course, *Al-Nahar* exclaims: "This was a beautiful sight. The soil has united what religions have separated. . . . The rich farmer sat next to the poor fellah. Soil is indeed the basis of democracy. It is great, this service of the Institute!" The writer ends: "The American University is earnestly delivering an important message to the Arab farmer in Lebanon and elsewhere. Do we not believe that it is our duty to share this responsibility? Or should we always be dependent upon others, and let the University do its work, while we, government and people, stand by as spectators?"

Mr. Najjar has written twenty-two pamphlets, of which more than 20,000 copies have been distributed to the farmers. Concerning the value of the pamphlets, the Director of Agriculture of Transjordan was moved to express himself thus: "This is the first useful thing done to the agriculture of this region. Those who have used this subject before have not used your practical method. The reading of your circulars is economy and its application is wealth. Kindly send us six numbers of each circular so that the agricultural agents of Transjordania may benefit."

In addition to the type of work described, the Institute of Rural Life has acted to improve livestock in the country by lending its prize Jersey bull to several villages. It has sought to increase egg production by distributing White Leghorn chickens (bought in 1939 from Bulgaria). In one village, Abadiyah, a marketing cooperative was started, and in 1939 total sales were increased 350 per cent over the previous year, with the number of members increasing from twenty to forty-five. The cooperative now regularly markets milk in Beirut, a new enterprise bringing new income to the farmer members. Mr. Najjar has been working with officials of the Syrian Government to develop legislation facilitating the further establishment of credit cooperatives among the peasant farmers.

4. THE CIVIC WELFARE LEAGUE

Since the development of the Village Welfare Service, the students of the American University have turned their attention to matters other than village welfare. The Village Welfare Service is now but one of four sections of the Civic Welfare League of the University, the other departments being the City Welfare Service, The Relief Committee, and the Finance Committee. The Relief Committee, the newest branch, adopted two Palestinian orphans, supervised the inoculation of refugees and Beirut school children, and contributed more than 100 Syrian pounds for the aid of sufferers in the terrible Turkish earthquake of the winter of 1939-40.

At a period when students in Beirut were terribly hard pressed for funds because of depreciation of currency and the added cost of travel in war time, it was deeply moving to see their self-sacrificing interest in a catastrophe which occurred in another country a thousand miles to the north.

The City Welfare Service, with its interest centered close at hand in the town of Beirut itself, can carry on its work throughout the school year. Its work is organized under separate committees, concerned with public health, a night school and volunteer teaching service, social, medical and educational work with the Al-Sour basket boys (hamals or porters). The Night School committee recently broadened its activities to take in fourteen other schools in the city where the same type of work is carried on. Much of this work is now being done in conjunction with groups from the Ecole Protestante, American Junior College, the British Syrian Training School and the American Mission. The influence of the City Welfare Service has begun to spread beyond the walls of the University.

The financing of all this extensive social service work is not a simple problem even though a large part of the work is done by volunteers. Consequently one section of the Civic Welfare League devotes itself to finance. A regular budget is worked out and a campaign for funds is carried on from November to April. With benefit cinemas, dances, plays, garden parties, miscellaneous canvasses, collection boxes, and finally in March, a great tag day, the students collect as much money as they can. The budget revised in February 1940 called for an expenditure of 2,100 Syrian pounds, exactly three times the sum estimated the previous fall. It was by far the largest budget ever proposed by the League, but it reflected the increased responsibility which the students felt in the war situation, as well as the greater need for their efforts. In spite of their own impoverished state, the volunteers had raised over twelve hundred pounds by February 1, 1940. This did not count a gift of $100 from an Arab group in Boston, nor did it include the funds provided from America by the Near East Foundation, which takes care of the permanent field work and pays the salaries of the permanent staff. The money was raised entirely among the students and teachers of the University.[4]

Twenty-one hundred Syrian pounds (the total budget) is approximately one thousand dollars. That is real money for students to raise even on a campus of comparable size in America. It is almost a fantastic amount when one considers the financial condition of the majority of the students at Beirut, many of whom have great difficulty in meeting their regular college expenses. The success of the finance committee's work is an evidence of the sincerity with which the students face the task which they have undertaken.

The influence of the Civic Welfare League is constantly growing. Members of the City Welfare, after gaining experience in the Beirut work, have started similar efforts in their home communities. Village Welfare workers, unable to serve in the regular camps, have undertaken to promote new work in untouched fields. In the summer of 1939, for example, courses in reading and writing were given by students working on their own initiative to more than five hundred people of the Plain of Sharon in Palestine.

Although the war made it necessary to curtail much of the field work of the Civic Welfare League in 1940-41, it not only continued its local activities but expanded them. In cooperation with the Beirut Y.W.C.A. and other organizations, additional educational and medical work was done in various parts of the city. The City Welfare Service opened new work with the numerous unemployed class developed as a result of war conditions. The students investigated worthy cases and raised funds with which to employ them in building a new athletic field adjoining the present stadium. The spirit of social service at Beirut declines to be daunted by the shadow of a world at war.

[4] No reports have been received about the budget for 1940-41. It must inevitably be smaller than that of the previous year, though substantial contributions have been made by other Arab groups in America.

XVIII. INTERNATIONALISM

I. COOPERATION FROM GOVERNMENTS

Reference has several times been made to the cordial relations which have existed between the University and the governments of states with which the institution has had contacts. Some of the more striking instances of this friendliness, however, have not been mentioned and deserve further notice.

Since the French mandate was established, the mandatory authorities have never attempted to force any regulations upon the University. They have exempted its imports of supplies from customs duties, its faculty from income taxes on salaries, the campus itself from land and other taxes, with very few minor exceptions.

Until very recently the University authorities have been permitted to select as teachers for the French sections desirable young Frenchmen who have come to Beirut and there enlisted in the colonial army for the purpose of fulfilling their requirements for military service. The French High Commissioner has then kindly permitted them to teach at the University in lieu of military service, their military instruction being condensed into the summer months.

Professional teachers from France who serve on the faculty at Beirut are granted by the French Ministry of Public Instruction the same credit toward promotion as they would receive were they teaching in an official French school in France itself. Similarly, faculty members of the University have been invited to assist in managing the French baccalauréat examinations and have been given equal authority with teachers in official French schools. In every way possible the government has accorded official recognition to the status of instruction at the University. The Haut Commissariat has regularly appointed a jury to examine graduates of the professional schools of the University for license to practice.

During the summer of 1940, when travel conditions in the Near East were greatly complicated by unusual restrictions imposed because of the war, it became apparent that unless these restrictions were eased it would be impossible for students to attend the University in the fall. Here indeed was a situation in which any lack of confidence in the institution would inevitably come to the surface. When, however, certificates of eligibility for admission were sent to prospective students by the University, these were in every case honored by the governments of Lebanon, Syria, Palestine, Transjordan, 'Iraq and Egypt, which granted not only police permits for leaving the country but visas for Lebanon as well. As a result, instead of the marked decrease in attendance which had been expected, a marked increase actually occurred. In May 1941 President Dodge reported an enrollment of 1,992 students, whereas the enrollment for the preceding year had totalled but 1,847. It is understandable that Dr. Dodge should write: "We were very much touched by the extreme kindness of the authorities, especially by the exceedingly generous spirit of the French officials at Beirut."[1]

For many years it has been the practice of the governments of the Near East to send to the University picked students whose expenses are borne by the State. The number has varied from year to year, with some states dropping out for a period (as in the case of Ethiopia) and others taking their places. Thus in 1928 there were fifty bursary students, from six countries. In 1936 there were thirty-seven bursaries from five countries. Three years later, in 1939, there were sixty-three bursaries, representing six countries, but three of the six were different from those of 1928. In 1940-41 a total of one hundred nine students was supported by seven governments. 'Iraq has always led in the number of bursaries granted, with 27 in 1928, 24 in 1936 and 77 in 1940. Yet nearly every year the 'Iraq Government has requested a larger number of graduates for government positions than the University can supply. It is apparent that there is no lack of appreciation of the value of an education at the American University of Beirut.

It is not alone the governments nearby with which the University has enjoyed friendly cooperation. In 1940 a bursary student was sent by the government of 'Oman all the way from that isolated country on the Persian Gulf coast of Arabia—the first boy,

[1] Personal letter, November 26, 1940.

incidentally, who has been known to leave that country to receive a higher education. The Ministry of Education of Iran has for several years supported a teacher of Persian in International College, and various consular representatives in Beirut have taught the languages of their homelands.

In reciprocal fashion the University has offered its facilities to foreign governments for the training of their consular representatives in the Arabic language. Especially pleasant relations of this sort have been enjoyed with the British Consular Service, which, by the end of the academic year 1938-39, had sent some thirteen probationer vice-consuls to the University. The appreciation of the British Foreign Service for this assistance was expressed in an interesting letter to Dean Brown from the British Consul General at Beirut:

"*Dear Professor Brown:*

I have just been informed by the Foreign Office that three Probationer Vice Consuls attached to my staff who were examined last December at the conclusion of their first year's Arabic studies have all passed with credit.

In expressing his satisfaction at the continued high level of proficiency which is achieved by successive years of Probationers here, Viscount Halifax directs me to transmit to yourself his thanks for the continued cooperation of the American University of Beirut to this end. It gives me much pleasure to forward His Lordship's message, for I am fully aware of the great debt we owe to you and to all those of your professors who take part in their instruction.

Yours sincerely,

(signed) G. T. HAVARD"

Other evidences of the esteem in which the University is held have come in the form of honors bestowed upon the administration and faculty members. Several of the latter have been decorated by the governments of various states and several have received personal messages of appreciation from the rulers of countries which have been aided by the research or advice of these men. President Dodge himself was, in 1927, given the Order of Merit of the Lebanese Republic and a few months later in that year was made Chevalier de la Légion d'Honneur by the official representative of the government of France, the High Commissioner. "In offering this high honour to President Dodge," said M. de Reffye at the presentation ceremony, "the French Government desires not only to honour the man himself but also to show that far from fearing American rivalry and competition in this country . . . France is happy to show its esteem for the work accomplished by the American University of Beirut, from which it has learned to expect efficient collaboration for the greatest good of Syria and Lebanon."[2]

Ten years later the Syrian Government bestowed upon President Dodge the Ordre de la Merite Syrien, and in the same year (1937) he was made Grand Officier de l'Ordre Royal du Phénix by the Greek Government.

University representatives have been asked to assist in many of the important activities and developments in Near Eastern states. For example Mr. Stewart, Treasurer of the University, was asked in 1936 to serve as an active member of the Beirut Municipal Council. Dr. Ingholt was asked for technical assistance to the Departments of Antiquities of both Turkey and Syria. President Dodge was appointed by the League of Nations in 1936 as one of its two members on the three-man Trustee Board for the Settlement of Assyrians of 'Iraq, a board which has done a remarkable work in the repatriation of nearly 9,000 Assyrians in the Jazirah district of Syria.[3] The League appointed Professor Walter H. Ritsher as alternate for President Dodge in case of the latter's absence from the country.

Such examples might be multiplied, but they are sufficient to show not only the way in which the University plays an active part in what might be called the extra-curricular life of the Near East, but also how well known and thoroughly appreciated is this service in Europe as well as in the Levant.

2. INTERNATIONAL ATHLETICS

Ever since the inauguration of competitive athletics in the Syrian Protestant College, games have played an important part in the

[2] Al-Kulliyah, XIII, 8:214 (June 1927).

[3] President Dodge has described the Settlement of the Assyrians in a detailed statement published as Special Article No. 10 by the Near East Service (Near East College Association).

building up of a wholesome student life. Association football has been the major sport at Beirut, with field hockey, track and field events, swimming, tennis and basketball all attracting considerable student devotion. American football is not played, for it is not adapted to the rocky soil of the campus and would require the importation of expensive equipment. Baseball has never been popular, perhaps because the specialized throwing skill was not developed early enough. Recently, however, soft-ball has gained in popularity.

Since the régime of Mr. Smurthwaite (1910-14) emphasis has been increasingly placed by successive physical directors on the development of sportsmanship through competitive athletics. The completion early in 1928 of the magnificent stadium between the campus and the sea[4] gave impetus to interscholastic competition and at the same time relieved other facilities for the use of an intensive intramural program. Now almost every able-bodied student in the University or International College takes part in some form of supervised athletics, with the outstanding performers being chosen for the Varsity teams.

After having a succession of competent American physical directors, the work was in 1934 put under the guidance of a graduate of the University, Abd-us-Sattar Tarabulsi, who had been for several years assistant to preceding directors. Mr. Tarabulsi, no mean athlete himself, also attended the Summer Coaching School at the University of Michigan.

To Americans the idea of competitive games is far from being unusual, but at an institution like the American University of Beirut the situation is definitely extraordinary. The unusual thing about the athletics there is not that they are so markedly successful, but that they can exist at all. Teamwork, cooperation, sportsmanship, have not in the past distinguished the singular individuality of the Near Eastern character, even when it was limited to one nation or one religious group. At the University these qualities must be developed in a mixture of nearly fifty nationalities and

[4] This stadium, donated by Mr. V. Everit Macy, had in large part to be blasted from the solid rock. One end is not fifty yards from the Mediterranean. It is one of the most beautifully situated athletic fields in the world.

thirty religious sects, many of which have not been noted for their friendly relations.

The writer will never forget an experience he had when serving as one of the two American instructors who accompanied a group of eighty students from Beirut to Cairo in April 1930. It was an invasion of Egypt, with its object the subjugation of the Egyptian National University in football, basketball, hockey, tennis and track. The invasion was timed to coincide with spring vacation and some of the team members were to be picked up en route, since they had gone home a short while before making the trip.

It was a motley crowd which boarded the single day coach reserved for their use. Had the car been stood on end it might have passed for the Tower of Babel. Arabic, English, Hebrew and French were the principal tongues audible and others were present. Space was at a premium and the aisle became an elongated bed as the extended trip wore on.

Moving south from Haifa one worry was on everyone's mind: "Will Cohen make the train?" Cohen was the star right wing who lived in Tel Aviv some distance from the line. He might miss the connection or his parents might not let him go. So when the train pulled into the junction, the tension was considerable. But Cohen was there and the shout which went up must have startled the good citizens of Lydda. He was lifted on shoulders and passed through the window of the train, his bag following. Joy was unconfined, for now the American University of Beirut might beat the Egyptians.

At that time Arab-Jewish feeling ran high (it burst into flame three months later) but to the Arab students Cohen was not a Jew—he was a team member from the American University and they liked him and needed him. Shortly before the train reached Kantara East, he was to be seen lying in the aisle with his head on the lap of a Moslem sheikh (another student) and sharing a sandwich with a Druze staffite.

All the Varsity teams are international in composition, but they are famous for their fine team work. Consider the line-up of the 1938-39 champion football team:

Sharabi (Captain)	Palestinian	Sleem	South American
Sheik el Ard	Syrian	Braggiotti	Cypriot
Abou Khadra	Palestinian	Katraghrasi	Syrian
Manougian	Armenian	Nahara	Lebanese
Muja'is	Lebanese	Barameda	Syrian
Alsagoff	Singapore	Antippas	Greek
Dirhalli	Palestinian		

On other teams have been Persians, Egyptians, 'Iraqi, Russians, Tranjordanians, Americans, even one boy from Bahrein. The fact that members of such a cosmopolitan group can work together and learn to depend on one another is a matter of no small significance to the world today.

For many years teams from the University have visited neighboring countries to play against school and club teams there. The trip to Egypt in 1930 was the most ambitious project to be undertaken up to that date, but it was so successful that it has been followed by numerous return visits as well as trips to Palestine, Transjordan, Cyprus and, in 1939, to Greece. The travelling teams have not only been international themselves but they have been, over a wide area, emissaries of international good will of whom the University can be justly proud.

3. ALUMNI

Some indication has previously been given of the important part which graduates of the University have had to play in the development of the Near East. The international distribution of alumni has not, however, been sufficiently stressed, for the figures are surprising. It is unfortunate that because of the war more recent statistics are not available, but those of 1934 provide an insight into the area of influence which, through its graduates, the University has acquired.

In 1934 the General Secretary of the Alumni Association, Mr. Shehadi, listed the distribution of verified living graduates as follows:

Beirut	486	Cyprus	13
Lebanon	202	Greece	13
Syria	150	England	14
Egypt	322	North America	160
Sudan	42	South America	39
'Iraq	110	Miscellaneous	50
Palestine and Transjordan	402		
Persia	28	*Total*	2,031

Under the miscellaneous heading were the following:

Algeria	India
Arabia	Jugoslavia
Asia Minor	Morocco
Australia	Philippine Islands
Belgium	Rumania
China	Russia
Ethiopia	Scotland
France	Senegal
Germany	Turkey
Gold Coast	

Of the miscellaneous list France led with seven graduates and the Philippines were next with six.

This record included only graduates who had been in communication with the Alumni Secretary, who admitted "that possibly there are several, if not many, mistakes and omissions . . . , for many of our graduates . . . do not send us their new addresses when they move . . . and a large number have not been heard from for many years."[5] At that time the total number of graduates since 1860 was listed as 2,724 and of them 374 were known to have died. Thus in the lists above, some 319 men were not accounted for. No account at all was taken of former students who did not graduate.

These lists did not include the 224 alumnae from the School of Nursing and Midwifery and 43 women from the other branches of the University. Their distribution might not have increased the number of countries in which graduates were represented but they would have swelled the total in several of them.

The alumni who are scattered over the world have maintained their interest in the University and in many cases have organized

[5] Alumni Bulletin (Al-Kulliyah), XX, 3:69 (February 1, 1934).

branches of the Alumni Association to strengthen their ties and to aid their alma mater. Into these branches they have drawn many of their compatriots who never attended the University but who have been so devoted to it that they have given considerable time and money to its welfare. It is estimated that alumni and their associates have made pledges and contributions to the University in money and gifts to the libraries to a value exceeding $200,000.

As listed in 1934 there were active branches of the Alumni Association in the following cities:

Cities	Country	Cities	Country
Beirut Zahleh Sidon Tripoli	Lebanon	Alexandria Cairo Mansourah	Egypt
Hama Homs Aleppo Damascus	Syria	Sao Paulo Rio de Janeiro	Brazil
Haifa Jaffa Jerusalem Nazareth Tul-Karm	Palestine	New York Chicago Detroit Boston Buffalo Youngstown Cleveland Pittsburgh Los Angeles San Francisco Sacramento	U.S.A.
Baghdad Mosul	'Iraq		
Khartoum	Sudan		

Since 1934 most of the branches in the United States have become inactive, but two have been added in Transjordan (Amman and Es-Salt) and one in Palestine (Nablus). The present Secretary of the Alumni Association, Khattar Akl, has his office on the campus at Beirut. The official representative of the alumni in the United States is Professor Philip Hitti of Princeton University, who has done much to organize the branches in both North and South America.

The active interest which alumni in so many lands preserve toward the American University of Beirut is a tribute to the fundamental quality of its influence. Truly international in its aims, its students, its faculty, its alumni, it merits the devotion of those sons and daughters who echo from the corners of the earth the song of their Alma Mater:

"From the islands of the ocean,
From the banks so green
Of the great Egyptian river,
Or from Palestine;
From the waters of Abana,
Pharpar Damascene,
We salute thee, Alma Mater,
Oriental Queen.

"Hail to thee! our Alma Mater
We would ever be
Worthy sons—Oh make us faithful,
Faithful e'er to thee!
Wheresoe'er the land that calls us,
E'en across the sea,
We'll salute thee, Alma Mater
Hail, oh Hail! to Thee."[6]

[6] These are the last two verses of the song, which is sung to the tune of the Cornell "Alma Mater." The words were composed by Dr. Henry Noble MacCracken, President of Vassar College, when he was a staffite at Beirut from 1900-03.

XIX. THE LIFE OF THE SPIRIT

I. RELIGIOUS PRINCIPLES

IN HIS INAUGURAL ADDRESS, delivered on June 28, 1923, President Dodge provided an excellent guide to an understanding of the view which the institution takes of its spiritual responsibilities. "We think of education," he said, "as training in every phase of life, and we shall strive to turn out a well-balanced type of manhood. Our University motto is: 'Ut vitam habeant et abundantius habeant,' and we glory in life:—life of the body, life of the mind, and that life which is set aflame by God.

"To develop the spiritual natures of our students," continued Mr. Dodge, "we do not propose to proselytise or to emphasize names and forms. To us Protestantism means religious freedom, and as a Protestant institution we wish to give our students freedom of worship and freedom of belief.

"We feel that religion is not an ulterior aim of education; it is not a quantity of tangible facts to be taught, or a creed to be subscribed to:—it is something much more fundamental; it is the consciousness of a spiritual power, controlling life and seeking good. Religion is not for the chapel alone, but can be found in the spirit of honest study, good sportsmanship, and consecration to the welfare of mankind. It must be learned in every phase of the university life.

"It is for the mosque, synagogue, or church, to provide the practical formalities of organized religion, but the school should join with them in fostering a consciousness of God, and a desire to live in accordance with God's moral purposes. Other influences usually determine membership in one sect or another, but education forms the inward motive to avoid evil and seek the good.

"The University does not have the negative aim of tearing her students from the formal affiliations and ceremonies of the ancient East, but rather the positive aim of sharing with them the spiritual experience of the growing West. The institution forms a link between East and West; a channel for the exchange of ideas between the two. Our University does not champion the cause of any one sect, but she does bind on her armour to champion the cause of the spiritual; of working with God. We wish every student to be religious.

"Men and women of all types of belief are to be found on our teaching and administrative staff. It is not the function of our institution to carry on a campaign in behalf of any one creed or intellectual belief, but rather to unite men of varied points of view, and help them to keep alive a vital faith in God, in the midst of the developments of this changing, modern world. Everywhere, today, the rising generations of men and women are drinking in the facts of modern science with an unquenchable thirst. The readjustment between new theories and old traditions is working havoc. Skepticism, agnosticism, and blank despair are let loose in the world.

"Our University must have no share in tearing down the intellectual structures of the past, so as to leave ruin in their place. It should be our part to respect the great historic dogmas of mankind, and to interpret them to the youth of our day in a language which they can understand, that they may know that God is still in His heaven, and that we still live and move and have our being with Him. It is not our part to destroy but to fulfill.

"We long to teach our students to regard the ideals of their parents with sympathy; to honor all who are charged with the official duties of their sects; to respect the motives for their ceremonies and rites; and to revere places of long-accustomed worship. At the same time we strive to vitalize it all in the light of our modern life, that religion may become something practical to the youth of our times; a real force in the regeneration of the human soul, and in the reconstruction of our war-ridden world.

"Religion seems to be a consciousness of God; a life of the spirit, manifesting itself in the conduct of each day, and it is when we wish to make this fact intelligible to our students that we hold before them an ideal personality, whose actions were so supremely guided by submission to the divine will and whose sacrifice blazed forth as a beacon to mankind. God forbid that our University should carry on a new crusade in eastern lands, but we do long to make every student as loving, as pure, and as unselfish as Jesus was. The solution of problems of race hatred and sectarian strife must be brotherly love. The way of attaining social decency and honest business is by pure conduct. The only answer to the world-wide question of poverty and wealth is unselfishness. How supremely this love, purity, and self-sacrifice are needed by our students, if they are to play their part in this Twentieth Century.

"At such a time as this strong men and strong women are needed to take their places at the front. Men and women, who are ready to pay the price and give their best; who are willing to live or die that good may triumph and that all may love each other more. The hopes of the world are in great lives freely given; sacrificed for humanity and for God.

"As I am called upon to represent the American University of Beirut, I pledge myself and my colleagues, to do our utmost to raise up students who will hear this call and answer with their lives."[1]

2. REGULAR RELIGIOUS SERVICES

Until 1915 all students of the Syrian Protestant College were required to attend daily chapel. In that year a change in the system was of necessity brought about, and ever since then the University has continued to practise the revised plan. All students must daily attend one of two morning services:—the definitely religious service held in the chapel or the "alternative exercises" of a non-religious character, held at the same time. Attendance at alternative exercises has never been large and in recent years it has become relatively infinitesimal. During 1938-39 there were but thirteen men, approximately one-half of one percent of the entire student body, who elected to attend them, and ironically enough the thirteen were the most vigorously anti-Jewish Moslems and anti-Arab Jews on the campus. One may imagine that they regretted their decision to avoid regular chapel.

The shadow of world events has fallen heavily upon the student body in the past few years with a resultant deepening of interest in religious matters. President Dodge reported recently in a letter

[1] Al-Kulliyah, IX, 8:128-30 (June 1923).

that so many students have elected to attend the daily chapel that it has been necessary to add fifty seats in the corners and aisles of the building. Since the autumn of 1938 attendance at a special Sunday evening service held in the West Hall auditorium, has been required for all English speaking students of International College and that meeting is regularly filled to capacity. It is an inspiring experience to hear these boys of many races and creeds join powerfully in singing the grand hymns of the Church. The music in daily chapel is greatly helped by the organ playing of Professor Kouguell and it is perhaps typical of the universal character of these Christian services that the music is thus led by a Russian Jew.

Each Sunday morning a regular church service is held in the chapel, but attendance at this is voluntary. Christian students are encouraged to attend the Sunday services of their own churches in the city just as they are on special holy days. But even the voluntary Sunday service is always well attended.

The celebration of holy days of the numerous religious sects cannot, of course, be recognized on the college calendar because it would bring about a vacation nearly every other day. Students are, however, excused from classes on good evidence of their attendance at special religious celebrations. During Ramadan, when Moslems are not supposed to take food between sunrise and sunset, special privileges are extended to Moslem students so that they may observe the fast—but they must regularly attend classes. President Dodge reported in 1938 that "for some reason few Muslim students enjoy Mosque services. On Muhammedan feast days the Arabian students attend (college) prayers wearing their Arab costumes."[2]

A spirit of great tolerance toward the religious observances of other groups has always marked the student body of the University. Some years ago, for example, at the celebration of the Prophet's birthday by the Moslem Society, the Greek Orthodox students, then the dominant religious group on the campus, played a surprise rôle. Quite unexpectedly, toward the close of the program, a Greek Orthodox leader mounted the rostrum and presented to the Mos-

[2] International College Annual Report (1937-38), p. 21.

lem Society a beautifully ornamented copy of the Koran together with a flag of green silk on which appeared, side by side, the Cross and the Crescent. The impression made on the student body was profound.

3. SPECIAL SERVICES

From early days it has been the custom at the University to hold each winter a series of special religious meetings to deepen the spiritual consciousness of the students and give them an opportunity to hear the Christian message delivered by men from outside the faculty. These meetings have been purely voluntary in attendance but they have nearly always filled the West Hall auditorium to capacity.

In recent years the leaders at these effective services have been such men as Dr. Henry Sloane Coffin (1935), Dr. John R. Mott (1937), Professor J. Seelye Bixler of Harvard Theological Seminary (1938), Dr. S. Ralph Harlow of Smith College (1939), Wilbert P. Smith, General Secretary of the Cairo Y.M.C.A. (1940), and the Reverend Alford Carleton, president of Aleppo College (1941). During the visits of these men, students have been given an opportunity for personal interviews with them to discuss the problems which are causing them concern. On the rare occasions when outside speakers have not been available, as was the case in 1936, members of the faculty have conducted the meetings.

In 1930 Dr. Daud A. Himadi of Ridgewood, New Jersey, a Pharmacy graduate in the class of 1897, promised to the University a gift of $250 to etablish a series of lectures to be given by leaders from different religious sects. In a letter written in 1932, Dr. Himadi, who was himself a Druze, explained that his purpose in making the gift was to advance the University as the epitome of a truly non-sectarian institution and "to reduce upon its platform the complex fractions of religious differences into one common denominator—the conception of one God, one creation, and the precepts of the Golden Rule. . . . The world," continued Dr. Himadi, "has schools and colleges galore for the study of science and arts in all their branches, but we have yet to build the institutions which inculcate the desired ideals which make for international peace and proper moral conduct. May the American University of Beirut become a brighter beacon unto the world in fulfilment of those objects which you have often proclaimed."[3]

The first series of the Himadi Lectures was given in April 1931 by Professor Irwin Edman of the Columbia University department of Philosophy, whose three fine addresses served as a general introduction to the later subjects of the Lectureships. Apparently the students were not the only ones to be impressed by the experience, for Dr. Edman himself devoted a chapter to his Beirut adventure in his delightful book "Philosopher's Holiday." He was particularly surprised to discover how completely he could feel at home with such a cosmopolitan student body, whose personal problems of adjustment proved nearly identical in pattern to those of American students of similar scholastic level.

The second Himadi lecturer was Sheikh Mustapha Abdul-Razik, Professor of Islamic Theology in the Egyptian National University at Cairo. Professor Abdul-Razik devoted two of his three lectures to "Religion as Seen by Islam" and "The Attitude and Meaning of Islam," while his first address was an analysis of the attitude of modern science toward religion and its origin. An exceedingly picturesque speaker in his flowing robes and turban, Professor Abdul-Razik proved the value of the Lectureship in the spirit of sympathy and friendliness between Christians and Moslems which he aroused.

The lecturer in 1933 was His Beatitude, Mar Ignatius Ifram I, Patriarch of the Syriac Orthodox Church, who gave in Arabic an analysis of the various branches of the Eastern Church. He was followed in 1934 by 'Arif Bey Al-Nakadi, one of the outstanding Druzes of Syria, who spoke on the Druzes. This distinguished speaker was a member of the Arab Academy of Learning, in Damascus, and Director of the Dawudiyyah School in 'Abeih.

Each of the lecturers in the short series made such a real contribution to the spiritual life of the campus that even though the Lectureships could not be longer continued, they proved themselves of great value to the University community. It is to be re-

[3] Al-Kulliyah, XIX, 1:17 (November 1932). Mr. Himadi hoped to endow the lectureship but the Depression prevented his doing so.

gretted that such a program could not have become a permanent part of the religious experience at Beirut.

4. THEOLOGICAL TRAINING

In 1891 the Theological Seminary was removed from the campus, and although it was later reestablished in Beirut as the Presbyterian Mission's School for Religious Workers, the relations between it and the Syrian Protestant College never became particularly close, though they were always cordial. In October of 1932, however, a union was brought about between the American Board's School of Religion, at that time conducted at Athens, Greece, and the Presbyterian School at Beirut. The resulting institution was called the Near East School of Theology, and a close connection with the University was immediately established. Arrangements were made whereby students of the School of Theology might, through a five year course, obtain the B.A. degree at the same time that they received their theological diplomas. Three of the full-time professors of the School were listed as lecturers on the faculty of Arts and Sciences of the University and their courses were granted academic credit by the University as electives.[4] During the year 1933-34 fifteen students took advantage of the joint course.

At the end of the first year of cooperation President Dodge reported on the excellent results which were already apparent. "This plan," he wrote, "has brought a very constructive element to the campus. In the past the Protestant pastors have not been university trained as a general rule. Hereafter it is hoped that the University students will gain a new respect for the ministry as a profession, and that the clergymen of the future will understand how to deal with men and women who are well educated."[5]

The experience with the Near East School of Theology was so successful that in 1938 a plan of cooperation was worked out between the University, the School of Theology, The American School of Oriental Research in Jerusalem and the Young Men's

[4] The three professors were William Gaius Greenslade, Principal of the School, Lutfi Levonian and George Michaelides, all outstanding men.

[5] Annual Report (1932-33), p. 16.

Christian Association in Jerusalem, whereby picked theological students from America might spend a year of study in the Holy Land without loss of credit and with very great advantage to their understanding of the Bible. It was proposed that such students might spend part of their year in Jerusalem, where they could attend the sessions of the American School of Oriental Research, and part in Beirut, where they could work both at the American University and the Near East School of Theology. The incidence of the war prevented the carrying out of this plan but it is open for development when travel again becomes possible.

In 1934 the Greek Orthodox Church planned the establishment of a theological school at Beirut for the entire Diocese of Antioch, probably the oldest branch of the entire Christian Church. In order to provide a much-needed secular education for the student priests, the Archbishop of Beirut asked the cooperation of the University. He asked for the reduction of tuition charges for a group of young priests who would spend part of their time in college classes and part in the seminary. This was at once agreed to, for here was a great challenge to the University to aid in the regeneration of the most ancient and influential church of the Near East, which for generations had suffered from lack of education in the priesthood.

The experiment began slowly with but two of the boys enrolled in the French School. In succeeding years the numbers increased and before long some fifteen boys were being sent as full-time boarding pupils whose room and board were paid by the Church. They became students of International College when that institution moved to Beirut, and the group of monks is now a familiar sight on the campus. "These boys," writes President Dodge, "have long black robes, round black caps and unshorn hair. They are . . . dedicated to the service of the Church, eligible for promotion to the higher clergy. As only a few other monks are being educated, it is inevitable that they will be given places of responsibility. The other boys do not make fun of their strange clothes, but respect them and realize how important they may become in the future."[6] The long hair proves something of a handicap in athletics, but the

[6] Annual Report, International College (1936-37), p. 10.

young priests do not permit it to interfere with participation therein. In every way these future leaders of the church of Silas, Barnabas, John Mark and Paul are regular members of the student body.

5. BROTHERHOOD

During the Great War all student organizations had to suspend their activities, and the very successful student Young Men's Christian Association was one of the first to be disbanded. Immediately after the Armistice, however, another religious body was set up, under the name of the West Hall Brotherhood. This society had as its stated purpose "to unite students and teachers of all religions in a religious brotherhood based on mutual respect and sympathy; to advance their spiritual welfare, to develop cooperation, and to promote social service; and all this without prejudice to the religious affiliations of any member."[7] As a motto typifying the attitude of the membership, the Brotherhood proposed the significant sentence: "The realm in which we share is vastly greater than that in which we differ." It is a motto which has shown its ability to breathe new life into the Near East.

The Brotherhood has from the beginning been concerned with the creative possibilities of religious interest, and from small beginnings with social service work its scope has constantly expanded until it has developed into and merged with the city and village welfare work of the Institute of Rural Life, whose startling influence has previously been described. The aim of the Brotherhood, like that of the University, has constantly been to give vitality to religion through opportunity for practical expression. The theoretical and intellectual development of it can safely be left to the increasingly popular courses in philosophy, the classes in religion and the regular religious exercises of the University.

Only through works, indeed, can a spiritual renaissance be effected in the Near East. It is a land where all too frequently religious formalism has been a tool for political intrigue, a cloak for personal aggrandizement, an excuse for racial fanaticism. Far too often the once living spirit of religious truth has slipped away from the empty shell of sectarian ritual, devotion to which but

[7] Quoted in Al-Kulliyah, X, 7:106 (May 1924).

seldom reaches the heart. Such empty dogmatism cannot be revitalized by added words or new doctrines. It must be suffused with a spirituality expressed in deeds, dramatized by unselfish service.

There is an urgent need for vitality in the spiritual life of the Near East, for within the past twenty years it has faced extinction. The new techniques of the West pouring in upon a mediaeval culture have torn great holes in that placid fabric. Upon the upper classes the conflict between science and religion has broken with a violence far greater than that of the slower adjustment which took place in the West. The result has been a tendency toward radical unbelief, cynicism, materialism and loss of moral stability. When even the peasants can suddenly hear the voices of the West cachinnating over loud speakers in the market place, the strain of adjustment to a new world becomes yet more intense.

President Dodge tells of seeing on the platform of a tramcar in Beirut an old Moslem trying to say his prayers. Hardly would he get himself faced toward Mecca when the tram would round a corner and the poor man would have to rearrange himself. In a very short time he was completely bewildered and looked piteously at his fellow passengers as if for aid which they could not give. He typifies the difficulty which Moslem tradition has had to face in an incredibly changing world.

Leaders of Moslem thought are realizing the dangers in the situation, and welcome what aid a western institution can give. In 1937 a young teacher from International College, himself a Moslem, visited Mecca where he was royally received by the King, the Crown Prince, the Vizier and notables from Mecca, Medinah, Jiddah and Taif. He had an opportunity to talk at length with the leading sheikh of Sa'udi Arabia, and frankly asked him whether or not there were objections to having sons of pious Moslems from Arabia go off to a Christian college at Beirut. The old man answered him: "Kena'an Effendi, if the American University will give these boys the strength of character which it is known to give, and will save them from the materialism and unbelief which is playing havoc in many so-called Christian lands today, we will call its name blessed. There is no objection to sending the boys if the University can thus strengthen our hands."

The reappearance of war has brought new strains into the framework of life erected in the past two decades. So-called Christian powers have been shown again to have feet of clay, though fortunately this time the issues of the war are perhaps more clearly understood in the Near East than they have been before. The Arab countries feel the pressure of events with deadly earnestness. At such a time, when students' minds are serious with the vision of dangers and hardships ahead, the University has an opportunity for moral influence which one can only pray may not be shattered. Faith is fostered by such a statement as that recently made by one of the Arab teachers: "The forces of evil are at work in the world, but they are fighting for transient things. We are toiling to establish the eternal things, and we shall prevail. The University is not in its buildings and equipment. It is in the spirit that we carry within our own being. This no man can destroy. And if we are driven from here, it is only to carry that spirit to ever-widening circles, to keep the flickering torch lighted in the midst of darkness, treachery and barbarism."[8]

President Dodge has voiced a feeling of equal optimism in a recent letter in which he described conditions at Beirut in the winter of 1940-41: "The fine spirit which exists among the teachers and students of many nationalities on our campus is such a contrast to the hostility in other places, that it makes one realize what a tremendous force for good an educational institution can be. It is encouraging to know that good-will and faith in spiritual things can live and even increase, regardless of what is going on in other parts of the world."

They can increase at Beirut because, in the American University, devotion to the things of the spirit is a fundamental part of the college life, given permanence through the experience of brotherhood and the practice of inter-racial, inter-religious, international cooperation. These are not subjects of conversation only;—they receive living expression in the activities of daily life on the campus.

[8] Quoted in Annual Report (1939-40), p. 23.

On the commencement platform a group of men and women, new graduates of the seventy-five year old University, stand ready to enter what to many a college graduate may seem an uncertain future. But with a fervor arising from an experience which few students in other lands have been privileged to live through, they sing with determination in their hearts:

These things shall be,—a loftier race
Than e'er the world hath known shall rise,
With flame of freedom in their souls,
And light of Knowledge in their eyes.

Nation with nation, land with land,
Unarmed shall live as comrades free;
In every heart and brain shall throb
The pulse of one fraternity.

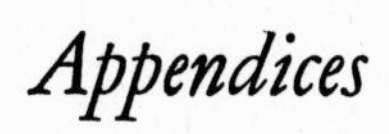

Appendices

APPENDIX A

CERTIFICATE OF INCORPORATION (CHARTER) OF THE SYRIAN PROTESTANT COLLEGE

We, the undersigned, William A. Booth, William E. Dodge, David Hoadley, and Simeon B. Chittenden, being citizens of the State of New York—and Abner Kingman and Joseph S. Ropes, being citizens of the State of Massachusetts—all being of full age and citizens of the United States of America, desirous of associating ourselves for benevolent, charitable, literary, scientific, and missionary purposes, in order to become a body politic and corporate in pursuance of the provisions of the Act of Legislature of the State of New York, entitled "An Act for the Incorporation of Benevolent, Charitable, Scientific, and Missionary Societies," passed April 12, 1848, and the Acts amendatory thereof, do hereby certify as follows:—

First—That the name or title by which said Society, hereby intended to be incorporated, shall be known in law, shall be, "The Trustees of the Syrian Protestant College."

Second—The particular business of said Society shall be to raise a fund for the purpose hereafter mentioned; to make, from time to time, such investments and reinvestments thereof as may seem to be most judicious; to collect and receive the income thereof, and apply the same and such portions of the principal fund, from time to time, as may be deemed necessary or expedient in establishing and maintaining, or assisting to establish or maintain, in Syria, or other adjacent countries, a college or other educational institution, which shall be self-governing and founded and conducted upon strictly Christian and Evangelical principles, but not sectarian.

The objects of the said Society shall be to aid the natives of Syria and other countries speaking the Arabic language, in obtaining in such college or educational institution a literary, scientific, or professional education.

Third—The number of the Trustees of said Society to manage the same, shall be six, four of whom shall be citizens of the State of New York.

Fourth—The names of the Trustees of said Society for the first year of its existence shall be William A. Booth, William E. Dodge, David Hoadley, and S. B. Chittenden, of the City of New York in the State of New York; and Abner Kingman and Joseph S. Ropes, of the City of Boston and State of Massachusetts.

Fifth—The business of said Society shall be conducted in the City and County of New York.

IN WITNESS WHEREOF, we have hereunto subscribed our names, at the City of New York, this fourteenth day of April, in the year of our Lord one thousand eight hundred and sixty-three.

(Signed)

William A. Booth
William E. Dodge
David Hoadley
S. B. Chittenden
Abner Kingman
Joseph S. Ropes

Boston, April 18th, 1863.

Acknowledged and signed before Mr. Frederic Bull, Notary Public for the State of New York, April 14, 1863.

By the Boston Trustees in the city of Boston, Suffolk County, Massachusetts, before Mr. Charles B. F. Adams, Commissioner for the State of New York, April 18th, 1863.

Certified and signed at the Office of the Secretary of State, Albany, New York, on the 24th of April 1863.

(Signed)
J. Wesley Smith
Deputy Secretary of State

(Signed)
Horatio Seymour,
Governor

(Signed)
Horatio Ballard,
Secretary of State

(Endorsed) I consent to and approve of the filing of this certificate, New York, April 22nd, 1863.

(Signed)
George G. Barnard
(Justice of the Supreme Court
First Judicial District)

Filed April 27th, 1863
Certified by

Henry W. Genet
Clerk of City and County of New York

This 4th day of May 1863

APPENDIX B

("Chapter 579")

An Act authorizing "The Trustees of the Syrian Protestant College," and "The Trustees of Robert College, of Constantinople," to take and hold real and personal estate.

(Passed May 4, 1864)

The people of the State of New York, represented in Senate and Assembly, do enact as follows:

Section 1. "The Trustees of the Syrian Protestant College," and "The Trustees of Robert College, of Constantinople," Societies incorporated under the General Act, entitled "An Act for the Incorporation of Benevolent, Charitable, Scientific, and Missionary Societies," passed April 12, 1848, shall, by their corporate names, respectively, be capable of taking and receiving by gift, purchase, devise, or bequest, subject to existing laws and of holding real and personal estate for the purposes of their incorporation, and for no other purpose, notwithstanding the value thereof, and the clear annual income thereof, may exceed the amounts specified in the second section of said General Act.

Section 2. This act shall take effect immediately.

APPENDIX C

PREAMBLE

Whereas, It is deemed essential for the promotion of Protestant Missions and Christian civilization in Syria to establish an institution where native youth may obtain in their own country and language, a literary and scientific education; and

Whereas, The said institution, with the title "The Syrian Protestant College" has been incorporated under the laws of the State of New York, in the United States of America; and

Whereas, It is the distinct purpose of the founders of this College to have it conducted on principles, strictly Protestant and evangelical, but not sectarian or such as to exclude students of any sect or nationality who will conform to its laws; designing also so to identify the College with the interests of the people, as to make it thoroughly indigenous, and entertaining the hope that, in the course of years the instruction of the institution may be wholly committed to competent evangelical natives; and

Whereas, Beirut or its vicinity is deemed the most eligible location for the College, both from the growing population and commercial importance of that city, and also from its central position in respect to the millions who speak the Arabic language throughout the East, and who, it is hoped, will ultimately be reached by influences flowing from this institution;

THEREFORE, For the general organization and management of "The Syrian Protestant College" there have been adopted the following

Constitution and By-Laws

APPENDIX D

BOARD OF MANAGERS

In accordance with the foregoing articles, the following gentlemen were constituted the "The Board of Managers of the Syrian Protestant College":

Reverend Daniel Bliss, D.D., President of the College, and ex-officio, President of the Board of Managers

George J. Eldridge, Esq., H.B.M. Consul General J. Augustus Johnson, Esq., U.S. Consul Reverend W. M. Thomson, D.D. Reverend C. V. A. Van Dyck, M.D. W. H. Whitehead, Esq. James Black, Esq. Henry Heald, Esq. Reverend Henry Harris Jessup	BEIRUT
E. T. Rogers, Esq., H.B.M. Consul Reverend S. Robson Reverend J. Crawford	DAMASCUS
Reverend J. E. Ford Reverend Wm. W. Eddy	SIDON
Noel Temple Moore, Esq., H.B.M. Consul	JERUSALEM
Reverend R. J. Dodds	LADAKIYEH
Reverend G. Brown	ALEPPO
Reverend S. H. Calhoun J. G. Scott, Esq. Reverend Wm. Bird	LEBANON
Reverend G. Lansing, Cairo Reverend John Hogg, Alexandria	EGYPT

APPENDIX E

UNIVERSITY OF THE STATE OF NEW YORK

Amendment to Charter of Syrian Protestant College

Having received a petition, made in conformity to law, and being satisfied that public interests will be promoted by such action, the Regents, by virtue of the authority conferred on them, hereby amend the Charter of the Syrian Protestant College by changing the number of Trustees from six to twelve.

IN WITNESS WHEREOF, the Regents grant this amendment to Charter, No. 1,783, under the seal of the University, at the Capitol in Albany, June 28th, 1906.

(Signed)
St. Clair McKelway
Vice-Chancellor

(Seal) (Signed)
A. S. Draper,
Commissioner of Education

Recorded and took effect, 4 P.M., June 28, 1906.

APPENDIX F

THE UNIVERSITY OF THE STATE OF NEW YORK

Amendment to Charter of the Syrian Protestant College

THIS INSTRUMENT WITNESSETH That the Regents of the University of the State of New York have amended the charter of the Syrian Protestant College, which was incorporated by a certificate executed on the 14th and 18th days of April 1863, and filed in the office of the Secretary of the State of New York, by changing the corporate name of said college to American University of Beirut and by making and enlarging its educational powers to be both college and university in character and scope, and to comprehend sanctioning, subject in all things to the rules, requirements and restrictions of the said Regents of the University, the establishing and maintaining of under-graduate and graduate college departments, professional, technical, vocational and other departments; the designation of any departments of the University as schools and with appropriate distinguishing names; the placing of any such departments under special directing management, auxiliary and subordinate to that of the University trustees; the affiliation with other approved organizations in educational work within the jurisdiction of the University; the conferring of suitable degrees, which or whose symbols are then registered by the Regents, upon duly qualified graduates from courses of instruction given by or under its supervision and directing control; the awarding of attesting certificates for meritorious educational work done under such supervision and control; and the giving or supervising of elementary and secondary instruction, preparatory for or in connection with higher grades of its educational work.

Granted November 18, 1920, by the Regents of the University of the State of New York, executed under their seal and recorded in their office. Number 2932.

(Seal) (Signed)
Pliny T. Sexton
Chancellor

(Signed)
John H. Finley
President of the University

APPENDIX G

THE UNIVERSITY OF THE STATE OF NEW YORK

Amendment to Charter of American University of Beirut

THIS INSTRUMENT WITNESSETH That the Regents of the University of the State of New York have amended the charter of American University of Beirut,—which was incorporated under the name of the Trustees of the Syrian Protestant College by a certificate of incorporation executed on the 14th and 18th days of April, 1863, and filed in the office of the Secretary of State of New York, which certificate of incorporation was amended by action of the Regents taken at their meeting on June 28, 1906, increasing the number of trustees from six to twelve, and again amended by the Regents on November 18, 1920, by changing the corporate name of said college to American University of Beirut and by making and enlarging its educational powers to be both college and university in character and scope,—by increasing the number of trustees of the corporation from twelve to fifteen, so that paragraph "Third" of such certificate of incorporation as amended will read as follows:

"*Third*: The number of the Trustees of said Society to manage the same, shall be fifteen, four of whom shall be citizens of the State of New York."

Granted May 16, 1941, by the Regents of the University of the State of New York executed under their seal and recorded in their office. Number 4754.

(Seal) (Signed)
Thomas J. Mangan
Chancellor

(Signed)
Ernest E. Cole
President of the University
and
Commissioner of Education

APPENDIX H

III *TREATY*

Clauses taken from the *Convention between the United States and France* (Treaty Series No. 695), signed at Paris, April 4, 1924, proclaimed August 13, 1924.

Article 6.—The Mandatory shall establish in Syria and the Lebanon a judicial system which shall assure to natives as well as to foreigners a complete guarantee of their rights. . . .

Article 8.—The Mandatory shall ensure to all complete freedom of conscience and the free exercise of all forms of worship which are consonant with public order and morality. No discrimination of any kind shall be made between the inhabitants of Syria and the Lebanon on the ground of differences of race, religion or language.

The Mandatory shall encourage public instruction, which shall be given through the medium of the native languages in use in the territory of Syria and the Lebanon.

The right of each community to maintain its own schools for the instruction and education of its own members in its own language, while conforming to such educational requirements of a general nature as the administration may impose, shall not be denied or impaired.

Article 10. The supervision exercised by the Mandatory over the religious missions in Syria and the Lebanon shall be limited to the maintenance of public order and good government; the activities of these religious missions shall in no way be restricted, nor shall their members be subjected to any restrictive measures on the ground of nationality provided that their activities are confined to the domain of religion.

The religious missions may also concern themselves with education and relief, subject to the general right of regulation and control by the Mandatory or of the local government, in regard to education, public instruction and charitable relief.

APPENDIX I

Agreement between Mr. Myron T. Herrick, Ambassador Extraordinary and Plenipotentiary of the United States of America to France,

and the President of the French Republic, M. Raymond Poincaré, Senator, President of the Council, Minister of Foreign Affairs.

Article 1.

Subject to the provisions of the present convention the United States consents to the administration by the French Republic, pursuant to the aforesaid mandate, of Syria and the Lebanon.

Article 2.

The United States and its nationals shall have and enjoy all the rights and benefits secured under the terms of the mandate to members of the League of Nations and their nationals, notwithstanding the fact that the United States is not a member of the League of Nations.

Article 3.

Vested American property rights in the mandated territory shall be respected and in no way impaired.

Article 5.

Subject to the provisions of any local laws for the maintenance of public order and public morals, the nationals of the United States will be permitted freely to establish and maintain educational, philanthropic and religious institutions in the mandated territory, to receive voluntary applicants and to teach in the *English language.*

Article 6.

Nothing contained in the present convention shall be affected by any modification which may be made in the terms of the mandate as recited above unless such modification shall have been assented to by the United States.

APPENDIX J

FOREIGN FACULTY AND STAFF—AMERICAN UNIVERSITY OF BEIRUT

NAME	GRADUATED FROM	YEARS AT BEIRUT
Acheson, Barclay	Macalester	1912-1914
Adams, Frederick H.	Wesleyan	1925-1927
Adams, Philip D.	Penn. State	1925-1927
Adams, Walter B.*	New York University	1890-1928
Agne, Royal C.	Heidelberg	1912-1915
Alexander, Charles	University of Pennsylvania	1930-1933
Allen, Dorothy	—	1919-1921
Allen, Sherman A.	Boston Tech.	1903-1906
Anderson, Joan	—	1928-1930
Anderson, Paul R.	Ohio Wesleyan	1928-1930
Anderson, Samuel M.	Nebraska	1903-1910
Appleton, H. S.	Harvard	1919-1920
Armstrong, James N.	Princeton	1920-1923
Atwood, John	—	1925-1926
Aubrey, Banquier M.	University of Michigan	1931-1933

NAME	GRADUATED FROM	YEARS AT BEIRUT
Avery, Bennett F.	University of Michigan	1926-1941
Avery, Margaret S.	University of Michigan	1926-1927
Bacon, Arthur A.	Dartmouth	1919-1940
Barnes, Edward*	Lafayette	1904-1906
Barnes, Elsa	—	1920-1922
Barr, Edgar E.	Catawba	1938-1941
Barraud, Eugene	—	1912-1913
Barrows, A. E.	Hastings	1901-1904
Bastress, Alfred W.	Penn. State	1922-1925
Bauwens, Doris	Dunbury	1930-1931
Baylor, Curtis H.	Emory, Johns Hopkins	1938-
Beal, K. Malcom	Dartmouth	1928-1931
Beall, Clarence	West Virginia	1909-1910
Beattie, Robert H.	Princeton	1885-1889
Beck, Edwin A.	Wooster	1900-1903
Belgrave, Richard	Cambridge	1934-1935
Benedict, Miriam	Boston	1926-1927
Bianquis, Philippe	Sorbonne	1924-
Billman, A. M.	Franklin and Marshall	1912-1915
Biros, Marc C.	France	1925-1930
Bisbee, George A.	Carnegie Tech.	1920-1921
Bixler, James	Miami	1926-1928
Bixler, J. Seelye	Amherst	1920-1922
Black, Robert	Dartmouth, Columbia	1935-1937
Blake, Kingsley	Yale	1931-1934
Blatchford, C. Hammond	Yale	1925-1928
Blish, Eleanor	Wisconsin	1929-1933
Blish, Zirian	Wisconsin	1930-1932
Bliss, Alice	Presbyterian Hospital	1920-1921
Bliss, Charles	Washington, D.C.	1891-1895
Bliss, Daniel*	Amherst	1864-1916
Bliss, Daniel	Amherst	1920-1923
Bliss, Frederick J.	Amherst	1880-1883
Bliss, Howard S.*	Amherst	1902-1920
Bliss, Virginia	Mt. Holyoke	1924-1929
Boardman, Eugene	Beloit	1932-1935
Boardman, Francis, Jr.	Williams	1938-1941
Boettiger, L. A.	Lawrence	1914-1917
Boettner, Marie A.	—	1933-1936
Booth, Maynard W.	Toronto	1924-1926

NAME	GRADUATED FROM	YEARS AT BEIRUT
Bowman, Harold L.	Coe	1910-1913
Boyle, Elizabeth	—	1915-1918
Brade, Lorna	Oxford	1934-
Breed, Eleanor	Pomona	1932-1934
Brigstocke, Richard W.	England	1872-1882
Bristol, W. E.	Vermont	1907-1910
Brouard, Perry deF.	Carleton	1927-1930
Brown, Julius A.	Dartmouth	1909-
Brown, J. B.	Princeton	1901-1903
Brown, N. I.	University of Dublin	1913-1914
Buchanan, J. R.	Edinburgh	1910-1914
Bucher, J. C.	Princeton	1890-1894
Buck, Norman S.	Yale	1913-1916
Bunker, P. R.	Oberlin	1920-1923
Burns, Norman	Yale	1929-1932
Burrows, Millar	Brown	1930-1932
Burrows, Robert B.	Emory, Yale	1937-1940
Burtnett, Ida	Hunter	1913-1915 1925-1931
Butler, C. C.	Oberlin	1913-1916
Byerly, Robert C.	Franklin and Marshall	1907-1910
Caillet, Lucie	—	1913-1914
Cain, W. C.	Albion	1920-1921
Calhoun, William	—	1874-1875
Camp, Jessie	—	1915-1918
Campbell, Charles S.	Yale	1938-1940
Campbell, Douglass	Oberlin	1930-1933
Campbell, Margaret	—	1916-1918
Cardwell, Viola E.	Syracuse, Toronto	1938-1941
Carhart, Charles L.	Yale	1910-1912
Carruthers, A. D.	Trinity, Cambridge	1904-1905
Chamorel, A.	France	1890-1896
Charbonnier, H. C.	France	1899-1908
Chase, Roland	Lafayette	1922-1923
Church, W. Randolph	Amherst	1926-1929
Clawson, Donald	Washington University (St. Louis)	1930-1934
Close, Harold W.	Princeton	1910-
Condé, Marlette	Columbia	1936-1937
Copeland, Paul W.	Whitman	1920-1921

NAME	GRADUATED FROM	YEARS AT BEIRUT
Corcoran, Dorothy	Smith	1931-1933
Corley, Douglas H.	Harvard	1919-1922
Cornud, André	France	1924-1933
Cox, Luther B.	South Carolina	1935-1937
Crane, Joshua B.	Brown	1876-1879
Crawford, Archie S.	Beloit	1921-
Crawford, J. Forrest	Wisconsin	1923-1927
Crawford, J. Stuart*	Westminster	1903-1939
Creighton, Roy L.	—	1928-1930
Crosby, Richard	Dartmouth	1937-1940
Cruikshank, W. Douglas	Toronto	1919-1938
Crump, Lela	Michigan	1931-1933
Cumin, René	France	1910-1911
Dale, Mary Bliss	—	1904-1923
Daleen, Irene O.	Chicago	1938-
Dana, C. A.	Montana	1907-1910
Daniels, Antoinette	Radcliffe, Yale	1933-1935
Davison, W. S.	Princeton	1906-1909
Dawe, Howard	Wittenberg	1930-1938
Day, Alfred Ely*	Illinois College	1889-1930
Day, Henry	American Univ. of Beirut	1927-1928
Dean, Prentice N.	Princeton	1920-1923
DeForest, David M.	Union and California	1930-1935
De Goumois, Marcel M.	France	1911-1912
Delaporte, René	France	1909-1910
Dennett, Daniel C.	Harvard	1931-1934
Dennis, Emery W.	Oklahoma City and California	1931-
Dennis, George H.	—	1920-1921
Derby, Margaret	—	1927-1931
Deuel, Wallace R.	Illinois	1926-1929
Deuth, Albert	Milwaukee	1935-1938
Deuth, Esther	Slayton	1936-1940
Deyo, A. L.	Williams	1908-1911
Dickerman, Watson B.	Dartmouth	1929-1932
Dight, Charles F.	Michigan	1883-1889
Distin, Hazel B.	Hartford Hospital	1923-1925
Dodd, Stuart C.	Princeton	1927-
Dodge, Bayard	Princeton, Union Theol. Semy.	1913-
Dodge, D. Stuart	Yale	1864-1873

NAME	GRADUATED FROM	YEARS AT BEIRUT
Domer, William	Ohio Wesleyan	1926-1927
Dorman, Harry G.	Harvard	1903-1941
Dorman, Harry G., Jr.	Harvard	1927-1930
Dow, Albert J.	Boston	1923-1925
Dray, Ada	—	1924-1926
Dray, Arthur*	Pennsylvania	1911-1926
Dray, Bertha	—	1927-1930
Drew, Marjory	—	1930-1932
DuBois, Philip A.	Union	1925-1928
Duffield, G. B.	Princeton	1904-1906
Dugan, Raymond S.	Amherst	1899-1902
Dulles, Nataline	Bryn Mawr	1921-1922
Dumontet, Georges	U. of Paris, Grenoble	1929-1939
Duncan, C. L.	Leland Stanford	1907-1910
Dunn, Alexander	Princeton, Union Theol. Semy.	1903-1904
Eddy, Ruth	—	1920-1921
Eddy, W. W.	Princeton	1911-1913
Edwards, Allen D.	Kalamazoo	1928-1931
Elam, Daniel	Whitman	1931-1933
Enzen, Edmond	France	1921-1925
Erdman, Frederick S.	Princeton	1924-1925
Erdman, Paul	Princeton	1894-1897
Ewald, Rose	—	1928-1930
Ewing, Thomas D.	Princeton	1921-1924
Fagerstrom, D. P.	Coe	1911-1914
Faust, Vincent B.	Franklin and Marshall	1925-1927
Favre, Marcel	France	1912-
Felton, Ralph A.	Southwestern	1907-1910
Fielding, Una	—	1928-1929
Finney, William P., Jr.	Princeton	1908-1911
Fisher, E. M.	Coe	1914-1917
Fisher, John C.	Princeton, L.I. Medical	1884-1889
Flater, E. Marjorie	Presbyterian Hospital	1939-1940
Fleming, James P.	St. Bonaventure	1937-1938
Foot, Harry W.	Denison	1926-1929
Forbes, William H.	Harvard	1923-1924
Fowler, A. B.	Princeton	1907-1910
Fowler, William	Glasgow	1936-

NAME	GRADUATED FROM	YEARS AT BEIRUT
Fox, C. L.	Princeton	1904-1907
Fox, Edward E.	Philadelphia Dental	1925-1930
Francis, Robert C.	Harvard	1923-1924
Fraser, John	Scotland	1869-1871
Fraser, Philip H.	Princeton	1899-1901
Fredericks, Mildred	—	1920-1921
Freidinger, William A.	Maryville	1908-1910
Frisbie, Charlotte	Hartford	1930-1932
Fuller, Millard	Oberlin	1920-1922
Furniss, Edgar S.	Coe	1911-1914
Galbraith, Margaret	Brandon, Manitoba	1932-1938
Gardner, O. F.	Princeton	1902-1904
Gidney, James B.	Dartmouth, Columbia	1938-1939
Gifford, B. S.	Ripon	1909-1912
Gilchrist, Alan	London	1935-1936
Gilmore, R. C.	Rochester	1920-1921
Giroux, Louis F.	Hamilton	1884-1887
Gleason, Mary L.	Smith	1937-1938
Glockler, Edwin	S.P.C.	1904-1908
Glover, Samuel P.	Pennsylvania	1885-1887
Goodale, Raymond H.	Wesleyan, Harvard	1926-1929
Goodhue, Joseph	Springfield	1902-1905
Graham, Ella T. (Mrs. Harris)	—	1922-1925
Graham, George F.	Whitman	1928-1932 1940-
Graham, Harris*	Michigan	1889-1922
Greene, Walter F.	Amherst	1914-1919
Greenslade, W. Gaius	Whitman	1933-
Greiner, Otto A.	Lafayette	1904-1907
Griffith, Andrus O.	Illinois	1923-1926
Guerne, Marius	France	1912-1914
Haege, Olive G.	Kansas, Columbia	1938-1941
Hall, David	Harvard	1920-1922
Hall, Harry H.	Union	1926-1929
Hall, Harvey P.	Union	1930-1933
Hall, Isaac	—	1875-1876
Hall, William H.*	Union	1896-1927
Hampel, Chester W.	Harvard	1936-

NAME	GRADUATED FROM	YEARS AT BEIRUT
Hanke, Lewis U.	Northwestern	1927-1930
Hannaford, H. D.	Wittenberg	1910-1913
Harris, Stanley E.	Princeton	1925-1929
Hartzler, John E.	Goshen, Hartford Theol. Semy.	1931-1932
Havens, Henry C.	Princeton	1892-1895
Helming, Vernon P.	Carleton	1925-1928
Hickman, Isaiah	—	1922-1926
Hinkhouse, Frederick J.	Parsons	1919-1921
Hinshaw, Horton	California	1928-1931
Hodgeman, Gertrude	—	1919-1920
Hoffman, W. S.	Penn. State	1913-1916
Holck, Harald G. O.	Copenhagen	1929-1934
Holmes, Lawrence	Wesleyan	1932-1935
Homma, Karl G.	Vienna	1932-1936
Hoskins, Franklin E.	Princeton	1883-1886
Houghton, C. Hubley	Harvard	1929-1931
Hudson, Ellis H.	James Milliken	1911-1914 1923-1924
Hudson, G. Donald	James Milliken	1926-1929
Hulbert, H. W.	Union Theol. Semy.	1885-1887
Hulbert, Kathryn	Connecticut	1921-1923
Hulbert, W. H.	Dartmouth	1919-1922
Hume, Willis F.	Oberlin, Harvard	1939-
Hurt, Arthur E.	Northwestern	1920-1921
Hutchinson, C. A.	Rochester	1920-1923
Hutton, John A.	Oxford	1934-1935
Hyde, Frederick S.	Amherst	1888-1891
Imer, Oscar	Lausanne	1901-1906
Ingholt, Harald	Copenhagen, Princeton	1931-1938
Ireland, Philip W.	Wesleyan	1925-1928
Irwin, Harry N.	Wooster	1905-1913
Jaeggi, Louis	—	1909-1912
Jessup, Anna	Elmira	1917-1922
Jessup, Frederick N.	Princeton	1897-1900
Jessup, Helen	—	1920-1921
Jessup, James S.	Amer. Univ. of Beirut	1935-1938
Jessup, Stuart D.	Yale	1899-1902
Jessup, Stuart D., Jr.	Yale	1925-1926

NAME	GRADUATED FROM	YEARS AT BEIRUT
Johnson, Robert L.	Amherst	1939-1941
Joy, Alfred H.	Oberlin	1904-1916
Kahrl, George M.	Wesleyan	1926-1928
Kappers, C. U. Ariens	Leyden	1929-1930
Kay, Thomas W.	Baltimore Medical School	1883-1888
Kerr, Stanley E.	Pennsylvania	1925-
Keye, William F.	Fargo	1913-1915
Kirk, Margaret	—	1930-1933
Klein, William C.	Princeton	1925-1928
Klutz, Lex W.	Davidson	1920-1923
Knepper, Frederick T.	Princeton	1922-1925
Knight, George	Cornell	1931-1933
Knox, John	Davidson	1930-1932
Knudsen, John	—	1925-1929
Kochenderfer, C. C.	Maryville	1907-1908
Krayer, Otto	Berlin	1934-1937
Krischner, D. Harald*	Graz	1928-1932
Krohn, Volmer	Stockholm	1898-1902
LaBrie, Annie	—	1908-1909
Ladd, Carolyn	Mt. Holyoke	1932-1938
Lair, H. P.	Southeastern	1909-1912
Laird, Edith M.	Queens College (Ontario)	1926-
Landon, Flora R.	Mary Fletcher Hospital	1923-1926
Lanphear, B. W.	Clark	1910-1911
Lazarre, S.	France	1919-1920
Leader, Ruth Anne	Columbia	1936-1940
Leary, Lewis G.	Rutgers	1900-1903
Leary, Lewis G., Jr.	Vermont	1928-1931
Leavitt, Leslie W.	Dartmouth	1916-1919 1928-
Leavitt, Russell W.	Dartmouth	1916-1919
Lebard, Raymond	France	1938-
LeClair, Charles R.	Pennsylvania	1936-1940
Ledgerwood, Wyatt W.	Parsons	1926-1929
Lee, Benton M.	Missouri	1924-1925
Leitzman, Jewel	Illinois, Chicago	1931-1932
Leslie, Amy Marion	—	1921-1922
Leuallen, Elliot E.	Philadelphia	1935-1937
Levonian, Lutfi	Woodbrooke (England)	1933-

NAME	GRADUATED FROM	YEARS AT BEIRUT
Lewis, Edwin R.	Harvard	1870-1882
Lewis, Walter S.	—	1879-1880
Linn, John G.	Hamilton, Columbia	1939-1941
Little, C. Roy	Carthage	1910-1913
Little, Theodora S.	—	1923-1924
Little, Mrs. Thomas	—	1913-1914
Loomis, C. W.	Amherst	1919-1920
Lukens, John N.	Princeton	1925-1927
Lund, E. Everett	California	1932-1937
Lyman, Katharine	Mt. Holyoke	1932-1936 1938-
MacCracken, Henry Noble	New York University	1900-1903
MacFarland, William E.	Acadia, Yale	1936-
MacFarlane, Andrew	Pennsylvania	1884-1885
MacGregor, Donald A.	Wisconsin	1924-1925
MacInnis, Florence B.	Deaconess Hospital (Boston)	1926-1929
MacIntosh, Elizabeth	—	1896-1908
MacNeal, C. S.	Lafayette	1919-1922
Maier, G. W. M.	Princeton	1902-1904
Malmstrom, Hilja I.	Radcliffe	1938-
Manchester, Edward W.	Wesleyan	1927-1930
March, Elisabeth	Wooster	1909-1913
Marsh, Elias	Harvard	1936-1937
Martin, W. W.	Union Theol. Semy.	1883-1885
Mayer, Edmund	Berlin	1936-
Maynard, Harrison A.	Washburn, Union	1937-
McBurney, Helen	—	1921-1924
McCall, William A.	—	1927-1928
McCann, E. C.	Wooster	1912-1915
McDougall, Winifred	Roosevelt Hospital	1931-1932
McGibeny, D. H.	Hamilton	1914-1915
McGrath, Sterling	Carleton	1934-1935
McKee, Paul H.	Wooster	1923-1925
McKennon, George E. (Miss)	Boston	1930-1934 1935-1938
McKown, Paul	Princeton	1920-1923
McLean, E. D.	Hamilton	1914-1915
Metzler, Sara A.	Mass. General Hospital	1922-1926
Michaelides, George	Columbia, Union Theol. Sem.	1933-1937
Micks, Henry W.	Union	1920-1922

NAME	GRADUATED FROM	YEARS AT BEIRUT
Miller, Geneva E.	Baker, Kansas, Western Reserve	1938-
Miller, George H.	Wooster	1910-1913 1932-
Miller, Lucius H.	Princeton	1899-1902
Miller, R. Stewart	Glasgow	1934-
Miner, Estelle	Roosevelt Hospital	1908-1914
Mitchell, Arthur	Yale	1894-1896
Mitchell, J. M.*	—	1898-1899
Moore, Franklin T.*	Princeton	1891-1915
Moore, J. Leonard	Princeton	1927-
Moore, S. C.	Wooster	1901-1904
Morgan, Harrison P.	Yale	1931-1934
Morris, R. P.	Cornell	1920-1921
Mossman, A. H.	Amherst	1920-1922
Moullet, Jules	France	1909-1912
Muard, Elie	Paris	1913-1914
Muller, Edouard	France	1906-1911
Muller, Robert	France	1908-1909
Munro, Donald	Harvard	1905-1910
Munson, J. P.	Oberlin	1913-1916
Murray, Cecil H.	—	1905-1906
Myers, Rena	Presbyterian Hospital	1936-
Napp, J. E.	Kalamazoo	1908-1911
Neal, Robert J.	Michigan	1883-1884
Nelson, Harold H.	Chicago	1904-1927
Nelson, W. S.	Amherst	1884-1885
Neumann, Kathryn M.	—	1923-1924
Nicely, J. W.	Princeton	1893-1903
Nicholls, Elsie	—	1919-1920
Nickoley, Edward F.*	Illinois	1900-1937
Nickoley, Emma R.	Illinois	1919-1925
Nickoley, Kathryn	Wells	1932-1937
Nurse, Frank L.	Chicago, McCormick Sem.	1906-1907
Nute, William	Yale	1917-1918
Oldfather, C. H.	Hanover	1912-1914
Oliver, Kenneth	Johns Hopkins	1928-
Omwake, R. H.	Princeton	1901-1904
Oppenheimer, Albert	—	1934-

NAME	GRADUATED FROM	YEARS AT BEIRUT
Osborne, Alice E.	N.Y. Post Graduate	1913-1916 1920-1923 1926-1929 1932-1939
Osborne, Ella	—	1920-1929
Ostrander, Marion Y.	Simmons	1926-1927
Packard, Frank E.	Amherst	1881-1884
Palmer, Sibyl	Wellesley	1929-1931
Parkhill, Elliott D.	Lenox, McCormick Sem.	1911-1914
Parr, Leland W.	Chicago	1923-1930
Patch, James A.	Boston Tech.	1900-1921
Patch, Ralph D.	Amherst	1927-1930
Paton, Lanice	Cornell	1907-1910
Pauly, Rudolph J.	Whitman	1920-1923 1927-
Pellegrin, Jean	—	1926-1929
Pellowe, Albert E.	Albion	1919-1921
Penningroth, Paul	Iowa	1928-1930
Penrose, Stephen B. L., Jr.	Whitman	1928-1931
Pernot, René	France	1925-1934
Perret, William	France	1921-1922
Perrine, Charles	Berea	1919-1921
Perrot, Léon	Paris	1938-
Perry, Harriet E.	Hahnemann Hospital	1921-1923
Peterson, Freda Al	Wisconsin	1939-1940
Pfeiffer, Timothy A.	Princeton	1939-1941
Pinkston, James O.	Harvard	1937-
Piper, Kenneth B.	Columbia	1920-1923
Plain, William B.	—	1925-1926
Pletcher, N. M.	Illinois	1901-1904
Plimpton, Fred F.	Harvard	1938-1941
Porter, Ellen L.	Michigan	1925-1927
Porter, Harvey*	Amherst	1870-1923
Post, George E.*	New York University	1869-1909
Potts, Francis M.	Illinois	1922-1925
Pulver, Jean A.	Neuchâtel	1922-1924
Ravenhill, Emily	—	1924-1927 1929-
Rea, William	Princeton	1934-1935

NAME	GRADUATED FROM	YEARS AT BEIRUT
Reed, Cass A.	Pomona, Union, Harvard	1934-1935
Reed, Robert B.	Princeton	1906-1918
Rhynbergen, Hendrika	Simmons	1929-1934
Riggs, Ernest W.	Princeton	1916-1918
Ritsher, Walter H.*	Beloit	1921-1924 1927-1939
Roberts, J. R.	Coe	1914-1917
Robinson, George L.	Princeton	1887-1890
Rogers, Ralph H.	Yale	1919-1921
Romig, E. F.	Franklin and Marshall	1913-1916
Rountree, Dorothy	—	1927-1930
Rouse, Mary W.	Smith	1920-1923
Rouse, Winifred	Smith	1921-1924
Rugh, A. Douglass	Oberlin	1931-1934
Russell, Harry K.	Virginia	1924-1927
St. John, Ancel	Rochester	1906-1909
Saunders, Gladys	Acadia	1934-1937
Saunders, Richard	Clark	1925-1928
Schauffler, William G.	Amherst	1890-1896
Schearrer, R. P.	Franklin and Marshall	1913-1916
Scherer, George H.	Drury	1907-1909
Schoonmaker, Oliver J.	Harvard	1906-1907
Schwenke, C. H.	Wooster	1903-1906
Scott, Arthur P.	Princeton	1904-1907
Scott, George T.	Princeton	1903-1906
Scudder, Delton	Wesleyan	1927-1928
Seelye, Laurens H.	Amherst	1919-1935
Selsam, Howard S.	Franklin and Marshall	1924-1927
Severac, Henri	France	1925-1926
Seybold, Sarah R.	Oneida, N.Y.	1923-1926
Seylaz, Albert	Lausanne	1937-
Shanklin, William M.	Delaware	1925-
Shawhan, Lucy M.	Post Graduate Hospital	1926-1929
Sheets, D. Ervin	West Virginia, Bethany	1927-1930
Shoemaker, Maude	Minnesota	1929-1934
Shuman, John W.	Geneva, Pittsburgh	1922-1923
Simpson, Ellen	—	1922-1925
Smallwood, J. W.	Oxford	1906-1907
Smith, Byron P.	Wooster	1910-
Smith, F. Tredwell	Harvard	1923-1924

NAME	GRADUATED FROM	YEARS AT BEIRUT
Smith, Henry Watson	Scotland	1917-1919 1922-1934
Smith, Jean	Roosevelt Hospital, N.Y.	1927-1933
Smith, Randolph B.	Harvard	1922-1925
Smock, Mary V.	Illinois	1926-1928
Smurthwaite, J. S.	England	1910-1914
Snyder, Harry R.	Lawrence	1927-1929
Snyder, Jeanette	Wells	1932-1936
Soltau, Roger	Cambridge	1930-
Souter, Charles E.	Cornell	1920-1923
Speller, H. M.	—	1920-1921
Sprague, Eleanor M.	Middlebury, Columbia	1937-1941
Stancliffe, Elsie	—	1922-
Stanford, Cleo	Amer. Univ. of Beirut	1936-1938
Stanwood, Mary	—	1936-1938 1939-
Staudt, Calvin K.	Franklin and Marshall	1919-1922
Steen, R. S.	Princeton	1901-1904
Stein, Joseph H.	Franklin and Marshall	1921-1924
Stephens, Charles D.*	England	1907-1913
Stevens, Wilma Faith	Coll. of Idaho, Presbyterian Hosp., N.Y.	1934-1939
Stewart, George B.	Princeton	1906-
Stewart, H. B.	Princeton	1908-1909
Stiver, Michael L.	Wisconsin	1926-1927
Stone, Robert	Springfield	1923-1926
Stoutenburg, W. F.*	—	1879-1881
Strong, Curtis C.	Whitman	1937-1938
Strutt, Caroline	—	1898-1908
Sturmer, Evelyn A.	Hartford Hospital	1935-1938
Sverdrup, George	Yale	1906-1907
Swaim, J. Carter	Washington and Jefferson	1927-1928
Swain, James R.	Princeton	1895-1898
Talbot, Lydia	—	1922-1926
Temple, Gertrude	California	1938-
Thaw, S. D.	Yale	1907-1908
Thèneaud, Franc P. G.	France	1926-1929
Thomas, Harry G.	U. of Denver, Nebraska	1920-1922
Tompkins, J. Butler	Wesleyan	1926-1929
Tompkins, L. Alva	Cornell	1925-1928

NAME	GRADUATED FROM	YEARS AT BEIRUT
Tower, J. Allen	Univ. of Washington	1928-1931
Turner, Edward L.	Chicago	1923-1936
Valla, M.	France	1931-
Vance, W. F.	Hanover	1908-1910
Van Dyck, Cornelius V. A.	Jefferson Medical	1867-1882
Van Dyck, Edward	Cairo	1870-1871
Van Dyck, Henry	—	1878-1879
Van Dyck, William T.*	New York University (Medical)	1880-1882 1915-1939
Van Dyke, G. Malcolm	Princeton	1923-1926
Van Zandt, Elsie	N.Y. Post Graduate Hospital	1910-1913
Van Zandt, Jane E.	N.Y. Post Graduate Hospital	1905-1940
Vauthrin, Dollie	Christ Hospital, Topeka	1922-1923
Veatch, Roy N.	Oregon	1922-1925
Veit, Ralph	Knox	1930-1933
Vincent, Jeanette C.	Johns Hopkins Hospital	1926-1928
Waddell, A. F.	Kansas	1914-1915
Wadsworth, George	Union	1914-1917
Walker, D. A.	—	1889-1892
Ward, E. St. John	Amherst	1911-1931
Warner, Robert	Ohio Wesleyan	1931-1935
Webb, Kenneth B.	Harvard	1925-1926
Webb, William D.	Earlham	1929-1932
Webster, Amy Frances	Oberlin	1919-1920
Webster, Charles A.	Toronto	1895-
Webster, Donald E.	Oberlin	1934-1935
Webster, Edgar H.	Chicago	1919-1920
Webster, Marjorie	Toronto	1923-1925
Weld, W. E.	Wooster	1903-1906
Wells, Franklin	Princeton	1888-1891
West, Alice (Mrs.)	—	1907-1925
West, Francis W.	Princeton	1921-1924
West, Margaret	Wilson	1916-1924
West, Robert H.*	Princeton	1883-1906
West, William A.	Princeton	1919-1921 1923-
White, Henry E.	Cornell	1924-1925
Whitney, Edwin P.	Pomona	1919-1922
Whittlesey, Raymond C.	Philomath (Oregon)	1921-1924

NAME	GRADUATED FROM	YEARS AT BEIRUT
Wible, E. T.	Kansas	1914-1915
Widmer, Robert	Paris	1931-
Willett, Herbert L.	Chicago	1913-1916
Williams, Helen M.	Roosevelt Hospital	1921-1923
Williams, Maynard Owen	Kalamazoo	1911-1914
Wilson, F. E.	Oberlin	1913-1916
Wilson, John A.	Princeton	1920-1923
Wisner, C. W.	Princeton	1896-1899
Wood, Dann L.	Union	1897-1900
Woodruff, Frank S.	Princeton	1885-1893
Wooster, Mary	Methodist Hospital, Indianapolis	1929-1932
Wortabet, Henry	—	1871-1872
Wortabet, John	New York University	1867-1882 1883-1890
Wright, Walter L., Jr.	Princeton	1921-1925
Wuerfel, Theodore T.	Michigan	1929-1932
Wuthier, Alexander	Lausanne	1911-
Yeiser, Frederick T.	Princeton	1923-1925
Young, Agnes	—	1927-1928

* Died in service

APPENDIX K

SYRIA

Statement by Dr. Bliss to the Versailles
Peace Conference, 1919

M. Clemenceau welcomed Dr. Bliss and called on him to make his statement.

Dr. Bliss then read the following statement.

"Mr. President, Gentlemen,

I shall not detain you long. My deep interest in the people of Syria, irrespective of race, creed, or condition, bred from a long residence among them —in fact I was born on Mt. Lebanon—is my only excuse for detaining you at all.

First, a preliminary word as to the people themselves. They are intelligent, able, hospitable and lovable, but with the sure defects of a long oppressed race; timidity, love of flattery, indirectness. They also have the defects characteristic of people who are face to face with the results of civilization without having passed through the process of modern civilization. They lack balance, they are easily discouraged, they lack political fairness, they do not easily recognize the limitations of their own rights. They must therefore be approached with sympathy, firmness and patience. They are capable of nobly responding to the right appeal. And they will grow into capacity for self-determination and independence.

My plea before this body on behalf of the people of Syria is this: that an Inter-Allied or a Neutral Commission, or a Mixed Commission, be sent to Syria at once—in order to give an opportunity to the people of Syria—including the Lebanon—to express in a perfectly untrammelled way their political wishes and aspirations, viz: as to what form of government they desire and as to what Power, if any, should be their Mandatory Protecting Power.

My plan is based upon the ground that the 12th point of President Wilson's 14 points and the declarations made by France and Great Britain in November 1918 have committed the Allies and the United States to the granting of such an opportunity of self-expression to the people freed from the Turkish yoke so to express themselves. The declaration is as follows:

'The aim which France and Great Britain have in view in waging in the East the war let loose upon the world by German ambition is to ensure the complete and final emancipation of all those peoples so long oppressed by Turks, and to establish national governments and administration which shall derive their authority from the initiative and free will of the peoples themselves. To realize this France and Great Britain are in agreement to encourage and assist the establishment of national governments in Syria and Mesopotamia, now liberated by the Allies, as also in those territories for whose liberation they are striving and to recognize those governments immediately they are effectively established. Far from wishing to impose on the peoples of these regions this or that institution, they have no other care than to assure, by their support and practical aid, the normal working of such governments and administrations as the peoples shall themselves have adopted; to guarantee impartial and even justice for all, to facilitate the economic development of the country by arousing and encouraging local initiative, to foster the spread of education, to put an end to those factions too long exploited by Turkish policy—such is the part which the two Allied Governments have set themselves to play in liberated territories.'

I maintain that such an opportunity of self-expression has not as yet been given. Up to the time I left Beirut, viz: January 9, 1919, the stringency of the censorship of the Press and of the Post Office, the difficulty of holding public or private meetings for the discussion of political problems and the great obstacles in travelling, had made it practically impossible for the people, suffering from centuries of intimidation, and now timid to a degree, to express their opinions, with any sort of freedom. It is true that a

Lebanese delegation has succeeded in reaching Paris and is here today. I know these gentlemen, several of whom are my pupils, but there are many other groups from the Lebanon, who would have gladly been here to speak for themselves and others had they been as fortunate as this group in being able to organize themselves and to find the means of travelling hither.

The point is this: Up to January 9th (the date of my leaving) no notice of any arrangements had been published anywhere in Syria, so far as I know, looking to anything like a general poll of the people of Syria (always including the Lebanon) or even anything like an attempt had been made to secure a widespread knowledge of public sentiment. I did hear more or less of a list of names that was being made up attached to various petitions in favor of this or that program, but although in a position to hear of any official or thorough or systematic general plan to ascertain the wishes of the people, no such report came to my knowledge. Many interested citizens of Beirut and the Lebanon were never approached for the purpose of ascertaining their political desires.

I therefore plead that the above mentioned Commission should be sent out as soon as possible by the Peace Conference, with ample powers given to them, and of course with the whole-hearted support granted to them by the French and British authorities now in Syria. The ascertaining of the desires of the people should proceed either without the presence of any foreign Power (and this is impracticable) or in the presence of both French and British authorities under whom Syria has been living for the past four months.

The people are easily frightened and intimidated even where there is nothing to fear from any source; hence these precautions. The advantage of knowing what the people wish would be a boon to the power eventually becoming the Mandatory Power as well as to the people of Syria. One word as to the work of the Commission. Their task will not be an easy one. They must approach it, in my opinion, in the spirit of large sympathy, infinite patience, frankness and good-will. In the hands of fair and open-minded men, resourceful, shrewd and generous—men who can make clear their honest purpose to a timid but intelligent people—very valuable results can be secured. The result of this enquiry will be, I am convinced, the discovery of the desire for the erection of a state or states looking eventually to complete independence but at present seeking the guardianship of a Mandatory Power.

Both the state or states and the Mandatory Power should be under the control of the League of Nations. Unless in this state or states there should be an absolute separation between religion and the state, most serious results must inevitably arise. The Government on the one hand, religion on the other, can best pursue their majestic tasks apart. Surely Oriental if not general history is making that abundantly clear.

One word more. Unless the Mandatory Power working under the League of Nations approaches its great task in the spirit of lofty service, her splendid opportunity to lead an aspiring people to independence will be forever lost. But once let the same superb spirit sustain her and the League of Nations as has animated the Allies and the United States in working together for the establishment of the freedom of the world, the task, though difficult will be accomplished."

APPENDIX L

THE BOARD OF TRUSTEES 1863-1941

William A. Booth, President	1863-1895
William E. Dodge, Sr., Treasurer	1863-1883
David Hoadley	1863-1873
Simeon B. Chittenden	1863-1883
Abner Kingman	1863-1878
Joseph S. Ropes	1863-1873
Alfred C. Post, M.D.	1873-1886
Alfred L. Dennis	1873-1890
D. Stuart Dodge, Secy., Treas., Pres.	1882-1922
William E. Dodge, Jr., Treasurer	1883-1903
Morris K. Jesup, President	1884-1908
Samuel S. Dennis, Secretary	1892-1919
Alexander Maitland	1895-1908
V. Everit Macy	1897-1922
C. C. Cuyler, Treasurer	1903-1909
Arthur Curtiss James, Vice-President	1906-1938
William M. Kingsley, Treasurer, President	1906-
Marcellus Hartley Dodge	1906-
Alfred E. Marling	1908-1935
William Fellowes Morgan	1908-1940
James S. Dennis, Secretary	1908-1914
Mrs. Morris K. Jesup	1912-1914
Francis Brown	1912-1916
Edward B. Cragin, M.D.	1913-1918
Eleanor de Graff Cuyler	1915-1933
William Adams Brown	1919-1921
Franklin A. Dorman, M.D.	1919-1927
James H. Post	1919-1938
Clarence Phelps Dodge	1921-1936
William S. Ladd, M.D.	1923-1941
Vanderbilt Webb, President	1923-
Mrs. Van Santvoord Merle-Smith	1923-1941
Acosta Nichols	1928-
William W. Patton	1936-
Loren H. Rockwell	1936-
Whitney C. Colby	1936-1940
Harold B. Hoskins, Vice-President	1938-
H. Irving Pratt, Jr., Treasurer	1939-1941
John W. Young	1940-
Lawrence C. Marshall, Treasurer	1941-

(In 1919, when the Near East College Association was established, Albert W. Staub, the American Director, became ex-officio secretary of the Board of Trustees)

APPENDIX M

STATISTICS OF STUDENTS BY NATIONALITIES

Nation	*1936*	*1937*	*1938*	*1939*	*1940*
Lebanon and Syria	779	813	902	866	1071
Palestine	265	295	419	417	374
'Iraq	119	145	166	204	223
Egypt	82	76	69	50	52
Cyprus	—	14	20	14	7
Iran	37	32	25	27	24
Turkey	11	11	13	19	18

Nation	*1936*	*1937*	*1938*	*1939*	*1940*
Transjordan	15	19	27	23	34
Arabia					
Hijaz	14	23	19	9	5
Kuwayt	—	3	2	2	1
Bahrein	1	10	7	2	—
Sudan	8	5	7	3	3
Zanzibar	4	1	1	1	—
India	2	1	3	2	—
Tanganyika	—	1	—	—	2
Abyssinia	1	1	—	—	—
Singapore	—	1	—	—	—
France	20	30	31	33	37
Switzerland	2	6	6	5	4
Bulgaria	11	10	3	3	—
Czechoslovakia	2	4	1	—	—
Jugoslavia	2	1	2	1	—
Lithuania	—	2	—	1	1
Albania	3	4	4	3	1
Great Britain	21	27	32	34	17
Hungary	1	—	—	—	—
Greece	19	15	18	15	12
Russia	10	2	—	1	3
Poland	5	7	10	6	5
Italy	3	2	5	5	5
Spain	1	—	2	—	—
Germany	6	5	8	10	9
Belgium	—	1	1	—	1
Austria	2	1	1	—	—
Latvia	1	1	1	1	1
Roumania	1	1	1	—	2
Malaya	3	—	2	1	—
Panama	1	1	—	1	1
Colombia	2	—	—	—	1
Peru	1	1	—	—	—
Brazil	2	5	3	4	3
San Domingo	2	1	—	—	—
Argentine	3	3	2	2	—
Equador	2	2	3	1	1
Mexico	2	3	3	3	2
Chile	2	2	5	5	2
Cuba	1	1	—	—	—
Honduras	2	2	2	1	1

Nation	*1936*	*1937*	*1938*	*1939*	*1940*
Canada	1	—	—	—	—
U.S.A.	72	113	104	71	64
Nansen	—	1	—	—	1
Japan	—	—	1	—	—
Guatemala	—	—	6	—	—
Tunisia	—	—	1	1	1
	1544	1705	1938	1847	1992

APPENDIX N

STATISTICS OF STUDENTS BY RELIGIOUS SECTS

Sect	*1937*	*1938*	*1939*	*1940*
Moslem	546	646	642	727
Jew	193	228	226	198
Deist	1	1	—	—
Druze	50	52	55	62
Bahai	8	6	10	8
Zoroastrian	—	1	—	—
Hindu	2	3	2	1
Freethinker	1	—	—	—
Buddhist	—	1	—	—
Greek Orthodox	330	379	358	379
Greek Catholic	47	45	39	48
Protestant	262	301	297	284
Maronite	71	79	53	84
Gregorian	61	63	57	54
Latin	76	94	84	100
Coptic Orthodox	24	13	2	12
Syriac Orthodox	14	13	10	12
Syriac Catholic	7	6	4	8
Chaldean Catholic	7	2	2	4
Armenian Catholic	4	5	6	9
Nestorian	—	—	—	2
Jacobite	1	—	—	—
	1705	1938	1847	1992

APPENDIX O

STATISTICS OF STUDENTS BY DEPARTMENTS

	1938	*1939*	*1940*
School of Medicine	117	115	114
School of Pharmacy	63	49	53
School of Dentistry	13	7	—
School of Nursing	68	72	71
School of Arts and Sciences	391	280	319
Total Number of University Students	652	523	557
Institute of Music	83	83	68
International College			
Elementary School	235	229	252
French School	400	337	416
English School	376	315	325
Intermediate Section			
Freshman	192	140	134
Sophomore*		158	170
Commerce*		53	55
Special*		9	15
Total, International College	1203	1241	1367
Total, University and International College	1938	1847	1992

* Transferred from Arts and Sciences in 1939.

APPENDIX P

STATISTICS OF PERSONNEL

By Nationalities

	1938	*1939*	*1940*
America	52	52	40
Great Britain	13	14	13
Greece	3	3	3
Russia	3	2	1
France	15	8	10
Bulgaria	1	1	—
Switzerland	3	5	5
Spain	1	1	1

	1938	1939	1940
Germany	2	2	2
Lebanon and Syria	178	195	198
Iran	4	1	1
Palestine	6	4	7
Egypt	4	3	3
Turkey	1	1	—
Czechoslovakia	—	1	1
	286	293	285

By Religious Sects

	1938	1939	1940
Greek Orthodox	49	57	56
Greek Catholic	8	9	8
Protestant	147	150	143
Gregorian	12	15	14
Syriac Orthodox	1	1	—
Latin	19	13	13
Maronite	11	11	11
Moslem	18	21	21
Druze	8	7	10
Bahai	4	2	2
Jew	9	7	7
	286	293	285

Index

INDEX